To/ Hugh.

"Happy Christmas".

With love

Trish xxx

December 92.

Cricket Cauldron

5op

D1461265

CRICKET CAULDRON

WITH HUTTON IN THE CARIBBEAN

ALEX BANNISTER

THE PAVILION LIBRARY

First published in Great Britain in 1954

Copyright © Alex Bannister 1954
Introduction copyright © Alex Bannister 1990

First published in the Pavilion Library in 1990 by
PAVILION BOOKS LIMITED
196 Shaftesbury Avenue
London WC2H 8JL

Series Editor: Steve Dobell

A CIP catalogue record for this book
is available from the British Library

ISBN 1 85145 462 4 Hbk
ISBN 1 85145 467 5 Pbk

Printed and bound in Great Britain by
Biddles Limited, Guildford

INTRODUCTION

Cricket Cauldron is the hard-to-believe story of an MCC tour to the West Indies which, at the time in 1954, held second place ranking in contentious controversy to Douglas Jardine's Bodyline rumpus.

At the end of three months of bickering rows, complaints, umpiring disputes, heat, volatile crowds, a bottle-throwing riot and an almost daily ration of bizarre happenings, MCC's captain and prime batsman, Len Hutton, was physically spent and mentally exhausted.

By his own reckoning his career was foreshortened by two years. In the following home season he missed two of four Tests, and many county matches, and only just recovered in time for the winter tour of Australia with 'Typhoon' Tyson and Co.

Hutton's West Indian experience was sandwiched between his double triumph of regaining (after nineteen years) and retaining the Ashes, but a case can be made that to draw 2-2 with such formidable opposition after disastrously losing the first two Tests was as fine a result as he achieved as England's unbeaten captain. An epic recovery of which there can be no doubt, but a private meeting of senior players, without Hutton's knowledge, played no small part in transforming demoralized losers into winners. To 'keep Len happy' they pledged renewed maximum effort and to lend more support to the younger players, who could scarcely have had a more difficult and testing start in international cricket.

Outplayed in the first half of the series, England decisively won the second against all logic. Such a tragedy that the action on the field was so often betrayed by a tension which Wisden rightly declared was created even before a ball was bowled.

Almost four generations on, it is hard to credit that an insistence by some writers that the 'cricket championship of the world' was at stake should generate fervour. Yet it did. Or that the exhortations by many of the white community to the visiting players that England *must* win should cause both irritation and pressure. Yet it did.

Oddly, since Hutton's captaincy and batting represented their best chance of fulfilled hopes, there was an element, seemingly cocooned in a time warp, who thought their world had fallen apart with England appointing a professional captain, and actually felt slighted that the West Indies were the first to have to play host to a non-amateur leader of MCC; one not even a member of the club!

There was also disappointment that MCC, at Hutton's instigation, asked for the number of social engagements to be cut to the minimum. It wasn't that he was anti-social, but his attitude and priorities were fashioned in the Yorkshire dressing-rooms of Sutcliffe, Bowes, Verity, Leyland and the rest and he saw only disadvantages in his players, especially the younger ones, being plied with strong drink and standing around, night after night, struggling with small talk, often to the same party goers and not all cricket enthusiasts.

He believed his first duty was to England, to win, and for the team to share his dedication. As J. M. Kilburn wrote, 'Victories were important to Hutton, he did not play in Test matches as a pastime.'

One rumour to stick was a supposed edict from the captain not to fraternize with opponents. Nonsense, replied Hutton.

A new dimension of concern arose, not totally unpredictable, when the series began; the old spectre of the standard of umpiring. *Wisden* reported: 'Convinced by the happenings on the field that the general standard of umpiring in the West Indies was not adequate for Test cricket, the touring team felt that the crowd atmosphere made the work of the men in the middle even harder than it should have been. The MCC players sympathized with the umpires threatened with physical violence, as marred the First and Third Tests. When, as the West Indies players admitted, the majority of disputed decisions, usually at moments of match crisis, went against

MCC, they wondered how in the circumstances any umpire could remain completely calm and controlled.

'To a man the MCC team recognized their responsibilities as ambassadors of sport, but, being human, the less phlegmatic did not always hide their annoyance and displeasure. In some instances only someone with the forbearance of the most highly trained diplomat could have been expected to preserve absolute sangfroid. Dramatic gestures of disappointment and untactful remarks, however understandable some of them were in the heat of the moment, caused resentment among West Indies officials, umpires and others.'

Of course there can be no excuse for intemperate behaviour on the field, but in these days of excessive displays of temper – it is scarcely necessary to list the instances – the public in general might not have been as shocked as it was in the 1950s. In truth, the worst of the incidents on the field in 1954 pale into insignificance beside the all too often rebellious behaviour sadly reflecting modern cricket times.

It was in the inflammatory moments that Hutton particularly rued the absence of the placid giant Alec Bedser. His deputy, Freddie Trueman, clearly arrived on the Test scene a tour too early, and a demanding one at that. Players considerably more experienced than Trueman could not hide their feelings.

Looking back I strongly believe Hutton and his team were let down by the Foreign Office. The sole briefing came from Viscount (then Sir Walter) Monckton on the eve of departure, which was fine as far as it went. But the true extent of the cultural and political changes then taking place in the scattered islands became evident only by bitter experience.

To be forewarned is to be forearmed. The next tourists to the West Indies, Australia, had nothing but a happy experience. So a lesson was learned.

But the FO might well have asked if the most meticulous preparation on the touchy situation in the West Indies could have avoided the extraordinary and unique episode when MCC's totally innocent captain was charged with 'insulting' Jamaica's Chief Minister, the flamboyant Mr Alex Bustamente. Hutton's understandable reaction was voiced in his book, *Fifty Years in Cricket* (Stanley Paul): 'The charge was so baseless that it is incredible it was ever made, and I cannot believe any touring captain anywhere has been obliged to endure such a blatant discourtesy.'

MCC's long-suffering player-manager Charles Palmer might well echo Hutton's complaint, for he was suddenly accosted by an irate official in the dressing-room and was lifted off his feet and shaken by the lapels of his jacket. His response deserves to be ranked as a classic in the annals of cricket. 'If you put me down,' he said mildly, 'I'll listen to what you have to say.'

Inevitably the team leadership was criticized, particularly by those the Atlantic Ocean away from the pressure-cooker atmosphere. Hutton, it was said, was not strong enough, though it would have been interesting to have witnessed the reaction of some of the old-style 'strong' leaders, and Palmer too conciliatory. Palmer was an oasis of common sense in every situation, and both manager and captain did all that could have been reasonably expected of them. In due course Hutton received a knighthood and Palmer held the highest offices in cricket, including the presidency of MCC.

The book was written from day to day as the drama unfolded. There was no time for second thoughts, no time for revision. (So much happened that the Reuter correspondent, Reg Hayter, exceeded his word quota half-way through the tour.) The pace was so hot that a foreword by the West Indies captain, Jeffrey Stollmeyer, planned to go alongside one by Hutton, did not arrive in time. Now, alas, Jeffrey is no longer with us, gunned down in 1989 by thugs attempting to steal from his beautiful home in Trinidad. By common consent he was one of Test cricket's finest captains, a batsman as graceful as Tom Graveney, and was always above the parochialism which often bedevilled the politics of the game.

He cared for cricket and the way it should be played, and if all shared his principles there would be no cauldrons in cricket!

Berkhamsted, 1989   Alex Bannister

CRICKET CAULDRON

WITH HUTTON IN THE CARIBBEAN

by

ALEX BANNISTER

With a Foreword by
LEN HUTTON
and a Preface by
C. H. PALMER

21 half-tone Illustrations

FOREWORD

I AM glad that an account of an unusual cricket tour is available to the sporting public of the British Empire so soon after its completion.

To many who did not witness any part of the 1954 tour of the West Indies by the M.C.C. sections of Mr. Bannister's book probably will seem far-fetched and strange. I am not in a position to comment on the events in the West Indies but they were strange indeed, and Mr. Bannister's factual report should give some idea of the difficulties faced by the M.C.C. players.

Having been on several tours with Alex Bannister, I can say from long acquaintance that he is not the type of journalist who draws on his imagination to colour his writing. In cricket circles he is accepted as one with the interest of the game at heart but also as a man not blinded by prejudices or inhibitions.

Our young cricketers, many of whom are serving their Test apprenticeship, should have developed considerably by their experience against the always-formidable opposition of the West Indies, who still have a great team, especially on their own wickets.

Naturally I was disappointed that England did not win the rubber, but I think all will agree that, by and large, the players did a fine job.

The future can be faced with confidence.

LEN HUTTON,
Captain of England.

PREFACE

MODERN cricket benefits and suffers from the great publicity it receives through the Press and the M.C.C. Team in the West Indies certainly created and received much publicity. Throughout my association with Alex Bannister on this tour I realized that in him was a news correspondent who had the interests of cricket at heart, who wished to present a fair picture to his readers, and I think he never resorted to "sensationalism" except when the events he described were "sensational". During the tour there were many incidents of interest which appeared to extend beyond mere cricket; there were many problems the import of which cricket followers everywhere may have had difficulty in assessing while the tour was in progress. All these in addition to the cricket itself the author has tried to present in a responsible way, mindful of the future development of the game.

C. H. PALMER
M.C.C. Player-Manager.

CONTENTS

CONTENTS

CHAPTER SIX

CHAPTER SEVEN

CHAPTER EIGHT

CHAPTER NINE

CHAPTER TEN

CHAPTER ELEVEN

CONTENTS

CHAPTER TWELVE

CHAPTER THIRTEEN

CHAPTER FOURTEEN

CHAPTER FIFTEEN

CHAPTER SIXTEEN

CHAPTER ONE

Hutton's out—Denis confounds all—Pyrrhic Pools victory—Trueman stutters—
Bermuda problems—Dinner 49s.—Shoe clean 3s. 6d.—Thirsty golf—Watson
sprains wrist—The knee again—Lock the terror—Too subtle for Ken.

"HUTTON . . . Hutton out first ball, sir!"
The immigration officer stamping my passport in the
lounge of the liner *Canonia* told me. Two members of the ship-to-
shore tender told me. So did the hansom cabby, a survivor of the
not so distant past when beautiful Bermuda could not boast of cars,
as his horses trotted sedately from the Customs Shed. The bell-hop
in the luxurious Bermudiana hotel confirmed the news.

"Hutton out first ball." Every man, woman and child of this
enchanting island seemed to be proudly rolling the four words
around their tongues as though they carried magic properties.
With the dramatic announcement went the obvious meaning:
"If nothing else happens at least we got Hutton out first
ball."

Twenty-four hours earlier a quiet-spoken man from the little
Yorkshire village of Pudsey (birthplace also of the county's celebrated John Tunnicliffe and Herbert Sutcliffe), a professional
cricketer by occupation, captain of England by popular acclaim and
a legendary figure wherever the game is played, was caught at the
wicket off the first ball of the first match played by any M.C.C.
side in Bermuda.

The incident will be recalled on the island for generations to
come. When it happened the home players were stunned into
momentary immobility. The shock came too quickly for them to
grasp its meaning, but when they did their joy was unrestrained.
There were cartwheels, whoops of delight and congratulations all
round—followed by no little dismay at the realization that the
champion's innings had been stillborn.

Peter Maudler, the Bermudian wicket-taker, must have felt
like H. C. Griffith, the West Indies fast bowler who shattered
Sir Donald Bradman's wicket some twenty years before. In a
voice vibrant with emotion Griffith roared, "I have bowled de
God."

The first-ball dismissal of England's captain was the second
major surprise of the tour, which included an experimental eight
days' cricket and ten days in all in Bermuda.

Some four days previously Denis Compton had confounded

everyone who knew him by being the first member of the team to arrive at London airport.

Throughout his distinguished career Denis has rarely caught a train, boat or aeroplane except by the skin of his teeth. Successive club secretaries, captains, tour managers and other worried organizers had vainly tried to contain their mounting anxiety until Denis made his inevitable last-second appearance.

His familiarity with the running-boards of trains gathering speed and the hoisting gangplank bordered on something out of this world. Yet here was the same Denis, bright and shining, first to reach Heathrow and with oceans of time to spare. Manager Charles Palmer was almost on the point of going home. He could only gaze and murmur, "Is my journey really necessary?"

He was to discover just how necessary his journey was. He had not long to wait.

Well might the hardy pioneers of cricket tours have been astonished had they been able to witness the smooth take-off of the strato-cruiser into the sombre clouds of an English December day. Not for the modern cricketer the agonies of the north Atlantic in midwinter—thoughts which were never far from the minds of Charles Bray (*Daily Herald*), Frank Rostron (*Daily Express*) and myself as we pitched and lurched our way from a fog-bound Liverpool to the embracing warmth of Bermuda's sunshine.

The M.C.C. team of 1953–54 were the first to travel from England by air, and the first in the modern era to have in Len Hutton a professional captain.

They arrived at Gander (Newfoundland) in snow a foot deep, 16 degrees of frost and a hotel temperature of 76. There they stayed for six hours, long enough for one to remember he had not posted his football pools coupon. He asked a postal official if it could be sent to England from there in time for the matches beginning five days afterwards. He was told it could but obviously no guarantee could be given that it would reach its destination within the time limit.

With bulldog persistence the cricketer had filled in the same permutation week in week out for more than ten years without even a penny dividend, and he was determined not to break his sequence.

Just ten days after posting, he heard from his wife that her copy showed eight lines of 21 points—for which the promoters were announcing a dividend of 63s. He saw himself richer by some £25.

He prepared to celebrate. In fact, he did celebrate, well in advance.

Alas! The next information from home carried the unhappy news that the coupon had not reached its address until the Monday after the games had been played.

Ever considerate, ever consoling to their faithful customers, the pools promoters returned the original investment of twelve shillings!

From Gander the next step was Bermuda, where the M.C.C. touched down on the same runway that had recently served the Queen and Sir Winston Churchill.

When the party left England Mr. Ronnie Aird, M.C.C. Secretary, described it as the strongest English combination sent overseas since the war, an opinion supported by Hutton. There were some doubters.

Still, mostly the feeling was of high optimism, brought about by the recovery of the Ashes from the Old Enemy. No doubt we were all rather inclined to under-estimate the undiminished strength of the West Indies who had already thrashed us in two post-war series.

We were tempted to gloss over the fact that the M.C.C. team contained several untried players, only one accredited opening batsman, no experienced slip fielder and no leg-spinner—the latter deficiency through the lack of suitable candidates rather than through any lapse by the committee.

A leg-break and googly bowler of the type and quality of Bruce Dooland would have been of infinite value. Unfortunately for England the man who in 1953 had been responsible for lifting Nottinghamshire from the bottom of the Championship table to a respectable place is an Australian, and therefore not eligible.

The greatest of all modern English bowlers, Alec Bedser, would also have made a vast difference but, with the sympathetic understanding of M.C.C., Alec had decided not to allow himself to be considered for the tour, a decision regretted in England but even more so in the lovely islands of the West Indies, a part of the world which he had never visited.

With a gruelling summer behind him and the prospect of more hard work in the English season of 1954 and the tour of Australia in the succeeding months—in other words 18 months' non-stop cricket—Alec pleaded to be allowed to rest at home.

Some said, wrongly in my opinion, that Bedser could have been nursed during the West Indies' tour by being played only in the Tests and more important matches. Alec needs at least eight games to reach his physical and bowling peak, and constant match practice to maintain his form.

I do not believe such an arrangement as suggested could have worked.

Also missing was fighting Bill Edrich, the man whose spirit and determination had helped England to regain the Ashes. I never understood why Bill was not invited for Australia in 1950–51 and, to my mind, his omission from the latest tour to West Indies was an equally grievous blunder.

Another whose absence surprised me was Reg Simpson, the Nottinghamshire captain and stylish opening batsman. I am sure he would have been an unqualified success in the West Indies. This opinion was shared by Frank Worrell, who had been in the same Commonwealth side in India until December.

Of the younger players not asked the two saddest omissions were Michael Colin Cowdrey (M.C.C.) from Oxford University and Kent, the most promising English batsman for years, and Robin Marlar, the Cambridge University and Sussex off-break bowler who for several years had performed prodigious feats in the best company.

Cowdrey's technique and ability is far advanced, and he needs only experience to become a batsman in the highest class.

Allowing for the strange absences of these four the team looked formidable enough. It consisted of:

> Len Hutton (Yorkshire), captain, aged 37.
> Trevor Bailey (Essex), vice-captain, aged 30.
> Peter May (Surrey), aged 23.
> Denis Compton (Middlesex), aged 35.
> Godfrey Evans (Kent), aged 33.
> Tom Graveney (Gloucestershire), aged 26.
> Jim Laker (Surrey), aged 31.
> Tony Lock (Surrey), aged 24.
> Willie Watson (Yorkshire), aged 33.
> Johnny Wardle (Yorkshire), aged 30.
> Freddie Trueman (Yorkshire), aged 22.
> Brian Statham (Yorkshire), aged 23.
> Alan Moss (Middlesex), aged 23.
> Dick Spooner (Warwickshire), aged 33.
> Ken Suttle (Sussex), aged 25.

Charles Palmer (34), the successful and popular secretary-captain of Leicestershire, continued in his dual capacity—this time as a player-manager. He intended to reverse the order of his role, being first a manager, then a player, but within a month he was in the second Test team.

Weeks before the players left England Hutton wrote to them individually asking them to make sure of being thoroughly fit for the work ahead. He hoped to avoid, as far as possible, the strains and illnesses which can ruin the prospects of a touring side. Hutton carried in his mind memories of the sad fortunes of the last M.C.C. team in the West Indies, the only M.C.C. side to make a tour without winning a first-class match.

Then, in 1948, Hutton had been flown out in response to an S O S from the captain, G. O. Allen. The selection of that injury-stricken team was said to be reduced to the simple process of taking the first eleven down to breakfast.

The M.C.C. cricketers, however, needed little encouragement to make themselves 100 per cent fit. Willie Watson turned out regularly for Sunderland in the First Division, Ken Suttle played outside-left for Betteshanger Colliery in the Kent League, Freddie Trueman and Johnnie Wardle practised in the indoor cricket sheds at Headingley and Brian Statham in the winter nets at Old Trafford.

The captain himself ran daily in the fields behind his Pudsey home, and the golf courses and squash courts up and down the country claimed the superfluous ounces of our touring cricketers.

Jim Laker, required as juror at the Old Bailey, London, was excused service. Privileged persons are these cricketers!

No previous M.C.C. party to the Caribbean enjoyed the advantage of using Bermuda as a stepping-stone although some indication of the strength of Bermudian cricket had been gained during a visit there by Sir Julian Cahn's team in 1933.

Sir Julian Cahn's side included players of the calibre of Walter Robins, Ian Peebles, Denis Morkel, the South African, Roger Blunt of New Zealand—all Test players—George Heane, captain of Nottinghamshire, and C. R. Maxwell, the Nottinghamshire and later Worcestershire wicketkeeper.

In the most exciting of finishes George Heane took a brilliant catch in front of the sight screen from a ball which looked to be sailing for six. Sir Julian Cahn's team won by three runs—to the undisguised relief of the Northumberland Fusiliers stationed on the island who had taken heavy bets on his team at odds of three to one.

In the absence of a turf wicket, however, the cricket found by Hutton and his men was of little value. The pitch consisted of a mat laid on a concrete base, which made timing difficult for the batsmen, and handicapped the fast bowlers even more. When the front foot made contact with the concrete the whole body jarred.

Trueman found himself compelled to deliver outside the matting strip. The wider he went the more trouble he met in trying to bowl straight. Moreover, he developed a "stutter" in his run-up which was not conquered for several matches.

Matting necessarily reduced the margin of skill between the

sides and, in such conditions, many English first-class county teams would have been hard pressed to beat Bermuda.

Quite the most disappointing feature of the three matches there was the poor public response. While the residents could not do too much for the M.C.C. off the field, few of them visited the cricket ground.

Some of the attendances were embarrassingly small and the crowd atmosphere so essential to bring out the best from many players never existed.

There were several causes. One was that the Somerset ground, the headquarters of the coloured Somers Isles League, is twelve or so miles from the centre of Hamilton, the capital of the island. The single taxi fare from Hamilton to Somerset was sixteen shillings, a not inconsiderable item even in an island of inflated costs.

Another factor was that most families were in the throes of Christmas shopping and many business men and their employees just could not spare the time to go to the cricket. Yuletide in Bermuda is celebrated more enthusiastically and spread over a longer period than I have experienced anywhere else. Bermuda is essentially a centre of social life.

That abundant interest in cricket exists in the island is beyond doubt and is proved by the presence of two strong leagues. The annual match between the representative sides from the two leagues is marked by a two days' public holiday and all the island attend.

Large sums of money change hands on the result and a star performer may find his bank balance suddenly lifted. In the inter-colony game Eugene Woods, who bowled so well against M.C.C., received £84 from admirers who rushed on the field and stuffed his pockets with notes.

For all that, the stranger, like myself, rightly or wrongly, could not escape the impression that local differences contributed to the sparse crowds. If future M.C.C. sides are to repeat their visit en route to the sterner cricket trials of the West Indies these differences must be composed.

After a first experience of Bermuda I have no doubt that the M.C.C. players would unanimously vote to repeat the Bermuda experiment with two qualifications—(a) that a grass pitch be laid, to provide adequate practice for the tour ahead; (b) the players are not swamped with tales of local cricket politics which to them are merely boring.

Whatever else it did the trip to Bermuda provided the M.C.C. cricketers with the opportunity of becoming accustomed to the intensity of the tropical sun. A few days later, when we disembarked from the 'plane at Jamaica, I appreciated what would have been the severity of the ordeal of arriving in such heat straight from the cold of England.

For the privilege of playing hosts to M.C.C. Bermuda paid a heavy cost. They had to meet the extra cost of the air fares from London to Bermuda, and Bermuda to Jamaica, compared with sea passages which would have been booked by the West Indies Board— a difference of almost £2,000.

This was paid by the Trade Development Board. Hotel costs and other incidentals must have been in the neighbourhood of £1,500 and the deficiency was made up by Mr. Stanhope Joel, the financier, who is reputed to enjoy a tax-free income of £130,000 a year.

The common joke among the players was that the gate receipts could not pay for the steaks (three dollars extra) which were devoured with understandable relish each night at dinner. A dinner which included steak cost 49 shillings. Prices of everything else were correspondingly high. Trevor Bailey found the charge for shoe-cleaning to be 3s. 6d. Subsequently the Army "spit-and-polish" became a favourite mode of cleaning.

Trevor also quickly acquired the island habit of using a low-powered motor-cycle for travel, which is the customary form of transportation in Bermuda where cars are a comparatively recent importation and a thirty-miles-an-hour speed limit is enforced. Such a speed limit is essential on the narrow and winding roads which were never built for the internal combustion engine.

Golf and bathing provided the favourite forms of relaxation for M.C.C.—bathing in the inviting clear blue waters and golf at the famous Mid Ocean club where the Big Three held their meeting.

A challenge golf match between a team raised by the Governor, Sir Alexander Hood, and the M.C.C. stood out as the highlight. According to the M.C.C. victory was theirs.

Around Christmas, however, golf in Bermuda is inclined to a character entirely its own. Once Charles Palmer and Denis Compton partnered in a four-ball game against opponents who drank five gins and tonic before lunch, beer, gin and tonic during the meal and Van Der Hum liqueur afterwards.

The game then began. At the second tee a gin and tonic was served to the home pair. Palmer and Compton took one sip of theirs before discreetly tossing it away when their opponents were looking elsewhere.

At the third hole the home pair opened a bottle of Van Der Hum which between them they emptied by the ninth. At the ninth they went into the club house, where they downed three more gins and tonic. At the tenth the caddy produced another gin and tonic and at the eleventh a bottle of brandy was uncorked. By the

sixteenth it was empty. And there the match ended abruptly with
Palmer and Compton the winners.

From time to time they had been pressed to share the refreshment but surreptitiously they emptied theirs into bunkers, the rough
and behind bushes.

The small but picturesque Somerset cricket ground was hewn
out of the side of a hill. On two sides the boundary consists of a
miniature cliff face which gives a neat little enclosure the suggestion
of a natural amphitheatre. Once Peter May pulled hard to the leg
boundary. The ball hit the wall with a thump but, instead of
signalling four, the umpire allowed only one run. He remained un-
convinced that the ball had rebounded from the wall.

Above the walls were placed tents—often unoccupied—and
opposite were rough wooden shacks, roof-covered with loose tar-
paulins and generously described as stands. The handsome white
pavilion dominated the scene.

In one corner of the ground a concrete strip had been put down
for net practice. When running for a ball in the outfield Willie
Watson slipped on the concrete and sprained his wrist. At the time
he felt little inconvenience, but later this seemingly innocent accident
caused him much pain and soreness.

The celebrated London surgeon, Mr. Bill Tucker, a Bermudian,
the man who looked after Denis Compton's knee, was at home at
the time and he attended Willie.

Bill Tucker, a Cambridge and England rugby footballer, is a
familiar friend to nearly all English sportsmen, as well as stage
celebrities. Of Denis Compton's knee he said to me one evening:
"With his knee Denis will never be one hundred per cent fit. We
must always remember he is only seventy-five per cent equipped to
play in first-class cricket."

The first of the three matches, a two-day practice affair, resulted
in an M.C.C. victory by an innings and 28 runs, Graveney and
Laker atoning for the Hutton duck.

The next two games were foolishly described as "Tests"—the
only Tests which have not been of first-class status. Bermuda drew
the first creditably, and rain washed out the last two days of the
second. By then M.C.C. had established a winning advantage,
having passed the Bermuda score with one wicket down.

On the mat Tony Lock was almost unplayable. In three innings
his analyses were 8—54, 1—13 and 7—35. What his figures would
have been had he been able to control the height of the ball after
pitching it is difficult to imagine.

He beat the bat almost as and when he wished but every other
ball went over the top of the stumps.

One of the best bowling performances in Bermuda was that of the loose-limbed eighteen-year-old jet-black pace bowler Eugene Woods, an £8-a-week hand on a local tug. In one spell Woods took five M.C.C. wickets for 19 runs—not bad for a boy who had played serious cricket for only eight months. A few weeks later the South Devon club, Paignton, engaged Woods as professional and coach.

Much of the credit for the good standard of cricket in Bermuda belonged to George Watson, the former Leicestershire and Kent batsman, and Corinthian footballer. Watson was the second Corinthian to join the paid ranks of Soccer, Frank Hartley, who signed for Tottenham Hotspur, having been the first.

Two months after Hartley turned pro Watson, an old Salopian, joined Charlton Athletic from whom he moved to Crystal Palace.

Watson had not been in Bermuda long when the M.C.C. arrived, but already he had made his mark. As a coach, what more could he ask than for a practical demonstration by some of the world's best exponents of the finer arts of cricket—such as field-placings and running between wickets?

Hutton struck an early and complete understanding with his new partner, Willie Watson. Their safe run-snatching immediately became one of the features of this all-Yorkshire partnership.

The umpiring in Bermuda caused little criticism, although I cannot believe umpires can do themselves full justice when they sit on shooting-sticks. As a result of this indulgence they were caught out of position to judge a possible run out.

Ken Suttle, the little Sussex left-hander, having received a first-baller in the opening innings against Bermuda, was the victim of one incident amusing to all but him.

The first ball sent down to him in the second innings went through to the wicketkeeper. A loud appeal came from behind the wicket and the umpire's raised finger gave disconsolate Suttle what, in cricket parlance, is called "a king pair". Peter May, the non-striker, seemed to share Suttle's obvious perplexity.

As Suttle made his exit the umpire asked the wicketkeeper what the appeal was for. "A catch," was the reply. "Oh! I gave him out l.b.w.," declared the umpire, who thereupon recalled Suttle, almost disappearing from view, to resume his innings. Actually the ball had flipped across Suttle's pads.

Suttle came back to the wicket and made ten runs before misfortune again overtook him. He hit the ball hard on to his thigh and was adjudged leg-before this time by the other umpire!

In the same game Dick Spooner, the Warwickshire wicketkeeper, failed to score in either innings. Next match, much to Dick's amusement, he was chosen for his batting, while Godfrey Evans kept wicket.

Christmas Day in Bermuda was notable for the hotel's "sleephead" breakfast for latecomers; the mid-day introduction to the local drink, the egg nog; dinner together in the evening; and later the hospitality of local families.

On Boxing Day it never ceased raining and washed out the cricket. Then on to Jamaica for the remarkable case of George Headley, surely a tale without parallel in cricket history.

CHAPTER TWO

The Headley case—Worrell injury—Mr. Bumper Man—Boycott threat—Holt's father cries—Attack on umpire's wife—Knife and pistol danger—The pitch guarded—Press attacks—Strange selections—Leaking covers—Leg-before decisions—Excess of zeal—Rudeness to Hutton—The Law steps in—The McCat—Firecrackers—And calypsos.

I DOUBT whether any outsider could pretend to uncover the real motive of the Jamaicans in bringing George Headley out of honourable "retirement" in the Birmingham League to do battle with the M.C.C.

Surely even in their most optimistic mood, the loyal subjects of "King George" could not expect the once-great batsman, now forty-four, with a tell-tale balding patch appearing on the crown of his crinkly head, to return to conquering deeds on the tough and ruthless fields of Test cricket. The lesson of George's post-war limitations had been provided on the Indian tour of 1948 when he scored two runs in his sole Test appearance.

A visitor could not escape the impression that Headley's presence had other and deeper significance. Whatever the reason, to expose such an illustrious figure to the saddest of all sights on a playing field—the formerly supreme artist struggling to hold his own long after he has passed his best—made a depressing spectacle.

Here was Headley, once spoken about in the same breath as Bradman and Hammond, the only scorer of a century in each innings of a Test at Lord's, trying to put back the years to meet the bold challenge of another generation represented by the confident young Freddie Trueman.

For many the emergence from the pavilion of the slight figure of Headley, his maroon cap at a precarious and a jaunty angle, provided a nostalgic moment. Yet I firmly believe his fervent admirers did him a disservice by exposing him to the ordeal which faced him.

The mere fact that over £1,000 had been subscribed to bring him to Jamaica placed Headley in a peculiar position and long before the Test I sensed that George gladly would have ducked out of his responsibilities.

Even when George practised at the nets every stroke he made brought a roar of appreciation from his courtiers. The crowds who thronged to the practices by the M.C.C. and West Indies players were easily the largest I have seen anywhere; in fact, Hutton had to seek police help to control them.

25

Headley's performances scarcely justified his inclusion in the first Test, although West Indies found themselves short of Frank Worrell, the vice-captain who, along with Sonny Ramadhin, the off-spinner, until December had toured India in the Commonwealth side managed by George Duckworth, the old Lancashire and England wicketkeeper.

Fielding slip to Sam Loxton, the Australian from Victoria, who can hurl down a ball at lively pace, Worrell failed to take a catch cleanly. A finger was badly dislocated and Worrell reported to Kingston an injured player. In this accident in far-away India the Headley supporters saw a heaven-sent opportunity to get George into the Test side, even though there was no shortage of class batsmen in the West Indies—such as Denis Atkinson, of Barbados, and Bruce Pairaudeau of British Guiana.

George had played four innings against M.C.C. He captained the Country Districts XI in a two-day game on the lovely ground at Chedwin Park, Spanish Town, and twice failed.

In the first innings he made one and in the second 12. In Headley's heyday the feat of Alan Moss who bagged his wicket twice in only three balls would have been hailed as stupendous. Not only was George twice dismissed cheaply but he misjudged a rising ball off a good length from Trueman—it was not a bumper as some declared—and was hit on the arm.

The injury kept Headley out of the first colony match and in the second, at Melbourne Park, he succumbed to his new and powerful adversary, Trueman, by now known as "Mr. Bumper Man".

Trueman kept Headley quiet for five balls and with the sixth tempted him by a short-pitcher. Headley rose to the bait and a hook went sailing into the ever-safe hands of Ken Suttle at deep fine-leg. Headley (five) had failed again.

What appeared to be his final chance came in the second innings. On paper he triumphed with an undefeated 53. The facts were that he gave chances from successive balls when 28, and took as long as four hours to get the runs. Not until the last ball before tea did he complete his half century.

Thus in four innings his scores were: 1, 12, 5 and 53 not out. His fans pointed to his arm injury to excuse his third failure, but, to the impartial observer, he had done little to justify a Test comeback. In his two Tests innings he made 16 and one, and gave away a fair proportion of that aggregate in the field.

Undisguised threats were made to dig up the pitch and boycott the Test if Headley was omitted. Lest anyone should pour scorn on this point let me refer to the experiences of Perry Burke, one of the Test umpires.

Burke found himself in the unhappy position of having to give out J. K. Holt, junior, leg-before when he was only six short of what would have been a maiden Test century. J. K. Holt, senior, himself a former International cricketer, was in tears as his son John palpably misjudged a straight ball from Brian Statham to which he offered no stroke. Holt prepared to duck to what he thought was a bumper. It was not.

Sections of the crowd, however, allowed their disappointment to run away with their balance. They became insensed. They argued that even if Holt was leg-before he should not have been given out. The umpire's wife was immediately slapped in the face by an irate spectator shouting "Let's take it out of his wife."

Standing on a station platform the same evening Perry Burke was accosted first by a man with a knife and later by another brandishing a pistol. On the Monday one of his sons was beaten up by a crowd of boys when on his way home from school, while Burke's father, also a Test umpire, now employed on the wharves, was told by stevedores, "We have a good mind to throw you into the water."

In view of all these happenings no chances were taken against accidents of any nature between dusk and dawn and two sentries patrolled the pitch each night of the Test.

The Jamaican crowd is noisy, demonstrative, cheerful at times, and always excited. On the Saturday evening of the Test Willie Watson, in the outfield, saw the start of an argument between two over-heated spectators. After being knocked down one of the contestants drew a pistol.

Immediately there was room for 500 more people at that particular area of the ground!

Whether the Selectors took heed of the boycott threats I cannot say but Headley found himself in the Test primarily, I believe, as a defensive unit—a batsman capable of keeping his end up if things went wrong.

The reaction of the other islands was prompt and to the point. "For sheer vulgar insularity this latest effusion takes the cake and in future everyone must understand we in British Guiana do not intend to take treatment of this kind lying down," thundered a B.G. paper.

The *Trinidad Guardian*, in a front-page article, wrote:

"Even charity can find no justification for the inclusion of the aged George Headley. To be uncharitable one might suggest that Messrs. Jeff Stollmeyer, Frank Worrell and Noel Nethersole (the selectors) have been perhaps over-impressed by

the public following which Headley still enjoys. Certainly his
selection could not be justified by his public showing. Or possibly
that Jamaica is trying to recover its 4,800 dollars investment"
(a reference to the public subscription opened to bring Headley
from England).

I have always wondered how in islands scattered so widely
apart and often with a distinct culture of their own, the West
Indies managed to get together an International side. Now, having
been to the West Indies, I am no wiser.

At Jamaica I was told by a highly educated man that he had
travelled *abroad* many times. "I have been to England and France,"
he said, "and to Barbados and Trinidad." To him they were all
foreign countries.

The English Press on tour were always referred to in Jamaica
as the Foreign Press. That was fair enough, but the habit of addres-
sing fellow West Indies people from other islands as foreigners
mystified me.

Up to the second Test West Indies' teams were chosen by the
captain, vice-captain and the resident Selector of the colony. Thus,
on a corresponding arrangement, if Great Britain fielded a representative football team and played a match, say in Cardiff, the
captain and vice-captain appointed by the full Selection Committee
would be augmented by the Welsh representative; in Glasgow by
the Scottish representative and so on. Just imagine the comments
which would be made if five or six Welshmen played at Cardiff
or five or six Irishmen at Belfast!

The big advantage enjoyed by the West Indies was that most
of the eleven picked themselves. Stollmeyer, Gomez, Worrell,
Weekes, Walcott and the calypso twins, Ramadhin and Valentine,
formed the permanent base upon which every side was built.

After the first Test the full complement of selectorial wisdom
descended on the lovely island of Barbados and sent for 14 players
to be available for the second Test. The cost of transporting so
many selectors and players to Barbados made nonsense of the Board's
plea that they could not afford to send the same two umpires around
for all the Tests.

The standard of umpiring provided the subject of much discussion and naturally, as in all countries, some of it was good
and some not so good.

Certainly the M.C.C. never experienced anything similar to
Patsy Hendren, the former Middlesex and England favourite, on
the Barbados ground over twenty years before.

The story was told to me by Major Rupert Howard, who

managed the 1946–47 M.C.C. team to Australia, as we stood talking under the George Challenor stand on the Kensington Oval ground on the eve of the second Test.

On going out to bat Patsy noticed that the umpire at the bowler's end stood at least a yard wide of the wicket.

"Here, you can't give a proper decision from there, you know," said Patsy; "you must be over the wicket."

"Oh, no, Mr. Hendren," came the confident reply, "I always stand here. I shall be all right."

Within a few minutes the ball struck Patsy on the left leg about a foot outside the leg stump. To Patsy's amazement, the bowler appealed for leg-before.

To his greater consternation his umpire friend gave him out, and as Patsy passed him on the way to the pavilion the smiling official tapped him on the arm and said, "See what I mean?"

The second colony match in Jamaica was spoiled by some unhappy decisions.

For example Holt was given not out when 47—caught at the wicket—and went on to score 152.

So confident was Godfrey Evans that he had made a legitimate catch that, as soon as he completed it, he turned his back on the proceedings and began chatting to a slip fieldsman already slumping to the ground. From eighty yards away but immediately in line with the wicket I heard an unmistakable click.

The umpire's decision dumbfounded the team and a young member of the team threw his cap on the ground in baffled annoyance.

Demonstrations of any kind are inexcusable on the cricket field. No matter how outrageous it might seem the decision of the umpire must be accepted without sign of outward disapproval.

I can, however, appreciate the mood of the fielders and bowlers, toiling on a beautiful wicket and under a scorching sun, when such a thing happens.

Already confidence had been sapped with other decisions and there had been the incident of the leaking covers at Melbourne Park.

After Jamaica had been dismissed for 187, M.C.C. looked forward to gaining a substantial lead on the same type of wicket the next day. Instead, they had to bat on a pitch just right for an off-spinner at one end. The tarpaulin covers had leaked at a spot length for an off-spinner.

A large wet patch could be seen there, but fortunately for M.C.C. the twenty-year-old Scarlett did not utilize it as well as Jim Laker would have done with his wider experience of field placings.

Scarlett, it is true, frequently found one or other of the edges of the bats of Laker, the night-watchman, Peter May and Denis Compton. Many streaky strokes went down to fine-leg, but Scarlett preferred to retain his close-set fielders in front of instead of square to and behind the wicket on the leg side. M.C.C. toiled all that Saturday but the crowd did not appreciate the sore handicap under which their batsmen were labouring.

I thought M.C.C. undeniably experienced the worst of the deal at Melbourne Park, but there could be few complaints about the umpiring in the first Test, at Sabina Park. A considerable amount of comment came from the first innings leg-before decisions against Compton and Graveney and that against Hutton in the second knock. All played forward.

In England, where the ball turns sharper, umpires are reluctant to give a batsman leg-before if, as he stretches forward, the ball hits the front leg. Yet, on the hard West Indies wickets where the turn is less appreciable, conceivably the ball would have carried on and hit the stumps. I think this is a point we must be prepared to concede.

One mistake probably was made—the important one of May being given out caught behind to Kentish, bowling leg theory, in the vital-for-both-sides pre-lunch period on the last day when the Test remained in the balance.

Instead of hitting the bat, the ball apparently snicked May's pad. Peter is too good a sportsman to pass comment but others in a sound position to judge were satisfied that the ball hit the pad and not bat.

Still, I sympathize fully with an umpire called upon to make one of the most difficult of all decisions—a catch on the leg side off a fast bowler. He hears a snick and sees the ball deflected on its course and is quite convinced the appeal is a good one. If he is wrong— well, it's just too bad. The last person to be blamed should be the umpire.

The behaviour of some of the younger members of the M.C.C. team received local criticism in Jamaica. One bowler frequently scowled and muttered at the batsman, and passed adverse comments on the fielding and catching ability of his team-mates.

Much of it was taken in good part and accepted as the excessive zeal and impetuosity of youth. Naturally opposing batsman were less inclined to take such an indulgent view.

Another bowler appealed with such frightening vigour that many felt he threatened to become too belligerent. In any case the members could not be rudely disturbed during their afternoon siestas by loud and persistent shouts. So the two young offenders were given some friendly but pointed advice by manager Charles

Palmer in his best ex-schoolmaster manner. They were told to eliminate all gesticulations which might cause offence.

All the occasions for complaint were not one-sided. Two off-the-field incidents left M.C.C. players hot with indignation. Denis Compton took two guests of Hutton into the pavilion because of the unavoidable absence of the England captain.

The tickets bore the customary words "not transferable" and Compton, who was merely acting as temporary host for his skipper, suffered the embarrassing experience of being shouted at and the tickets being torn into shreds in front of his face by an official who did not wait for an explanation.

Again, a gateman refused Hutton permission to take two guests into Melbourne Park, where the second colony match was played. That the captain of England should be subjected to such a humiliation was a disgrace and it would be idle to pretend differences did not exist.

Fortunately there was still much to laugh about. In full view of the crowd at the first colony match a white-helmeted policeman chased a man up a tree just inside the ground. Up and up they climbed until the pursued was in the topmost branches. The policeman then took a swish with his cane which persuaded his quarry of the disadvantages of his position. He came slowly down, literally into the arms of the Law.

There was the "McCat" dance, named after Clifford McWatt, the British Guiana wicketkeeper and left-handed batsman who had five "lives" in his first innings against England. He was promptly re-christened McCat, for fairly obvious reasons.

In the dance the male shuffles forward and, in the manner of a batsman, stoops and shapes as if about to receive a ball.

The next movement is an imaginary square-cut—McWatt's favourite stroke—and his partner shuffles in the direction of the hit and leaps with her hands and arms raised to take a catch.

Needless to add, she drops the chance and then goes through movements indicating acute anguish which might well have been copied from the English fieldsmen.

Clifford, aged thirty, a paymaster, served in England with the R.A.F. during the war, and was a more than useful member of the West Indies side.

I dread to think what would happen if the solemnity of Lord's was disturbed by the letting off of firecrackers every time a batsman hit a boundary.

Yet that happened regularly at Sabina Park until the patience of the bowlers became exhausted, and they appealed for the practice to stop. The din strained the nervous system, particularly when a stroke of especial brilliance was celebrated with the firing of two crackers! And there were a lot of good shots from both sides.

About 12,000 spectators could be accommodated inside Sabina Park and a few more hundreds perched in the tops of the surrounding swaying palm and coconut trees. A roaring trade was done also by the occupants of a house overlooking the ground.

Their balcony was as jam-packed as any London Underground train during the rush hours. The overflow, itself amounting to two or three hundred, found space on the corrugated iron roof. It was estimated that the takings would just about enable the owner to pay for the repairs to his roof!

The coconut-tree population in the West Indies reminded me of the M.C.C.'s one-day match at Colombo en route to Australia in 1950. An enterprising man charged half a rupee—half the admission price to the ground—for the right to climb his ladder into the trees from which could be obtained a clear, if high-altitude, view of the game.

His customers had not reckoned on being asked for another half rupee to be allowed the privilege of descending the ladder and returning to *terra firma*!

Dominating the background of Sabina Park were the Blue Mountains, their peaks crowned with wisps of cloud, while hovering overhead all the time were huge black John Crows, a species of vulture.

To kill one of these ghastly looking birds of prey is an offence punishable by law. As scavengers they are regarded as invaluable for clearing away rotting carcasses of other birds and animals.

Tony Lock and Freddie Trueman saw one John Crow begin a meal on a dead dog. That was enough to curb even their high spirits for the remainder of the day.

Jamaica is an island of barking dogs who caused members of the M.C.C. team to lose many hours of sleep. I have never had the misfortune to listen to so many dogs barking at once. They started about 10 p.m. and kept up the cacophony until dawn when the cockerels took over!

M.C.C. players at the time thought the Jamaicans had trained their dogs and fowls in the best interests of Jamaican and West Indies cricket. They recalled the legend of the factories overlooking the Bramall Lane cricket ground at Sheffield where the chimneys are said to be stoked up specially high when visiting teams go in to bat against Yorkshire.

Hospitality by Jamaicans and English families in residence on the island was overwhelming and the Cricket Association arranged, for both West Indies and English players, a wonderful Sunday tour by car to Tower Isle, one of the luxury hotels on the north coast.

At lunch a cake was cut and a calypso sung in honour of the M.C.C. team. The calypso, of five verses and a chorus, went like this: .

> Here's a thing that is known universally,
> Cricket is a game that must go on in history,
> And a thing that will live in our memory
> It's the visit of the English Test Team to show supremacy.

> *Chorus :* We welcome you here to Jamaica
> The land of rum, sunshine and water
> Where all the folks greet you with a smile
> When you are staying at Tower Isle.

> They played a match against Jamaica
> And beat them off with great honour
> Now they are waiting patiently
> To show West Indies supremacy.

> *Chorus :* We welcome you, etc.

> Willie Watson a real fine man
> Made a brilliant one sixty one
> The thing that's brilliant about his score
> He hit two sixes and seventeen fours.

> *Chorus—*

> Lennie Hutton that English skipper
> He's known throughout the world as a real good cricketer
> His determination with the M.C.C.
> Is to lead them always to victory.

> *Chorus—*

> Gentlemen all let me say these words to you
> And hope that the wishes of the West Indies will come through
> While we are under the flag red, white and blue
> Be loving, be kind, be honest and be true.

> *Chorus—*

From Tower Isle the party motored for tea to Shaw Park, another romantic spot 500 feet above Ocho Rios Bay.

The view here is almost out of this world. In its different way, the only sight comparable in my various travels was the Victoria Falls in Southern Rhodesia.

CHAPTER THREE

ENGLAND'S defeat in the first Test was complete, decisive
and shattering, all the more disappointing considering the rich
promise shown in the preparatory matches, which were notable
for the quick and smooth adjustment the majority of the players
made to the new conditions.

To send a cricketer overseas for the first time is always in the
nature of a gamble. English players, for example, find that in
hotter climes the ball travels faster through the clearer air than at
home. To meet the new situation they must sharpen their reactions
and movements. Some never settle down to the change.

A number of celebrated batsmen, able to make a profusion of
runs on the slower turning wickets of England and expected to
amass stacks of runs on some of the batting paradises abroad, have
been utter failures.

The early days of a tour always bring extra anxiety for a captain
and Hutton, who had been to Jamaica with Yorkshire in 1936, and
joined G. O. Allen's team in the West Indies in 1948, was full of
advice for the younger players.

Optimistic he may have been in England, and in public, but,
pointing to the scorching West Indies sun one day, he told his men,
"That fellow up there shining all day is the best bowler out here."

Hutton meant that the fierce tropical sun was likely to tire out a
batsman just as quickly as could a bowler. On this account I think
future touring teams from England should be provided with a
wider, better-fitting cap, something on the Australian style.

Scarcely once did an English fieldsman chase the ball without
his cap falling off. The same thing happened in the first two
post-war tours of Australia, and again in South Africa in
1948–49.

Hutton, dissatisfied with the present style, appeared at Antigua
with a cap of his own design, specially made at Bradford. He told
me it afforded him more protection from the sun and was distinctly
cooler.

34

This may seem an irrelevant point but, even though a player might not be accustomed to wearing one at home, to go capless in the West Indies is courting trouble unnecessarily.

At Sabina Park, Jamaica, the dipping sun after tea added to the difficulties of fielders at one end. For a vital second they might lose sight of the leather against the eye-searing ball of fire in the sky. On the Saturday of the first Test, for instance, when England lost their hard-won advantage in a disastrous hour after tea, the first of five chances given by McWatt would normally have meant a simple catch to old-fashioned point.

Clifford, attempting to kill a Trueman bumper, cocked up the ball but, in the glare of the setting sun, Watson lost it. A golden chance had gone begging. That was the beginning of England's decline—and subsequent fall.

To counter the weariness caused by the heat each player was issued with two salt tablets a day. Peter May, during his century innings at Melbourne Park, suffered from cramp in his hand brought about by gripping the bat tightly, and physical tiredness alone cost Watson his wicket just before the close of play on the fifth day of the first Test.

A few minutes earlier this highly trained athlete had asked Peter May, his partner, to take the bowling and not run as he himself was "all in". Peter then hit a long ball into the outfield, and they just had to take three runs. Willie, exhausted, was out next ball.

Watson enjoyed the distinction of making the maiden century of the tour, in the first colony match, and as a makeshift opener he settled down to his job with remarkable assurance.

Few players are equipped with such calm temperament and approach for the big occasion as the softly spoken Watson, whose father and brother were also professional footballers but, unlike him, not first-class cricketers as well. Watson moves with such an easy grace in the field that his pace is misleading. At first he appears to be travelling no faster than at a comfortable trot, but those who have tried to keep abreast with him know different.

Should Watson make the next tour to Australia, he intends to finish his Soccer career, which, as his future clearly lies in cricket, is a sensible decision.

For a long time Watson felt his chances of developing were retarded by batting at number five or six where usually he faced one of two tasks—to pull the side round with defence after a bad start, or improve on a good position with fast scoring.

All the great batsmen have occupied a position in the first four in the order where they can settle down immediately to play their own game and building, or trying to build, the foundation stones of the innings.

In his early days for Yorkshire Watson often lost his wicket in the 20's or 30's. Thinking over his cricket, as Willie always does, he decided his defence needed tightening. The only place to do that was in the middle.

So, for three years, he concentrated on improving his defence and he rarely allowed himself the luxury of attacking strokes. Finally he was satisfied that he could keep the ball out of his wicket as well as most top-class batsmen. From that moment he began to use his strokes freely again. And he has plenty, as the West Indies bowlers and crowds soon discovered.

The massacre of Valentine by Watson and Graveney in the first colony match was one of the most violent I have ever seen against a bowler who began the series needing only seven wickets to become the youngest to take 100 Test wickets. In three overs Valentine was clouted for 37 runs, including three gigantic sixes, two by Graveney and the other by Watson, whose mighty hit cleared the sightscreen and a wall ten yards behind that and some ten feet higher. The ball sailed high out of the ground.

While this assault was taking place, on Hutton's orders, Ramadhin, the other member of the famous West Indies spinning combination, sat disconsolate and perhaps fearful. Denis Compton put his arm round Ramadhin's shoulder and jocularly said: "There, Sonny, take a look. The shape of things to come." Denis could have kicked himself as soon as he said it. Slightly superstitious by nature, he realized he was tempting the fates. He was.

Valentine, with figures of 0—99 and a sore finger, retired to the outfield to think over things and no doubt he wished at that precise moment that he was nearer Walsall, for whom he plays in the Birmingham League, than Kingston, Jamaica.

He who laughs last is said to laugh longest and the laugh which Valentine and Ramadhin enjoyed as English wickets crashed to their spin and flight in the first innings of the Test must have been both long and loud.

The question is asked again and again, Why should Valentine be hammered with almost contemptuous ease in one game and yet sweep through the same opposition in the next, on a pitch just as hard and true?

The answer, I am sure, lies in that one was a colony match and the other a Test. Is not that one of the major obsessions of cricket?

To see so many English cricketers in action a Test might be defined as an encounter where all thoughts of enjoyment for players and spectators is cast aside; where all ideas of striking the ball with purpose are eschewed; where the occasion is made a grinding bore and the elementary fact that cricket was invented as a pastime and a game is forgotten.

To many groundsmen, with Mr. Bert Lock, of Kennington Oval, a shining exception, a Test affords the opportunity to make a bowler want to commit suicide; to legislators it is essentially the opportunity to bring in the cash.

The brilliant display of Tom Graveney in the colony match raised hopes that he would justify on the tour all the promise he had shown. Surely, with his ability, he should make large numbers of runs consistently. I think he will do so when he learns to concentrate naturally. At the slant of his career his lapses in concentration were too free and often. Then followed a period when he strained too hard, and as yet he has still not attained a happy medium.

A natural games-player, he strikes the ball superbly with a high-sweeping back lift, and among English cricketers he is the outstanding golfer.

In Tom's apprenticeship years he was advised by Andy Wilson, the Gloucestershire wicketkeeper and county coach, to put away his golf clubs, in order to help his back play at cricket.

For two years Tom did do so, which was a big sacrifice for a lad so keen on both that, when leaving school, he could have taken up golf professionally.

Yet there are times when I think the best advice which could be given to Tom would be to put golf in the background again for the next few years or so. For him these are still important and formulative years.

To get to the top is hard enough, but to stay there is harder still. The demands upon the top-class cricketer are many-sided and heavy.

Golf is a wonderful and pleasant relaxation, but one which should never be allowed to interfere with a professional cricketer's career. I am not suggesting that it does in Tom's case, but I often wonder whether he is not too good a golfer. . . .

D. R. Jardine, who captained England in Australia in 1932–33, commandeered the clubs of the then-junior member of the party—Freddie Brown, a future England captain.

During the West Indies tour Graveney sent a birthday cable to the Henleaze, Bristol, home of Mr. Sid Brookman, his eighty-year-old father-in-law, telling him to keep his pads clean. This was no joke.

Mr. Brookman still plays for Bristol Schoolmasters and the Wanderers and is insulted if anyone suggests he might require someone to run his runs for him. He fields at mid-off and has saved, and helped to win, a number of matches. He even goes on tour with the two teams, and remains a fine figure of a man who has always looked after himself.

On entering big cricket, Graveney, like Watson, had to tighten his defence. He received plenty of advice and coaching at the county nets but he found he learned most at the winter indoor school, where his duty was to try and teach young boys how to bat correctly. In helping others, he helped himself more than he ever realized at the time.

Graveney is one in whom England places her trust for the future. Another is Peter May, ex-Cambridge University and Surrey. Like Alec and Eric Bedser, Tom Dollery, Percy Chapman and Harold Wolton, Peter hails from Berkshire, the county which provided the 1953 champions of the Minor Counties.

For two brothers to be in separate county championship teams in the same season as were Peter May for Surrey and his brother for Berkshire probably constitutes yet another cricket record. More than once they have scored centuries on the same day.

If all goes well May is likely to be captain of England within the next few years—Trevor Bailey looks to be Hutton's natural successor, with Peter following Trevor into the vice-captaincy.

At the beginning of the West Indies tour Peter revealed a weakness on the leg stump—trying to turn the ball square instead of pushing it in the direction of mid-on. Hutton advised him, among others, to take guard outside the leg stump.

Apart from anything else, Hutton thinks this could have a psychological effect on umpires.

In time Peter May will probably become more and more an on-side player because he has rather large feet. He is, therefore, rather slower in movement than the best off-side batsmen.

This is no idle theory. Most of the best off-side batsmen have small feet. Bradman's boots, which can be seen in the Imperial Cricket Museum, were only size 7. Hammond used $8\frac{1}{2}$—and he was a very big man—and Hutton 8.

Of the young bowlers by far the most impressive were Brian Statham, who became known as "Greyhound" or "Whippet" because of his leanness and his long stride, and Tony Lock. Hutton was also very pleased with the way Alan Moss (Amos the Prophet or "Quito"—a Mosquito) gave of his best at every situation. The man who, whether successful or not, tries his hardest from first to last ball, makes a captain's job much easier. Such men go down in the records as "good tourists".

At the first practice in Jamaica the old Glamorgan and Sussex bowler Jack Mercer, one of the grandest raconteurs in the game, who now divides his time between coaching Northamptonshire cricketers in the summer and Jamaican players in the winter, predicted that Statham would be the best of the fast bowlers.

Among other things Jack noticed that Statham touched down lightly with his front foot and ran a long way in his follow through. The experienced Mercer declared that Brian was less liable to strain himself on the concrete hard pitches of the West Indies than those who landed heavily and followed through only a few steps.

Brian learned the hard way—on the heartbreaking pitches of India. He knew that in the West Indies his main hope was to bowl straight and maintain a length.

Without those two qualities, which are elementary enough but doubly important in the Caribbean, a bowler stands no chance to prosper.

The West Indies batsmen are eagle-eyed, quick-footed and, trusting the pitch implicitly, love to attack the bowling. They usually grip the bat low down and are brilliant cutters and hookers, and when driving do not bother to get to the pitch of the ball—it is not necessary as in England.

In 1951 Brian and his Lancashire colleague, Roy Tattersall, were flown out to Australia. They began on the 100 degrees plus heat of Renmark (South Australia), coming straight from the depths of an English winter. Statham found he could scarcely breathe.

Next winter, 1951–52, Brian and Fred Ridgway, of Kent, bowled their hearts out in India but never had a chance against the Indians in England the following summer, when Fred Trueman used the wet and flying pitches to establish his reputation with 29 wickets in the series.

Statham has not been given many Test opportunities at home, and after he had bowled out Hutton in the opening overs of his first Whitsun Roses match the England captain was set a poser by his seven-year-old son John.

"Why," asked John of his father, "isn't Statham in the England team? He bowled you out, didn't he, Daddie?"

As the precious shine lasts little more than three overs in the West Indies, to waste the opportunities which comes every 65 overs by failing to make the batsman play at every ball is a cardinal sin.

The essence of the new ball attack anywhere in the world must be to keep it up to the bat, but nowhere is this more essential than in the West Indies. If the ball moves in flight it has a fair chance of finding the edge of the bat.

Without the devastating speed of Trueman, Statham and Moss

made the batsmen play at more balls. Moss, one of the four pace men in the first Test, did not have the privilege of using the new ball.

By the time he went on he could not even read the maker's name on it and, in assessing his performance, this should not be overlooked.

In Jamaica Moss impressed others besides Hutton. Not because Moss dismissed him twice in the Combined Parishes game, but by his sustained aggression in the nets he also attracted the attention of George Headley.

At the moment of delivery Moss bends back his body in a bow-like arch. This habit was responsible for his making anything but an auspicious start to the tour. After dropping a slip catch off Michael Frederick from Trueman's second ball of the match Alan crashed to the ground with a nasty thump as he went to bowl his first ball.

Another young pace bowler who has taken Len Hutton's eye is Peter Loader, of Surrey. Frank Worrell came from India full of praise for Loader who, said Worrell, was the best bowler on the Commonwealth side.

With Statham, Moss and Lock showing up well and Trevor Bailey soon appraising the new conditions and playing on the temperamental weakness of the West Indies batsmen in their dislike of being tied down for any length of time Hutton, in those early days, had every chance to view the prospects of his attack with confidence.

Against the name of Freddie Trueman remained the biggest question mark. Few can doubt that a great future could lie ahead for Trueman if he could harness accuracy to his speed. He is strong and built on the lines of a battleship. His shoulders are wide and powerful like those of Lindwall and Miller and the West Indies pair, Esmond Kentish and Frank King.

Unhappily at times in the two-day game at Innswood and in the first innings of the opening colony match, at Sabina Park, his direction was anywhere but near the stumps. Moreover, his bumper was too wasteful and expensive to be considered anything but in the nature of a gift to the batsman. He bowled it so often that this legitimate weapon of the fast bowler lost its surprise.

In the second innings Trueman suddenly found a length and with the pitch still retaining its pace—one of the factors which deceived England into playing four pace men in the Test—he and Statham skittled out Jamaica. As a result M.C.C. gained an impressive victory by an innings.

Some knowledgeable West Indies folk said that Trueman's speed had not been seen at Sabina Park since the halcyon days c

"Manny" Martindale. He had won a new reputation overnight, and Hutton had gained a notable tactical triumph.

On winning the toss Hutton had sent in Jamaica. His reasons for this seemingly surprising move were, one, that if anything might be extracted from the pitch it would be in the first hour or so, and two, that if M.C.C. batted first and made a large total Jamaica would be left with no alternative but to play for a draw.

This would keep the M.C.C. side in the field for some gruelling days. As it happened, the pitch gave bowlers little help at the start but in the end everything went right for Hutton and his men.

At first Trueman's bumpers were received with angry booing, but the crowd soon realized these short balls carried the minimum of danger to the batsman's person and, in fact, provided a fruitful source of run-getting and their reaction was less vigorous. · A Kingston pantomime carried this typical rhyme to the tune of "What shall we do with the drunken sailor?":

> What shall we do with Freddie Trueman,
> What shall we do with Freddie Trueman,
> Freddie's bowling bumpers.

> *Chorus :* Heads down, for up she rises,
>   Heads down, for up she rises,
>   He's still bowling bumpers.

> Four hundred odd the scoreboard rises
> Four hundred odd the scoreboard rises
> And he's still bowling bumpers.

> Ram and Val have some fine surprises
> M.C.C. gwine open their eyeses
> M.C.C. gwine open their eyeses
> Early in the morning.

Though it may have been a joke for pantomime audiences, the fact that Goodridge, one of the Jamaican fast bowlers, sent down four bumpers in one over, which must have been perilously close to offending the law of persistency, had not passed unnoticed.

I imagine there were many who feared a "bumping war" to be on hand. Jeff Stollmeyer, the West Indies captain, arranged a meeting with Len Hutton and manager Charles Palmer ostensibly to talk about such laws as covering the pitch, mowing the outfield and other technicalities.

The West Indies preferred to have the option of taking the new ball after 200 runs instead of 65 overs. Apparently Mr. Billy Griffith, the assistant secretary of M.C.C., and Mr. Cyril Merry, secretary of the West Indies Board of Control, had discussed the matter and agreed on 65 overs, but never put it in writing. The West Indies conceded the points.

Then, after hours of discussion and when the meeting was about to break up, Stollmeyer introduced the delicate subject of bumpers. I gather he would have liked the number employed in any one over to be restricted to one, and when the last Test arrived the issue was left in the hands of the umpires, who decided to permit two an over.

Meanwhile, Stollmeyer ran into other difficulties. Two pre-Test practice matches were played by the West Indies Test players against local opposition.

In the second Frank King, the fast bowler, hurt his back, which meant that the team would be short of one of the two best batsmen, Worrell, and their fastest bowler, King. Neither was fit to play.

A deputy for King was ready-made in the person of Esmond Kentish, thirty-six-year-old Government clerk, who had played against England in the corresponding Test of 1948. Stripped, Esmond has back muscles which would make a physical culture expert's eyes shine with appreciation. In the two colony matches he bowled steadily and intelligently without suggesting he would be destined to play a leading role in one of the worst collapses in living memory.

Michael Frederick, chosen as an opening partner to Stollmeyer, must have created a record by playing in eight consecutive innings against England and M.C.C. He began in the Combined Parishes match, continued in the two colony fixtures, and finished with two innings in the Test, and finally, at the end of the tour, captained the Montego Bay Eleven against the M.C.C. and was told to stand by for the fifth Test.

When the M.C.C. played their first game outside Jamaica in the Leeward Islands something seemed wrong when the familiar figure of Frederick did not emerge from the pavilion and walk to the crease to take first ball. Whether the M.C.C. grew more tired of Frederick than he did of them is a moot point, but it was inevitable each should become a little weary of the other.

Frederick has English associations—he married a Derbyshire girl and played with no little distinction for Derbyshire during a business course in England—but eight innings in a row . . . !

An engineer on a sugar plantation Frederick, during those eight successive appearances, won his way from playing in a two-day match to a place in the Test side.

In the first game he presented Alan Moss, who had little right to be in the slips anyway, with a reasonable catch. Alan missed it.

Instead of being out for a duck, Frederick went on to 84—and none could complain he did not play a very fair innings. In the second knock he scored 40. He was chosen for Jamaica, for whom he hit 60 in the first innings. When he had made only five, however, he should have been caught by Trevor Bailey in the slips.

In his next three innings against M.C.C. Frederick made 10, 58 and 30 and he was in the Test side.

I am sure he owed much to the inability of the M.C.C. players to hold their catches close to the wicket. Early on the fieldsmen took up English positions and, with the ball travelling faster through the air, they were a split second late in their judgment.

The weakness of the team in fastening on to catches was a shock and a source of worry to Hutton. Even Tony Lock, who, in England, must rank as one of the best in the world, was as culpable as the rest.

One of the features of the first Jamaican match was the sparkling stroke-play of Ken Rickards who, like Headley, had been brought by public subscription from England where he plays for a Lancashire League club. On this form he was an obvious candidate for the Tests, but he slumped badly in the second colony game, and such inconsistency hardly merited his gaining a place.

Ever since the startling success of Statham and Trueman in the second innings of the first Jamaican fixture the four M.C.C. team selectors, Hutton, Palmer, Bailey and Compton, had flirted with the idea of utilizing what was thought to be the certain pace of the pitch by playing all four fast bowlers—Trueman, Statham, Moss and Bailey.

Such a gamble on speed meant two things—the omission of Laker and a dangerously long tail. Laker is an off-spinner who can take the utmost advantage of a turning pitch and a batsman who began the series with the very useful Test average of nearly 30.

In 1948 Laker was by far England's most successful bowler in the West Indies where in four Tests he created a record by taking 18 wickets, more than any other English bowler on a tour of the Caribbean.

Laker, the ex-bank clerk who was born in Bradford and after the war went to Surrey on the recommendation of the Army, has a knack of producing better batting form for England than for his county. Invariably, too, his scores have been worth many more than their paper value.

Moreover, Laker had not been on the losing side for England in the eleven Tests in which he had appeared since the disastrous defeat from Australia at Leeds in July 1948.

In retrospect, to play four pace men and weaken the already

slender batting resources after the Big Five of Hutton, Watson, May, Compton and Graveney was a big mistake.

True, Bailey had already given a further example of his monumental patience by taking 230 minutes to make 78 against the bowling of sugar-plantation employees at Chedwin Park, Innswood —on such occasions his team-mates refer to him as "Thunder-Bat".

After him, however, little could be expected from the soft and fleshy middle and tail batting. Evans was palpably out of form and troubled by a cyst just below his left shoulder, which had to be removed as soon as the Test was over.

In his two innings in Jamaica he had been out for ducks, which was enough to challenge even the happy Evans' philosophy.

Tony Lock, permanent holder of the number eleven position for Surrey, found himself elevated to number eight for England, with Statham, Trueman and Moss below him.

Perhaps Hutton banked on winning the toss—he had lost it five times in a row to Lindsay Hassett, Australia's captain, in 1953—batting first, and making a total sufficient at least to be an insurance against losing the match.

What would have happened had England won the toss and batted first is pure conjecture but, in spite of the extraordinary and inexplicable collapse which followed the West Indies opening score, I think England would have made a solid total.

The pitch was never as fast as during the colony game. Shorn of grass, it shone like the polished floor of a house-proud wife—the apple of the eye of the groundsman and of his barefooted staff.

As he stood at the crease, the batsman's reflection could clearly be seen on the pitch.

In the now-familiar pattern of Test cricket, the West Indies proceeded with correctness and circumspection to consolidate their advantage in batting first. They started anything but well. Frederick mistimed an intended hook off Statham, and was neatly caught by Graveney running from slip to fine-leg. Frederick thus ended his maiden Test venture with a duck. Many others, Hutton among them, appreciated his feelings.

Only Stollmeyer, still a fine upstanding player and one of the best in the world on the leg—was that why so many balls were bowled to him on that side?—followed Frederick back to the pavilion that first day which produced 168 runs and a position of stalemate.

Next morning the game flared into life. John K. Holt, junior—his father, with the same initials, played first-class cricket for Jamaica a decade before him—swayed in front of a straight ball from Statham and was leg-before. By a mere margin of six runs he missed joining the select band of cricketers who have scored a century on their first Test appearance.

Weekes, the "Caribbean butcher" who so often carves up the best bowling, was tied down by Tony Lock and, as so often happens, Tony paved the way for another to get the wicket.

In frustration Weekes tried to cut Alan Moss from the off stump and was bowled, a good wicket for Alan to claim as his first in Test cricket. Alan opened his account in the first-class game by dismissing the celebrated Cyril Washbrook himself, a success which must have given justifiable pleasure to E. M. Wellings, the cricket writer of the London *Evening News*, whose newspaper inaugurated a coaching scheme in which Alan was discovered among many other promising youngsters.

The departure of Holt left Headley to play out some dangerous few overs before lunch and none of the excited crowd could have been prepared for the sight of the English fieldsmen retiring to deep positions and Statham bowling a slow dolly down the leg stump, which "King George" gratefully pushed for a score-opening single.

At an England team conference the suggestion was approved and planned for Headley, in affectionate recognition of his past record and performances, to be presented with a single to get off the mark. Unfortunately in the almost barefisted business which followed, the significance of this sentimental gesture tended to be forgotten—particularly by the writer in the *Daily Gleaner* who *demanded* (his italics not mine) that English cricketers should play the game. What evidence he had to suggest they were other than sportsmen still escapes me.

By tea-time on the second day England's interest in the game was very much alive. The West Indies, 331 for six, had to face the new ball at once and a total in the region of 380—not gigantic by Caribbean pitch standards—could be envisaged with some reason and expectation.

To England's dismay the next boisterous, crazy and incredible hour, in which McWatt and Gomez added 60, lifted the West Indies into a commanding position.

If ever a team had to endure a hour of bitter torment the England eleven did in that hour.

If ever a captain had to suffer a nightmarish frustration of seeing a situation fast slipping out of control Len Hutton did. If ever two young bowlers went through a heartbreaking experience Brian Statham and Freddie Trueman did.

Not unnaturally the crowd reached a fever-heat of excitement as snicked hits sailed for four, catches were dropped, and as runs came in rich and unchecked profusion.

From England's viewpoint the simple tragedy lay in that Trueman and Statham bowled exceedingly well, but, in all, five catches, each presented by wicketkeeper Clifford McWatt, were missed.

When 14 McWatt stretched tip-toe, with the bat protecting his nose, as he tried to get on top of a bouncer from Trueman. The ball went off the splice of the bat in a gentle arc but, as I said before, Willie Watson, fielding in the gulley, lost it in the sun and seemed to be frozen into a state of immobility.

Had Watson not been blinded by the sun he scarcely could have missed the simplest of catches.

McWatt square cut the next delivery with shattering force through Watson's hands, the ball leaving the bat with the speed of a bullet from a gun.

The next three chances given by McWatt were offered at the other end where the fieldsmen could not complain of confusion caused by the searing rays of the sun, which at that end was behind them. Of the three chances Hutton's was the most comfortable to take but it went to his left side where, because of his shortened arm and restricted movement, he is handicapped a little in the field.

Had Trueman or Bailey caught either of the other two they would have done extremely well.

Hutton came in for criticism for allowing the McWatt-Gomez stand to bloom and prosper. A change of bowling, introducing the spinners, might have done the trick.

Yet the mind of Hutton, which has bred the most perfect batting technique in the world, could not believe that such a transgression of all the laws of batsmanship could continue indefinitely.

As it happened it went on long enough for the razor-edge balance of the match to tilt definitely in favour of the West Indies. Hutton's major mistake was in not plugging the hole through which went McWatt's favourite square slash. Hutton's failure to close the gap cost many runs.

Gerry Gomez, a notoriously bad starter, had one unforgettable over from Statham. Two boundaries to the sightscreen—behind the wicketkeeper—gave him eight runs and a third four was disputed by both Hutton and Compton. Compton, though impeded by a boy selling peanuts—inside the wire fences surrounding the boundary—stopped the ball with his foot and threw in while the batsmen were completing their second run. The square-leg umpire, however, immediately informed his colleague to signal a four.

Compton complained that the ball had not crossed the line, but the umpire remained adamant on the point. Denis looked upon the umpire's unwillingness to change his decision as a slur on his own honesty, and was upset.

What remained of the West Indies innings was mopped up with efficiency on the third morning, and England began the task of chasing a score of 417 without undue pessimism.

The wicket was good, the outfield fast and, in spite of the shock of Watson leaving to a straight ball from Gomez, lunch was enjoyed in a peaceful frame of mind. Tea was a less pleasant interval.

The afternoon of the Great Collapse began when Hutton dragged a Valentine ball well wide of his off stump on to his wicket. Compton was leg-before stretching forward, as was Graveney to Ramadhin at the other end, May gave a simple catch off a long hop and, although Bailey, as usual, propped up one end, the slide went on unchecked.

Once again England had failed dismally to class slow bowling. Without being able to turn the ball very much, by flight and variance of pace Valentine and the dapper little East Indian, Sonny Ramadhin, had deceived and beaten leaden-footed English batsmen.

On such a pitch a total of 170 represented ghastly failure, for which neither excuse nor explanation could be accepted.

Then came a surprise. Even though England were 208 behind Jeffrey Stollmeyer did not enforce the follow-on. When he went into the England dressing-room to break the news that West Indies would bat again a discreet silence greeted his announcement, but as soon as the door closed behind him a cheer of relief went up. At least England had gained some breathing space to reorganize her shattered and demoralized force. The English players thought Stollmeyer had blundered and they were confident of their chances of at least saving the game.

Time became a factor, and Stollmeyer, who was booed by large sections of the crowd both when he went in to bat and when he returned to the pavilion, knew the risk he was taking. In fact, he could have received no more forceful reminder than by the leg-theory tactics employed against him at the start of the innings. Success brings its responsibilities.

The captain's lot, like that of the policeman, is not always happy. He has to stand or fall by his decision. Rarely does he enjoy any credit for successful strategy but he gets plenty of blame when he is wrong. Stollmeyer did not breathe freely until the last English wicket fell.

Jeffrey shared a room with Michael Frederick in the South Camp Road Hotel, Kingston, and most of the night preceding the last day of the Test Frederick was troubled by a cough. At breakfast he apologized to his captain for having disturbed his night's rest.

"That's all right," replied Stollmeyer, "with the game in such a position as it is, I shouldn't have slept a wink anyway."

In making the decision Stollmeyer had the support of his team. Three main reasons prompted him to bat again. They were:

(1) He was afraid of the possibility of West Indies having to make 200 or so on a turning wicket in the fourth innings and having to face Tony Lock, for whom he had the greatest respect.

(2) He could not persuade himself to believe that England possibly could bat so badly in the second innings.

(3) Sonny Ramadhin was worried by a sore spinning finger and, without rest, might not be so effective.

Had Hutton been in Stollmeyer's position I doubt whether he would have been as cautious. Hutton is naturally a careful man in everything but he reckons that a team enforcing a follow-on has a definite psychological advantage.

The attitude of the Jamaican public to Stollmeyer was one of surprised hostility. They saw England in full flight and wanted to continue the chase so as to make the kill swift and certain. So small was the attendance that they virtually boycotted the last day.

On the final morning four women went through the entrance gate dressed in severe and unrelieved black. In explanation they said, "We are in mourning for West Indian cricket killed by Jeff Stollmeyer." Several hours later West Indian cricket looked a healthy enough corpse and certainly much more alive than the man who died on return from his annual holiday.

A friend arrived to console the widow.

"Would you like to see poor Tom?" he was asked.

He said he would. After gazing reverently at his friend's lifeless body and searching desperately for some words of comfort, he remarked, "Isn't he brown?"

"Yes," answered the widow, "his holiday did him good!"

Stollmeyer's worst moments must have occurred during the opening partnership of 130 by Hutton and Watson and the second-wicket stand of 90 by Watson and May.

Just before the close of the fifth evening Stollmeyer, apparently in desperation, went on himself—to the accompaniment of the now-customary cries of derision.

As was to happen again the experiment of his donkey-drop leg-breaks and googlies produced the desired result. Watson lost his wicket through the type of stroke which only a tired man could make but he had accomplished a great job with his second century in Test cricket.

Then Hutton courted fate by sticking to his chosen order—Graveney at number four instead of Compton—and not sending in a nightwatchman, but all was well and by the close England were almost half-way to their target of 457 runs to win. Still eight wickets were left.

All the England team felt that the further 230 needed for victory in the five hours of the last day would be well within the compass of their powers, provided May and Graveney could survive the opening onslaught when the West Indies would go all out for an early break-through.

Next day the young pair were never in trouble and, without taking risks, scored 27 in the first half-hour. During that period Stollmeyer set an orthodox field and the bowlers attacked. Eleven overs were sent down.

Obviously Stollmeyer could not allow England to continue at such a pace and he then put into operation the much-discussed and always criticized leg-theory form of bowling, the object of which is the devastatingly simple one of preventing the opposition from scoring and so wasting time. A parallel in Soccer is that of a team in the lead kicking out to touch on every conceivable occasion.

Viewed in the afterlight of events the fears of the West Indies captain seemed groundless, but it is as well to remember that in the pre-lunch period, with some four hours of the game left, his first task was to save his side from defeat.

Leg-theory is no recent invention. As far back as 1921 Warwick Armstrong, the Australian captain, used it, and there have been two instances of its employment by England against Australia since the Second World War—at Trent Bridge, Nottingham, in 1948, and at Headingley, Leeds, in 1953.

The West Indies bowled it at Bradford in 1950 against Yorkshire —it is interesting to note that Stollmeyer was the captain on that occasion—and again in India in 1951.

As Sir Donald Bradman repeatedly has pointed out no team can expect a monopoly of tactics and England were in no position to complain when Stollmeyer switched to leg-theory at Kingston.

Not a single bleat of protest could be made. Hutton had used precisely the same tactics in the West Indies second innings. The methods of Trevor Bailey and Esmond Kentish were as similar as the Bedser twins are identical to each other.

Both bowled their medium to fast deliveries twelve to eighteen inches outside the leg stump to an on-side field which, to the batsman, must have appeared to be as crowded as Speaker's Corner in Hyde Park on a Sunday afternoon.

No particular skill or merit is required from the bowler other than the patience and accuracy to concentrate for long stretches outside the batsman's legs.

Unless prepared to take impossible risks, the batsman has no means of countering leg-theory. When well set Everton Weekes moved over to the leg side and thumped two boundaries through the deserted covers, but the balls were both short and within reach.

Against accurate leg-theory a batsman is no more free than a handcuffed prisoner. He is not in physical danger, but unless this type of bowling is abandoned altogether by tacit agreement of captains recognizing it as an affront to the spirit and traditions of the game, it could be the eventual ruination of cricket. Fortunately neither Stollmeyer nor Hutton used leg-theory again in the series, and the united protest of the Press undoubtedly had its effect.

For the spectator who has paid good money to see a contest of skill between the leading exponents of two countries nothing more baffling or anger-provoking could be imagined than the sight of ball after ball, unmolested by the bat, thudding to the wicket-keeper standing back.

My view is that leg-theory is the most polished and advanced plan yet devised by the misplaced genius of man to empty cricket grounds.

Not content to waste time with leg-theory some modern captains go a step farther with open and deliberate time-wasting tactics which would put a schoolboy to shame. Those who saw England's methods during the last day at Leeds in 1953 will understand what I mean.

Some proudly refer to the practice of taking every possible chance to hold up the game as gamesmanship. Others would use an old-fashioned and stronger word.

The fielding captain passes the word round and from that moment play almost ceases. The stagnation is complete. Lengthy deliberations which frequently result in no change whatever being made in the field placings take place between bowler and captain, and the fielders change over as if they would be penalized for walking at a normal pace.

This is what E. W. Swanton of the *Daily Telegraph* had to comment on the subject:

"Closely allied with this evil (leg-theory) is another, the slowing down of the game by the fielding side by dilatory changing over and lengthy conferences between captain and bowler. There is a natural rhythm of the game of cricket which a cricketer recognizes, and he knows when it is being tampered with, with malice aforethought. Bluntly speaking, this is sharp practice too."

Other English correspondents covering the tour were equally strong in their unbiased condemnation of negative tactics. Speaking of leg-theory Charles Bray of the *Daily Herald* wrote:

"If we are not careful this negative method which restricts scoring just as much as Larwood's 'bodyline' did will be adopted by all accurate fast medium bowlers."

Ross Hall of the *Daily Mirror* made this comment:

"Cricket is a farce when players like Weekes and May, two of the liveliest stroke-makers in the game, are throttled unfairly. I suggest that Hutton and Stollmeyer play by themselves and we can all sleep while each other bowls a yard outside the other's leg stump."

Hutton's plan to stop leg-theory is to play timeless Tests. Certainly in the interests of his side the bowler would be forced to bowl straight but I think Len would be alone in his idea.

Yet the outcome of Stollmeyer's use of negative bowling was to open the door to a West Indies victory. Such a prospect could have been only secondary in his mind when he started it as a worried captain not unmindful of the fact that a hostile crowd would make him the scapegoat for a defeat.

The negative bowling slowed May and Graveney to 23 in the next hour, and practically washed out any hopes of England winning, until May, in sheer desperation, reached for a ball outside his leg stump and was given out caught at the wicket.

That was the beginning of the end. Next to go was Compton, who left the gap between bat and pad to a well-flighted off-break from Ramadhin. Denis felt his failure so acutely that he sat with his head in his hands in the dressing-room in an inconsolable attitude for the next hour. If his supporters are disappointed at such moments the player himself is doubly so.

Soon Graveney, in glancing Kentish, was superbly caught by Weekes at leg slip and, apart from a lively last-wicket stand between Bailey and Moss, *which produced 31 out of 39 for the last seven wickets*, that was the end of England's resistance.

From the third wicket onwards the collapse was recorded thus: 3—277, 4—282, 5—282, 6—282, 7—282, 8—283, 9—285, 10—316.

England's eclipse was complete and the 150 extra police who had been ordered to go to the ground in case of emergency should the

West Indies have been beaten and the crowd attempted to show their displeasure with Stollmeyer, for not enforcing a follow-on, found their task no more arduous than clearing a passage for the conquering West Indies cricketers.

And the biggest hero of all was Jeffrey Stollmeyer. . . .

In the first important Test West Indies had triumphed with a vengeance, and as an England player remarked, "and with a passenger, too". Still, a side which muffs its catches and suffers two major batting collapses cannot hope or deserve deliverance from defeat.

So Hutton, who had begun the tour with the highest expectations, accepted the first of the several bitter pills which he was destined to have to swallow.

THE FIRST TEST

Played at Sabina Park, Kingston, Jamaica, January 15, 16, 18, 19, 20, 21. *West Indies won by* 140 *runs.*

WEST INDIES

First Innings

M. Frederick c Graveney b Statham		..	..	0
J. B. Stollmeyer lbw b Statham	..	..	..	60
J. K. Holt Jnr. lbw b Statham	..	..	..	94
E. D. Weekes b Moss ..	..	..	..	55
C. L. Walcott b Lock ..	..	..	..	65
G. A. Headley c Graveney b Lock	..	..	..	16
G. E. Gomez not out ..	..	..	..	47
C. McWatt b Lock	..	..	..	54
S. Ramadhin b Trueman	..	..	..	7
E. S. Kentish b Statham	..	..	..	0
A. L. Valentine b Trueman ..	..	..	..	0
Extras (b 9, lb 4, w 1, nb 5)	..	..	..	19
Total			..	417

Bowling Analysis

			O.	M.	R.	W.
B. Statham	..	..	36	6	90	4
F. S. Trueman	..	..	34·4	8	107	2
A. Moss	..	..	26	5	84	1
T. E. Bailey	..	..	16	4	36	0
G. A. Lock	..	..	41	14	76	3
D. C. S. Compton	..	..	2	1	5	0

ENGLAND

First Innings

W. Watson b Gomez	3
L. Hutton b Valentine	24
P. B. H. May c Headley b Ramadhin	31
D. C. S. Compton lbw b Valentine	12
T. Graveney lbw b Ramadhin	16
T. E. Bailey not out	28
T. G. Evans c Kentish b Valentine	10
G. A. Lock b Ramadhin	4
B. Statham b Ramadhin	8
F. S. Trueman c McWatt b Gomez	18
A. Moss b Gomez	0
Extras (b 9, lb 2, w 1, nb 4)	16
Total	170

Bowling Analysis

	O.	M.	R.	W.
E. S. Kentish	14	4	23	0
G. E. Gomez	9·2	3	16	3
S. Ramadhin	35	14	65	4
A. L. Valentine	31	10	50	3

WEST INDIES

Second Innings

M. Frederick lbw b Statham	30
J. B. Stollmeyer c Evans b Bailey	8
J. K. Holt Jnr. lbw b Moss	1
E. D. Weekes not out	90
C. L. Walcott c Bailey b Lock	25
G. A. Headley b Lock	1
G. E. Gomez lbw b Statham	3
C. McWatt not out	36
Extras (b 8, lb 6, nb 1)	15
Total (six wickets dec.)	209

Bowling Analysis

	O.	M.	R.	W.
B. Statham	17	2	50	2
F. S. Trueman	6	0	32	0
T. E. Bailey	20	4	46	1
A. Moss	10	0	30	1
G. A. Lock	14	2	36	2

ENGLAND

SECOND INNINGS

W. Watson c and b Stollmeyer	116
L. Hutton lbw b Gomez	56
P. B. H. May c McWatt b Kentish	69
D. C. S. Compton b Ramadhin	2
T. Graveney c Weekes b Kentish	34
T. Bailey not out	15
T. G. Evans b Kentish	0
G. A. Lock b Kentish	0
B. Statham lbw b Ramadhin	1
F. S. Trueman b Kentish	1
A. Moss run out	16
Extras (b 4, lb 1, nb 1)	6
Total	316

BOWLING ANALYSIS

	O.	M.	R.	W.
E. S. Kentish	25	0	49	5
G. E. Gomez	30	8	63	1
S. Ramadhin	35·3	12	88	2
A. L. Valentine	25	6	71	0
G. A. Headley	5	0	23	0
C. L. Walcott	2	1	4	0
J. B. Stollmeyer	3	0	12	1

CHAPTER FOUR

ON the eve of sailing for England in April 1951, the South African cricketers attended a farewell party at Cape Town. As they were leaving skipper Dudley Nourse was taken aside by Dr. Malan, the Premier, who said:

"Well, Mr. Nourse, I hope you enjoyed your stay and will take back with you a good impression of our country."

A flabbergasted Nourse stammered an incoherent reply.

One can well imagine the mind of Dr. Malan grappling with problems even more complex than cricket but any Governor or Administrator in the British West Indies who betrayed such absent-minded ignorance of the game would find his term of office more than exacting.

Forewarned, Governors usually arrive in the West Indies red-eyed and study-worn, having spent the voyage mugging every volume of *Wisden* they can find.

In West Indies company failure to converse in the language of cricket and with the expert's insight might prove a handicap even the most able Governor could not overcome.

The average West Indian's deep passion and devotion to cricket is reflected in many ways. During the M.C.C. stay in the lovely island of Barbados the ceremony of granting Ministerial status—the most advanced system of Government to be found in any English colony—was performed with the dignity befitting an epoch-making occasion.

Yet the hour of the ceremony was advanced in order not to conflict with the start of the M.C.C. match with the colony.

Sir Robert Arundell, the Governor, in his address to the House of Legislature, said:

"This ceremony which, in most countries, would have occasioned the greatest possible interest, if not excitement, had to be fixed at this early hour so as not to interfere with the cricket. The presence in the island of the visiting M.C.C. is a happy augury, for no game can have had so much influence upon the characters of our peoples. Indeed, Viscount Hailsham once used the game of cricket to illustrate his arguments on the subject of cabinet responsibility when he wrote:

'Like the rules of cricket the correct interpretation of the conventions of cabinet government has always been open to argument. This is because the institution, like the game, depends for its efficient working as much upon sentiments of honour and considerations of political convenience, as upon formal rules and regulations, and has evolved slowly and naturally through the centuries, remaining still in a state of development today.' "

Note the words used by the Governor: "*had to be fixed* at this early hour".

As they heard these sentiments the Honourable Grantley Adams, the Premier, and his four new Ministers looked as profound as Jeffrey Stollmeyer in the final moment of deciding not to enforce the follow-on.

The Governor, the Serjeant-at-Arms, the Marshal bearing the Mace, the Ministers and members filed out of the Council Chamber with slow dignity.

I then heard this snatch of whispered conversation: Masculine Voice, "Now we can go to the cricket." Feminine Voice, "Man, that's all you think about—cricket."

At Antigua, the Governor of the Leeward Islands, Sir Kenneth Blackburn, decreed a two-days' public holiday for the M.C.C. stay. A member of the Legislative Council told me, "We thought we might just as well make it official, for everybody would have stopped work in any case."

Even the local newspapers ceased publication.

Apart from winning the match by an innings, the M.C.C. achieved several notable feats in Antigua. In exchange for an up-to-date appraisal of affairs manager Charles Palmer taught the Colonial Secretary's wife how to whistle through her teeth with a finger in the opposite corners of her mouth, in the manner of the Cockney born and bred—before becoming Secretary of Leicestershire Charles was a dignified schoolmaster in Bromsgrove (Worcestershire)—and Johnny Wardle so won the hearts of the crowd with his clowning, bowling and big hitting that they christened him the "Duke of Antigua".

When he and Tom Graveney were batting together each had a section of the crowd rooting for him. Johnny's fans were on one side of the screen and Tom's on the other.

Cheers and counter-cheers rang out every time either hit the ball, although Johnny seemed to have in extra support most of the boys in the trees and the auxiliary crowd taking a long-distance view from a nearby hill.

Antigua is the only centre where I have seen convicts employed on the ground. Dressed in their white prison uniforms they rolled the pitch with rare enthusiasm during the intervals between innings, and before the day's play began.

The fact that the game opened on a sticky wicket was due not to their taking revenge on society but to leaking covers.

On winning the toss Hutton sent the Leeward Islanders in to bat and they lost their first four batsmen for two leg-byes.

In Antigua, where Nelson once had a dockyard, they prefer the emblem of a painted duck to a round nought for scoreboard purposes and, as the Islands' team Nos. 1, 2, 3 and 4 were out without scoring, the board presented an interesting and unusual spectacle.

Ken Suttle, who was out first ball, was duly presented with a photograph showing the duck against his name.

On his return to the dressing-room Suttle struggling to find form had walked into skipper Hutton. With the customary set countenance and grave voice, Len said: "Bad luck, Ken. You had a straight ball first ball." For a moment Ken looked pained but when he saw the twinkle in his captain's eye he soon broke into his usual cheery grin.

To be a first-class cricketer a man must be able to take any amount of leg-pulling both when he is doing well and when not so well.

Did not Kipling speak of those "twin impostors—triumph and disaster"?

But for a spirited innings of 20 by Eddy, the Islands' XI would not have reached anything like their meagre total of 38. Johnny Wardle, who took five for nine, further bemused already baffled batsmen by using his "Chinaman"—the left-arm bowler's off-break.

I shall not readily forget the sight of England's leading professional cricketers lining up in front of the pavilion after the game in the manner of winning competitors in the annual school sports.

The winners were called upon to go forward to receive bats as prizes. Hutton was awarded one for his batting, Wardle and Laker one each for bowling, and Dick Spooner one for wicket-keeping. While the players stood in line on the brown earth and surrounded by hundreds of admiring locals, a ceremony lasting an hour, in which at least a dozen people spoke, went on from the pavilion steps.

Had the M.C.C. realized that this might occur they would probably have done something to bring the game to an earlier finish.

Rather than disappoint the 10,000 crowd, many of whom had travelled from other Islands specially to watch the game, Hutton had decided not to bring the game to a close until approximately four o'clock, but the time schedule went astray when, for the second

time, Eddy batted very well and was helped by Dr. Ross, ex-
captain of London University cricket team. Hutton was half an
hour out in his timing.

The colourful people of the West Indies have a gift for picturesque phrasing, and they adopt the most comical names. That of a
champion steel band (the instruments are made from disused oil
drums) which played at the cocktail party given to the team by the
Administrator of Antigua was "Brute Force".

The delicacy of their touch and the sweet rhythm emanating
from these grotesque-looking instruments belied such a title. It is no
exaggeration to say that anyone blindfolded and not knowing what
type of band he was hearing might easily think he was listening to a
high-class string orchestra.

CHAPTER FIVE

Crisis in the Caribbean—Wrong policy—"Hit de ball, man"—Demonstrations
—Rush of blood—Palmer mystery—The "boob" ball—"Shy" Lock again—
The throw must go—Discipline attacks—Wild rumours—Moral obliquity!—
Denis decides—But was he out?—Run outs remarkable—Walcott's weakness—
Bake Fuh Bake—A toss-up—Secret history.

LEN HUTTON took over the captaincy of England in 1952
with the blessing and warm approval of the overwhelming
majority of cricketers, critics and the public. The appointment of a
professional captain was hailed as the start of a new and better
era of English cricket.

In his first year as England's leader, Hutton brought about the
overpowering of the Indians, who suffered three crushing defeats.
Next summer he achieved the greater triumph of leading England
in the regaining of the "Ashes" from Australia after twenty years.

Not a pipsqueak of protest could be heard when he was selected
to captain the visiting M.C.C. team against the West Indies, who
had never been beaten in their own country. His appointment was
accepted as in the natural order of things—the best man had been
chosen for the job, said everyone. No obvious challenger for the
position could be seen anywhere.

A few months later the man who, as a conquering captain, had
waved so proudly to the cheering crowds massed in front of the
Pavilion at The Oval faced a major crisis. Len Hutton never looked
trouble so squarely in the face as he did at Barbados, that tiny speck
on the Caribbean seas. Never was his hold on the reins of leadership
so insecure; never was he the target for such harsh and adverse
criticism.

Nearly everything that could have gone wrong for Hutton had
done so. Much was beyond his control but not everything.

The no-balling by both umpires of Tony Lock for throwing in
the colony match was one problem. Then came charges against the
conduct of the team off the field. Furthermore, Len himself was not
well—and he lost the toss again in the Barbados Test.

Yet Hutton was a captain wedded to a false strategy, and he
cannot escape the prime responsibility, through the mistaken tactics
which, by order or example, he directed in the first innings, for
England's second Test defeat in succession.

Hutton believed that on the perfect wickets of the West Indies
the leading batsmen had no need to take risks; his view was that if
they defended their wickets successfully, automatically the runs

would follow. In other words he advocated a policy of "digging in" and "grafting" for runs rather than one of attack. He argued that, by a policy of attrition, Ramadhin and Valentine, the calypso twins, could be worn down.

Few unhappier sequels could have been possible. On the Black Tuesday of the Test the West Indies took the new ball after 65 overs with only 77 runs scored and at the end of the day all England had to show for five hours of toil on a perfect wicket with a fast outfield was 128 runs and seven wickets lost. These runs had been painfully extracted from no fewer than 114 overs.

Long after the main events are forgotten I shall remember two incidents which served to show the depths to which English batting degenerated. I saw John Goddard, the deposed West Indies captain, but still the skipper of Barbados, standing at the top of the gangway in the George ("Lord Runs Come") Challenor stand, trying to convince a doubting circle of friends on the merits of Hutton's batting.

"I tell you," John was saying, "he *is* a great batsman. You should have seen the double-century he scored against us on a sticky wicket at The Oval in 1950. The man you are watching today is not the real Hutton."

I also recall with some pain the spectacle of knots of coloured enthusiasts calling out to the M.C.C. players, as they returned to the Marine Hotel, "Hit de ball next time, man."

What the thoughts of Denis Compton and Tom Graveney must have been I would not care to imagine. Both wanted to hit the ball, but they had to abide by instructions.

Graveney played aggressively at the first three balls bowled to him in the first innings, but Len went down the wicket before the next ball and told him to be careful, indicating by sign that the right approach was to play down the line and play safe. Graveney then retired into his shell and for the next two hours he did nothing but defend. Then, as is so often the case, on receiving a slow full toss, he patted it gently back to the bowler. He had been so tucked up in defence that he could not untie himself in time to hit the ball as it deserved.

Compton, also receiving his skipper's injunction to "keep his nut down", gently lifted a short-pitched ball, preciously near to being a long hop, straight to King at square-leg.

During the afternoon two crowd demonstrations were made against the slow batting and each time Hutton drew away from the wicket and waited for the noise to abate. If his concentration was disturbed he was entitled to do so.

Now Kensington Oval holds a maximum of 10,000 spectators

and, with admission charges ranging from 1s. 9d. to 8s., the Barbados Cricket Association can make only a modest contribution to the £45,000 required to cover the cost of the tour—the West Indies pay all expenses and take all the profits. Jamaica and Trinidad are the profit-making centres but, if the Barbadians lack numbers, they do not lack the capacity to produce a loud volume of noise over a long period.

In the midst of England's lamentable batting performance sections of the crowd chanted, calypso style, "We want money back" and "We want cricket." Others slow hand-clapped.

Most of the hubbub came from the stand set aside for schoolboys who eventually became quite a nuisance. On subsequent days, when play was much brighter, these boys still protested. Not only for the sake of the batsmen trying to concentrate but in the interests of spectators trying to follow the game in peace they should have been checked.

The crowd's demonstrations have been put forward as an excuse, by those in search of a reason, for the extraordinary end to Hutton's innings. After batting with the grimmest determination and caution for four hours, twenty-six minutes, Hutton suddenly lashed out, hit two boundaries, and was caught in the same sensational over off a terrific skier.

I cannot believe a seasoned performer like Hutton, who has years of Test and County Cricket behind him and is familiar with the moods of crowds, would be so upset by a demonstration to throw away his wicket. The fact was, however, that Hutton lashed out in desperation as though number eleven had joined him instead of the dependable Charles Palmer.

Another theory was that Hutton was broken in spirit on Graveney's dismissal, and he certainly gave every evidence of being acutely disappointed. As Graveney made the shot Hutton slumped on the handle of his bat as if he could not believe his eyes.

Yet Hutton, throughout his career, has attempted little without the support of a solid motive. In the colony match on the same ground for instance he gave a striking example of the thoroughness of his cricket brain.

Having a chill on the liver, he was forced to bat low down in the order and, because of this, he reasoned that John Goddard would set a defensive off-side field to him in order to get at his tail-end partners.

Before play began, Hutton practised pulling balls well outside the off stump to the mid wicket and on sides. Seeing this, Johnny Wardle, his Yorkshire colleague, turned to Tony Lock and said:

"I've never seen Len do that before. I expect he's practising to go in lower down." Len was doing precisely that and, after perfecting his pull, he went to the wicket and beat Goddard's off-side field with a brilliant innings which took M.C.C.'s score to within 16 of the Barbados total of 398.

Manager Palmer commented, "If that's the way Len bats when he has a cold we must make sure he always has one."

It is a curious fact that another opening batsman, Reg Simpson, captain of Nottinghamshire, has the reputation for playing better with a cold than without one. Reg suffered from one of the vicious streaming variety when he collected a beautiful century before lunch for Gents v. Players at Scarborough in 1953.

I am inclined to the view that the explanation of Hutton's "rush of blood" was simple enough—he thought the time had come when it was imperative to try and knock Valentine off his length. He had just pulled Valentine savagely for four and driven him over cover-point for another four with suspiciously near a mishit.

In the excitement and drama of Hutton's dismissal two important points tended to be overlooked. First, Ramadhin showed exceptional judgment in making a fine catch; secondly, the hit was made directly into the wind which held back the ball considerably.

If Len had tackled half-volleys with the same venom as he launched into Valentine that final over I have no doubt he would have reached his first century of the tour long before he was out so dramatically.

The method of Hutton's dismissal, when England were still desperately short of runs, made even less sense in view of the way Charles Palmer, playing in his maiden Test, showed he was quite capable of staying at the wicket.

Indeed, of the unhappy English batsmen taking stock of their position at the end of the day only "Papa" Palmer, as he was called in the West Indies, could claim to have fallen to a genuinely good ball—one from Ramadhin which left him at the last second and was snapped up by an equally impressive slip catch by a diving Clyde Walcott.

Through the necessity to strengthen the core of the batting and to reinforce the second line of attack, Palmer's inclusion in the Test side had been probable rather than possible, and I could not understand why the four Selectors did not play him in the colony match which preceded the Test.

Before then Palmer had batted twice only and each time he was the victim of dubious leg-before decisions. Obviously his chief need was match practice. Half an hour in the middle is worth days of net practice.

On the eve of the Test Palmer indulged in a long and concentrated net practice against the team's leading bowlers, and, although the sight of an M.C.C. practice properly organized was a refreshing change—bowlers like Trueman often seemed to monopolize batting time in front of out-of-form batsmen such as Dick Spooner—it was inadequate.

For some unaccountable reason Hutton, having agreed to Palmer's inclusion, ignored him as a bowler in the long West Indies first innings (427 minutes and 125·1 overs) and until the 35th over of the second innings.

Surely a spell from the accurate Palmer would have relieved the sorely-pressed four-man attack of Statham, Lock, Laker and Bailey—particularly as Bailey, in stopping a power-drive from Walcott, fractured the third finger of his bowling hand.

The extent of the injury was not known until an X-ray examination the same evening, but Bailey continued playing in no little pain.

Almost as soon as he went on in the second innings Palmer deceived and beat Frankie Worrell with a leg-break which turned so much it must have pitched in one of the several big pot-holes appearing on the pitch. An equally surprised Godfrey Evans, accustomed to Palmer only as a medium-pace seam bowler, failed to accept a possible stumping chance. Godfrey kept wicket several degrees below his best all through the Test, but I think he was still feeling the effects of the cyst operation.

Surely, however, Hutton accepted Palmer's secondary role in the team as one of a change bowler capable of sealing down one end with the chance of snatching a wicket? Yet, of the 222 overs sent down by England, Palmer's contribution was a mere five, the same number as Compton in the first innings. Whereas Palmer caused one definite chance and conceded only 15 runs 29 were knocked off Compton.

The wisdom of experimenting for at least a few overs with a change bowler was amply proved by the West Indies captain, Stollmeyer, who used seven bowlers in the first innings and eight in the second. I can well imagine Hutton retaliating with an envious comment on his rival's extra resources.

Stollmeyer himself secured two valuable wickets in the second innings—in fact he turned the match—by getting Compton and Bailey with his high-tossed leg-breaks and googlies. Jeffrey, however, throws the ball too high in the air for him to be a deadly bowler and Bailey's stroke in hitting a full toss straight into the hands of square-leg—the ball went off the top edge of the bat—was the worst (in his own opinion) he had made for three years.

Still, Stollmeyer was only repeating what he had done against

India the previous year and against England in the second innings of the first Test. Even so, I would not class Stollmeyer as being any better a bowler than Tom Graveney, who should not neglect his leg-breaks and googlies. Still, "Stollies Dollies", as Frank Rostron christened them, are bowled with a high arm action and often bounce off the hard wickets at an awkward height.

Hutton, with his perfectionist's outlook on cricket, probably cannot reconcile himself to the fact that the second or third change bowler is always capable of snatching a wicket and breaking a partnership.

In any case the bad ball takes a wicket more often than is generally admitted or appreciated. This was demonstrated several times over during England's first innings.

Alec Bedser, who thinks deeper about cricket than the average bowler, purposely sends down what he graphically describes as his "boob" ball, which is either a tempting full toss or a short-pitched one under normal speed.

Alec has enjoyed striking success with it, particularly against batsmen whose prime thought is to play out time before the close or just before an interval.

When a batsman has concentrated on defence for hours, he has to re-organize his wits to hit a bad ball when it arrives and for him to make a mess of an attacking stroke is not unusual. Graveney found this to his cost in the first innings when Ramadhin supplied him with a soft full toss which he patted gently back to the grateful little East Indian.

Hutton's task in trying to restrict the West Indies total to reasonable limits, after they had recovered from the shock of losing three wickets for 25 runs, was grievously handicapped by the failure of Tony Lock, the Surrey left-arm spinner, to find form anywhere approaching the standard he set in England.

Tony began the Test under the personal cloud of having been no-balled for throwing by the Test umpires, Harold Walcott, Clyde's uncle, and Jordan. The fact that both had called him for the same alleged offence was important—they obviously agreed that his faster ball was an unfair delivery. Having also been no-balled for throwing once in the first Test, at Kingston, Lock realized he was a marked bowler.

He knew the faster ball with which he secured many of his wickets—some have put it as high as 25 per cent—had to be withdrawn from his attacking armoury.

The first time umpire Walcott no-balled Lock in the Barbados fixture produced a strange scene. With his faster ball Lock shattered the stumps of Sobers, the young left-hander, and the call did not seem to have been made until after Sobers had attempted his hurried but unsuccessful defensive jab. Sobers walked away not realizing he was still entitled to stay. Neither he nor Dick Spooner, the M.C.C. wicketkeeper, heard the umpire's call.

Lock was plainly put out by the incident and he went over to register his complaint to his captain. Hutton heard him, then walked across to umpire Walcott. Hutton knew better than anyone that he could do nothing about the decision, but he knew that his action gave time for Lock to simmer down and regain his composure.

Hutton rightly protested to umpire Walcott that the call came too late—most people agreed it was made a split second after the ball hit the wicket—and umpire Walcott, whose efficiency was seldom questioned, replied simply, "I'm sorry."

Walcott again no-balled Lock for throwing and, in the last over of the day, umpire Jordan also "called" him, which meant both umpires had given a clear warning that they looked upon Lock's faster delivery as transgressing the laws.

Who, of the English party, could say, with hand on heart, he was surprised at the turn of events? Only that day I had received a letter from an International player commenting on Tony's faster ball and suggesting he cut it out.

Ever since Lock began using it in 1952 it has caused suspicion. The winter before that he spent coaching and bowling in an indoor school at Croydon, Surrey, where the roof of the net was unusually low. There Tony acquired the habit of a lower trajectory and next spring, when he used the faster ball in the nets, almost the whole of the Oval staff forecast he would not be allowed to bowl it in county cricket.

Later that season Fred Price, the former Middlesex and England wicketkeeper, a man who is not afraid to translate opinion into deed, no-balled Lock at The Oval for throwing. Price was subjected to almost hysterical disapproval by the crowd. The old Middlesex-Surrey feud was said to be at the bottom of it all. Of course, that was unadulterated nonsense.

Instead of the matter coming to a head there and then, Tony was allowed to continue to bowl his faster ball. Apparently no other umpire saw anything wrong.

Now, I hold the deepest admiration for English umpires, all of whom have played in good-class cricket, and they properly enjoy a high professional reputation. Rightly they show very great reluctance to prejudice the future prospects of a young player, particularly that of a professional, by taking any such drastic action against him as to no-ball him for throwing.

In Lock's case, both the Surrey committee and the player himself should have seen the warning light after Fred Price's action. On this important issue they should not have been content to allow matters to slide. It was not something which could be conveniently ignored, but a matter to be tackled straightforwardly in the triple interests of England, Surrey and Tony Lock. To be no-balled on a "foreign field" was a severe shock for Lock and his team.

I take the view that umpires already have too much responsibility without having to decide in a period of a few fleeting seconds whether a bowler's action comes under the definition of a throw or a jerk—the crux of the legitimacy is contained in the position of the elbow in the final act of delivery.

A way out of the difficulty would be the formation of a panel of experts to study border-line cases. Umpires could report suspects and the members of the panel would be able to watch the bowler from every angle (which is most important) and over a long period of matches. If, at the end of the trial period, they were convinced that the bowler's action was unfair, they could warn him to change his style. Should he fail to do so the remedy would be simple and effective.

At least, a young bowler representing his country, thousands of miles away from home, would be spared the indignity and embarrassment of being no-balled for throwing.

Denis Compton, captain the next day in the absence of the indisposed Hutton, took Tony aside before the resumption of play and, in effect, said: "Don't try to bowl your faster ball today, Tony. What you do in the Test is your business and that of your captain, but today I would prefer you not to risk a scene by bowling your fast ball."

Lock accepted the advice and there were no scenes. Again, before the second Test opened, Len Hutton spoke to him specially about the matter. Len told him not to use his faster ball unless and until he himself asked him to do so.

In the two innings Lock sent down 74 overs and Len did not once ask him to bowl his faster ball! Apparently Hutton preferred diplomacy to the chance of more trouble but I wonder how much it affected Lock's bowling in the match?

Anyone who has played or watched cricket for any length of time instinctively recognizes an unfair delivery without the assistance of a definition in words. With his considerable natural ability of spin and flight, lined to a usually reliable length, Lock is too good a bowler to employ any doubtful method, and I hope we have seen the last of a faster ball which must always be suspect.

Fortunately for England and Hutton, Lock has never bowled

as badly as he did in the second Test when his aggregate was one wicket (that of wicketkeeper Clifford McWatt) for 216 runs.

The fact that for hours Lock bowled into the wind might serve as some explanation for his dropping short of length. It does not excuse his bowling down the leg side when Hutton had set a circle of defensive fielders on the opposite side of the wicket.

Moreover, he could not decide whether to bowl over or round the wicket and so unsettled was he that he changed half a dozen times in as many overs.

As the West Indies opening batsman, John Holt, commented during his second innings century, "As soon as I saw Tony go round the wicket I knew there were runs to be had."

In Jamaica Hutton arranged for Lock to call on Wilfred Rhodes the next time Surrey visited Yorkshire and I hope Tony will remain faithful to the appointment for he could do with some guidance in the important art of field-placing. All young bowlers run into the same difficulty.

Hutton certainly had his worries on the field. They also began to accumulate in other directions. When the fortunes of the team were at their lowest ebb—on the Tuesday of the first innings at Barbados—Ross Hall of the *Daily Mirror*, on his first cricket tour, accused the team of bad off-the-field behaviour and not backing up their captain. A few days earlier, at Barbados, the same paper had reported that Hutton was to be flown home for an operation for stones in the kidneys.

The reaction of Mrs. Hutton at her Pudsey home, on reading this information, can be imagined. Immediately she was telephoned by commiserating friends while Charles Palmer, the M.C.C. manager, received a long-distance call from Bruce Harris of the *Evening Standard*, London. Hutton's first words were : "Ask Bruce to telephone my wife and re-assure her that I'm all right and there's no thought of an operation. I have a slight chill on the liver, that's all."

Every England team to tour Australia since 1924 has been the victim of a charge of bad behaviour off the field:

Even the Australians do not escape. Last year in England Lindsay Hassett's men were similarly accused.

The majority of people probably dismiss such stories as unworthy of notice but there must always be a minority who believe that no smoke exists without fire. The number prepared to pass on fairy tales as gospel is quite extraordinary. Many of the English and white residents of each colony are to blame for the piffle and gossip which is spread around, and was a direct contribution to the unhappy atmosphere which developed.

As soon as the team arrived at a new place in the West Indies

they would be greeted with the inevitable and heartfelt plea of:
"You've simply got to win. We are counting on you. Don't let us
down whatever you do."

Believe me, any disappointment English people and the white
races abroad suffer from an indifferent display by England is small
compared with that of the players. Hutton, for instance, slept
scarcely a wink throughout the Barbados Test of 1954, and batsmen
who have travelled thousands of miles to represent their country but
get out to unworthy strokes are often visited by bitter self-reproach.
Many are the cricketers who spends the small hours playing over
and over again the stroke to which he fell.

Fantastic rumours swept Barbados. For example, all-night
parties were supposed to have been held by players who staggered
to the Kensington Oval direct from a club.

Possibly some players were seen at night clubs but these were
always the men not playing in the current match.

Had it been otherwise, however, what would the self-righteous
critics demand from healthy young men in the evenings? Should
they be in bed by 10 p.m. punctually each night and be tucked in
by the manager? The Indians in England in 1946 tried the roll-call
system and went to bed like docile lambs at the same time. As soon
as the manager's back was turned they went out again!

Hutton, like all sensible captains, relied on the self-discipline
and commonsense of his men, and he was not let down.

I, for one, have not seen a team try harder and to put down the
defeats in the first two Tests to anything but the inescapable fact
that the West Indies, lucky to win the toss twice and to escape the
penalty of many offered catches, were the better side is completely
wrong. To suggest that England lacked determination or were
physically ruined by loose-living only minimizes the splendid
achievements of a powerful combination.

I saw one fierce diatribe advocating that M.C.C. should institute
an inquiry into the team. I am sure the results of any such inquiry
would prove singularly disappointing to many.

To lose to the West Indies on their own wickets, before their own
crowds and under their own burning sun, cannot be considered a
disgrace.

What is ignored or overlooked by stay-at-home critics is the
difference in the conditions which must favour men used to them, as
obviously are the West Indies cricketers in their own sunny lands.
Not all English players are able to accustom themselves to the
glare from the sky or the greater speed through the air of the
ball.

How else can the fielding lapses of Tony Lock be explained? In

England he is known as one of the outstanding fielders and catchers in the game, but in the West Indies he dropped catches and fumbled and misfielded like a novice. Towards the end, however, when thoroughly accustomed to the different light, he was the old and familiarly brilliant Lock.

Suggestions that the tour was in turmoil, team spirit had gone to the dogs, players were on the verge of mutiny and so on, were amusing to begin with, because the team found difficulty in believing that such irresponsible fiction could be swallowed.

Manager Palmer and captain Hutton made formal denials, but they wondered if the voice of denial was as strong as the voice of accusation and condemnation.

From the start of the tour official engagements were cut down to the minimum in each colony. Usually they were restricted to three cocktail parties beginning at 6.30 p.m. and ending well in time for dinner, which was served at the hotels not later than 8 p.m.

The first cocktail party, given by the Governor of the Island on the team's arrival, took place a day or so before the match, the local cricket club invariably gave the second and the M.C.C. reciprocated after each Test was over by a cocktail party at which they could say "Thank You" and bid farewells to all those who had looked after them during their stay.

The M.C.C. team held its own "club" meeting on Saturday evenings throughout the tour. For a number of years now this has been the custom of all M.C.C. touring teams. The first toast is "wives and sweethearts" and the second "absent friends". Cricket is forgotten temporarily while the players enjoy themselves and, among other things, fine each other for alleged offences during the preceding week, such as not drinking with the left hand on a Saturday or not wearing an M.C.C. touring tie to breakfast on Monday. Altogether the outcome is the promotion of team spirit.

In a letter to *The Times* on the subject of M.C.C. behaviour Commander C. B. Fry wrote:

"In regard to criticism of recent events in the West Indies it may be interesting to recall that Mr. J. A. Spender, eminent editor of the old *Westminster Gazette*, caused a boldly-lettered notice to be posted in his sports department saying, 'Failure of a first-class batsman to score is not to be represented as an instance of extreme moral obliquity.'"

In my opinion Hutton did not emerge from the Barbados Test with an enhanced reputation as a tactician, and the critics on the spot, as was their right, did not pull their punches. That was fair enough. Others, thousands of miles from the scene of operation, chipped in with their own versions.

One columnist excitedly called for Alec Bedser to be flown out. To bolster the batting? Truly the batting, not the attack, which had to battle on the hardest wickets in the world, was the main cause of failure.

Just before the second Test at Barbados the local *Advocate* carried a full column of letters sent to the London *Evening Standard* debating whether Denis Compton should hold a place in the England side. Denis, being an old campaigner, was not unduly upset to know that only 50 per cent were for him, but I wonder if the anti-Comptons realized under what handicap Denis plays in top-class cricket—and, moreover, will willingly do so until a better number four is produced.

At the end of the second Test Denis went to have one of his periodical check-ups on his knee which had pained him in his innings of 93.

After examining the X-ray on the knee, the doctor said to Denis, "You can't play cricket with this knee."

"But I do," replied Denis.

"Then you'll have to take a month's rest."

"Sorry, I'm playing in two days' time," answered Denis. He did, in the next game, against British Guiana at Georgetown.

I mention this to refute the inference of lack of guts in the side. Shortly after Compton's knee operation in 1950—the third on his right knee—Mr. Bill Tucker, the surgeon, showed an X-ray plate of the knee to a fellow physician without mentioning to whom the knee belonged.

"What do you think of this fellow's chances of playing sport?" he asked.

"He hasn't a chance in a thousand," was the emphatic reply.

"Well, he does play. That knee belongs to Denis Compton."

Denis has done his best for England since, but I doubt whether he would have played had there been a sixth Test last summer against Australia. Still, like May and Graveney, he re-discovered himself in the second innings of the second Test in the West Indies, when he was allowed to play his natural game.

Things had gone too far to prevent eventual defeat. That, unhappily, was the logical sequence to the first innings flop and the series of dropped catches, but the change of attitude and outlook which came over the leading batsmen afterwards had to be seen to be appreciated. Those who saw the change certainly did not lack appreciation.

England needed 281 to win on the last day, in five hours with

seven wickets intact, and had not rain interfered—the start was
delayed by 51 minutes and a further 20 minutes were lost after
lunch—I would not have put it beyond the powers of Compton and
Graveney to have won the match.

All went well until Compton's innings ended cruelly only seven
short of what would have been his first Test century since he took one
off South Africa at Trent Bridge, Nottingham, in 1951, and he
batted as near his vintage form of 1947 as he will ever get again.

No one who saw Denis take ten runs from one over by Frank
Worrell, with shots which left the stroke-loving West Indies crowd
gasping with admiration, could write him off as finished.

May had also batted beautifully and afterwards McWatt, the
wicketkeeper, told me he thought May's driving off the back foot
was as powerful as Walcott's. I cannot think of higher praise, but
good as May's was I think McWatt was being over generous.

For the first time during the match genuine and prolonged
applause greeted England's batting. Certainly, with the exception of
Watson and Compton, all the front-rank batsmen went out to
attacking strokes for which they could have no regret.

Compton, it seems, was unlucky. When he was given out cries
of "Oh no!" went up from the fielders close enough to judge and
there were apologies amid the champagne after the game. Neither
side would want to obtain a wicket unfairly, and nobody less than
Jeff Stollmeyer who, like his predecessor, John Goddard, is a first-
class sportsman, but it was singularly unfortunate that the two vital
wickets in the first two Tests—Peter May's in the second innings
at Kingston and Denis Compton's at Bridgetown—should be en-
shrouded with doubt.

A second collapse of the middle batsmen was more than disappointing. This time they could not say they had not been given a
good start and, with five wickets vanishing for 23, the West Indies
gained their second victory with 96 minutes to spare. England could
find no consolation in realizing that they lost the first Test to the
West Indies without Worrell, and the second to them without
Everton Weekes.

In the first innings at Bridgetown Worrell was beaten second
ball by Statham, again England's best bowler, and in the second he
experienced a very shaky start. When he recovered, he played the
lesser role in a partnership of 221 with John Holt, the Jamaican.

They were eight short of the second wicket record of 228 by
Karl Nunes and George Headley in 1929–30 at Kingston when
Holt, off the second ball of the fifth morning, gave Statham a return
catch.

For Worrell to accept the secondary role in a long partnership suggests tremendous form by his partner. Such was the case, as is shown by the figures of Holt's innings: 50 in 95 minutes; 100 in 172; 150 in 250, with one six and 25 fours.

A strange and unhappy coincidence for Stollmeyer came in his being run out twice, which must be unique for a Test opening batsman. In the first innings Stollmeyer pushed Statham to the open space at mid-on and apparently called "Two!" whereas Holt shouted "One!"

Both calls were drowned in the noise of the crowd, with the result that the two men finished at the same end. Watson added to the general confusion by returning the ball to that same end, but, fortunately for England, Statham, the bowler, was tall enough to catch it. He had all the time in the world to throw it to the wicketkeeper and Stollmeyer was run out by the length of the pitch.

In the second innings Stollmeyer and Holt also found themselves all mixed up over a run. Stollmeyer appeared to be at fault this time.

He played the stroke, called, then stopped, by which time Holt had started off and arrived in the middle of the pitch where his captain stood transfixed. Stollmeyer could not get back and Holt could not get there. The fielder, again Watson, made an accurate and swift return.

The question arose at once—not was either out but which was out? Stollmeyer and Holt stood in uncertainty in the middle of the wicket, undecided whether they had crossed. If they had Holt was the run-out victim. Umpire Walcott decided they had not crossed. Stollmeyer had to go.

Clyde Walcott's double century was naturally the cause of great jubilation on his home ground, especially after he had been caught second ball in the second innings of the colony game.

With the help of Bruce Pairaudeau, of British Guiana, and then Denis Atkinson, of Barbados—Denis married John Goddard's niece and is spoken of as a future captain of the West Indies—Clyde pulled the West Indies out of the direst trouble.

The feature of his play which I admired so much was his absolute refusal to allow the position to upset his natural bent for aggression. He knew Hutton had to set an attacking field which left gaps in front of the wicket and he accepted the challenge with a counter-attack. How well he succeeded is history.

Walcott does everything in a big way. He is a giant in size and his stature on the field is no smaller. He has prodigious strength in his forearms and a capacity to force the good-length ball straight past the bowler or in the direction of mid-on. Sometimes the bat seems a puny weapon in his massive hands, but he can use it for a delicately timed leg-glance as well as a power drive.

For a big man he is surprisingly athletic and agile in the slips, where he takes nine out of every ten reachable catches.

In England's second innings at Bridgetown Walcott dropped a very hot chance off Compton and when the M.C.C. party reached Atkinson air-strip at British Guiana, Hutton, asked by local reporters to comment on Walcott as a cricketer, declared with a twinkle in his eye that England had found Walcott's weakness—meaning his slip catching. Walcott, there at the time, enjoyed the by-play.

Unfortunately for Hutton it was reported in good faith under the heading: "The M.C.C. have found Walcott's measure says skipper Hutton." This of the man who had just trounced England's bowling for 220 runs!

The M.C.C. bowlers were surprised at the information when they read their papers next morning at breakfast.

Clyde is a good sport and very popular with all teams. In the Barbados match Jim Laker bet him he would get off the mark with a stroke past Walcott at slip. Jim was out for a duck, so that he had to pay. This was Jim's second debt of the innings. He had also wagered with his Surrey colleague, Peter May, that of the pair he would score more runs. Both made 0—but Jim had lost his bet.

Nevertheless Walcott might have been out at 76 and certainly should have been at 90 when he pushed back a catch to bowler Lock which was nowhere near as hard as it looked from the ringside. The Lock of home standards would assuredly have taken the chance. In actual terms of runs it cost 130.

Walcott hit a six, and 28 fours by him raced over an outfield which was lightning fast. He needed only to tickle a slow ball from Lock and beat the inner fielders to score a boundary, one of the facts which made England's opening effort so miserable.

Bruce Pairaudeau, who wears glasses, is an attractive free-scoring batsman with many agreeable strokes in the arc from square-cover to mid-off. He played for Burnley while on an accountancy course at Manchester and finished second in the batting averages of the strong Lancashire League.

"The cold nearly killed me while I waited for buses," he told me once. That is not surprising for a man who comes from British Guiana which is only nine degrees from the equator.

The qualities of patience and aggression Pairaudeau showed in the different phases of his innings made the choice of Headley in preference to him in the first Test all the more puzzling.

Denis Atkinson, who deservedly won his place in the Test by

scoring a fine 151 in the colony game, toured India and Australia without marked success, but, in England, he would be a definite asset as an all-rounder. His off-breaks and capacity for bowling for long stretches would be invaluable on English wickets, he is a fine forcing batsman and, as a perfect athlete, an excellent fieldsman anywhere.

The West Indies attack again revolved around Ramadhin and Valentine and the saddest commentary on England's first innings batting on a perfect wicket which did not take spin is to be found in their bowling figures:

	O.	M.	R.	W.
Ramadhin	53	30	50	4
Valentine	51·5	30	61	3

Without attempting to under-rate the Terrible Twins of Spin I say that should never have happened. This was proved in the second innings, when the pitch gave them some measure of assistance. Their figures then were:

	O.	M.	R.	W.
Ramadhin	37	17	71	3
Valentine	39	18	87	0

So England were two down with three to play and Peter May's reply to the question on the immigration entry card on arrival, "What is the purpose of your visit?", went wrong. He had written, "To win the Second Test." Another England player had a simple answer for the question, "Married State?" He simply wrote "Happy."

The last time Jim Laker had been on a losing Test side was against Australia at Leeds in 1948. Since then he had played 11 times for England but now the tide of his fortunes had turned.

As only to be expected the Islands were jubilant and a postscript to the Test arrived in this amusing rhyme, written in the West Indies idiom by Cuffle de Poole, Junior, and appearing in the *Advocate*, Georgetown, British Guiana:

Whulaw, whulay! Lookah daw, lookah day!
It happan pan Kensin'tun Oval ouk key,
In Bridgeturg, Bubaydus, de odda day,
A team uv crickitahs from "Hoam" did cum,
Wid a blare ah trumpet an' beatin' ah drum,
Faith-tuh-Gawd! dey didn't expeck such a lickin' from
Jeff and his boys. Lookah, pass dah Munggay.

Tink bowt a team wid Hutton, Graveney,
Palmer and Lock, Compton and Bailey,
Statham an' Evans, an' Watson, good deah,
Doan fugget Laker, he also did play,
Hoi, whu' youh doin'? Go easy Oi pray,
Loike yuh seems to fugget dah is moi Munggay,
An' yuh kayan be drinkin' bake fuh bake wid me.

Jeff got run owt, nought. Worrell too got a "globe",
Um wuz 25 for 3 when y'ung Teddy Hobe—
Hoi! muh mowt slip Ah really means Holt,
Lef' afta' mekin' eleven. Dah wuz a helluva jolt,
To the Windian soide;
Then in came Cloyde—
Two hunnud and twenty he dash in deh robe.

Jeff's boys made a powerful three-eighty-three,
For tha' furst innings. De M.C.C.,
Reploied widh one-eighty-one, an' Cap'n Jeffrey,
Went in widh Holt and wuz run ouk agen,
Ouk agen
Read when
Jeff again sent in the English-men,
The oukt come of the match is now history.

Four-nointy-foive to win,
C'ud the M.C.C. bring
Home the bacon? Boi jing,
Dey c'u'dn't! Dey lost by one-eighty-three,
T'anks to lucky Cap'n Jeffrey.

Munggay is a brand of rum and "bake fuh bake" means glass for glass. The last line "T'anks to lucky Cap'n Jeffrey" is, of course, a reference to his winning the toss for the second successive time. Hutton had lost the toss for seven times in a row—five to Lindsay Hassett and two to Stollmeyer.

It is the privilege of the home captain to spin the coin and five times Hutton heard Hassett successfully call tails. Little wonder when Stollmeyer tossed the coin in the air Hutton also called tails. Before the Test at Barbados Compton implored his captain to go for heads. When Hutton returned and confessed to have remained faithful to tails Compton went outside, with Moss as witness, to make twelve calls. Of the twelve he called heads correctly eight times.

The story is told of the county skipper who lost the toss seventeen times running. Downhearted but not disheartened, he spent hours in his garden tossing and re-tossing the coin to try and discover the secret of successful calling or tossing.

On the assumption that most captains called "Heads" he worked out the amount of height needed for the coin to come down "Tails".

Next day when his rival captain called "Heads" he flipped the coin perfectly for it to land "Tails". It came down "Heads". Once more ——shire were in the field!

Jeffrey Stollmeyer told me of a remarkable incident in which he and Vijay Hazare, the Indian captain, figured in the previous Test series in the West Indies.

Stollmeyer tossed, thought Hazare had called incorrectly, and said, "We'll bat."

To his astonishment Hazare replied: "How can you make the decision, Jeffrey? I won the toss."

Stollmeyer was certain that Hazare, not himself, had made the mistake but, knowing Hazare to be too good a sportsman to try on anything underhand, conceded the right to his rival.

Who said cricketers are not diplomats?

THE SECOND TEST

Played at Bridgetown, Barbados, February 6, 8, 9, 10, 11, 12.
West Indies won by 181 runs.

WEST INDIES

FIRST INNINGS

Holt c Graveney b Bailey	11
Stollmeyer run out	0
Worrell b Statham	0
Walcott st Evans b Laker	220
Pairaudeau c Hutton b Laker	71
Gomez lbw b Statham	7
Atkinson c Evans b Laker	53
McWatt lbw b Lock	11
Ramadhin b Statham	1
King b Laker	5
Valentine not out	0
Extras (lb 2, nb 2)	4
Total	383

BOWLING ANALYSIS

	O.	M.	R.	W.
Statham	27	6	90	3
Bailey	22	6	63	1
Lock	41	9	116	1
Laker	30·1	6	81	4
Compton	5	0	29	0

ENGLAND

FIRST INNINGS

Hutton c Ramadhin b Valentine	72
Watson st McWatt b Ramadhin	6
May c King b Ramadhin	7
Compton c King b Valentine	13
Graveney c and b Ramadhin	15
Palmer c Walcott b Ramadhin	22
Bailey c McWatt b Atkinson	28
Evans b Gomez	10
Laker c Gomez b Atkinson	1
Lock not out	0
Statham c Holt b Valentine	3
Extras (b 4)	4
Total	181

BOWLING ANALYSIS

	O.	M.	R.	W.
King	14	6	28	0
Gomez	13	8	10	1
Worrell	9	2	21	0
Atkinson	9	7	5	2
Ramadhin	53	30	50	4
Valentine	51·5	30	61	3
Stollmeyer	1	0	2	0

WEST INDIES

SECOND INNINGS

Stollmeyer run out	28
Holt c and b Statham	166
Worrell not out	76
Walcott not out	17
Extras (b 5)	5
Total (for two wickets dec.)	292

BOWLING ANALYSIS

	O.	M.	R.	W.
Statham	15	1	49	1
Bailey	12	1	48	0
Laker	30	13	62	0
Lock	33	17	100	0
Palmer	5	1	15	0
Compton	1	0	13	0

ENGLAND

SECOND INNINGS

Hutton c Worrell b Ramadhin	..	..	..		77
Watson c McWatt b King	..	..	..	..	0
May c Walcott b Gomez	..	..	..	..	62
Compton lbw b Stollmeyer	..	..	..	..	93
Graveney not out	..	..	..	..	64
Palmer c Gomez b Atkinson	..	..	..	..	0
Bailey c (sub) Hunte b Stollmeyer	..	..	..	4
Evans b Ramadhin	..	..	..	..	5
Laker lbw b Ramadhin	..	..	..	..	0
Lock b King	..	..	..	..	0
Statham b Gomez	..	..	..	..	0
Extras (b 6, lb 1, w 1)	..	..	..	..	8
Total ..	..	..	..	..	313

BOWLING ANALYSIS

	O.	M.	R.	W.
King	18	6	56	2
Atkinson	23	10	35	1
Ramadhin	37	17	71	3
Valentine	39	18	87	0
Walcott	2	0	4	0
Stollmeyer	6	1	14	2
Gomez	13.4	3	28	2
Worrell	1	0	10	0

CHAPTER SIX

ON leaving Barbados one consolation was that everything might
have been worse for Hutton and his men.

For one thing M.C.C. escaped the indignity of losing the colony
game with Barbados by the barest of margins.

When Freddie Trueman, the last man in, went to the wicket
rolling up his sleeves with his customary and commendable air of
purpose, M.C.C. were twelve runs short of victory, and John
Goddard having started a collapse, Barbados were right on their
toes.

Goddard, still more than a useful off-spin bowler, immediately
rapped Alan Moss on the pad and appealed. At the end of the over
the umpire spoke to Alan. "Good job you snicked that ball first," he
said, "otherwise I should have given you out leg-before."

Alan kept a sensible silence for he alone knew that, in fact, the
ball hit the pad first and the bat second.

Three leg-byes off the pads of Alan Moss brought the winning
runs and Trueman, who had done all the striking in the last stand,
observed, "I shut my eyes and when I opened them again we had
won."

Barbados fielded several promising young players, including de
Pieza, a wicketkeeper, Griffith, a left-hand batsman, the son of the
famous fast bowler—how often the M.C.C. encountered cricketing
sons of illustrious cricketing fathers—and Sobers, a left-arm spinner
of no little skill.

For M.C.C. the happiest feature was the return to form of Ken
Suttle, the twenty-five-year-old Sussex left-hander, who up till then
had experienced a discouraging run of low scores. To his credit he
accepted his misfortunes in good heart and, when Hutton was taken
ill and Compton, the acting captain, called for a volunteer to open
with Watson, Suttle asked to be given the job. His second innings of
62 was a far better knock than the bigger score of 96 he made in the
first innings. This proved that Ken had benefited from a form-
finding experience.

When scoring one of his seven centuries last year, for Sussex
against Middlesex at Lord's, Suttle had made a deep impression on
Sir Pelham Warner. He is a bundle of energy, an incessant talker and
enjoys life to the full.

One of the best swimmers in the team, he pulled a drowning girl out of the sea at Bridgetown. Willie Watson, Dick Spooner, Ken Suttle and Reg Hayter, Reuter's correspondent, were playing beach football at the Accra Beach Club when Suttle heard cries of distress from the bather's companion. He brought the girl ashore with the assistance of Spooner. That night, at the player's club meeting, he was "fined" sixpence for posing as a hero!

A magnificent fieldsman, Suttle took several deep-field catches with aplomb. There are some outfielders who position themselves so well and remain so calm and assured that the catch, no matter how high or difficult, appears a certainty from the moment it leaves the bat. Ken is one of that type of outfielder.

Kensington Oval has at least two claims to distinction. First are the drink waiters. For years, crowds at Kensington have wagered on the first of the two to arrive at the pavilion gate on their return from serving refreshment to the players. Naturally, the waiters are not ignorant of the situation and, with the broadest of grins, first one then the other takes the lead to cheers and groans. Usually the race finishes in the deadest of dead heats. I could find no confirmation for the story that the waiters themselves do a little side-betting!

Jim Laker, in his second county match for Surrey, discovered that not always are the drinks taken on the field so soft and innocent as so many people assume. Towards the end of his fine career Alf Gover, the Surrey fast bowler, liked a pick-me-up of a tot of whiskey taken to him on the field, and a special glass was always earmarked for him.

One day, unaware of the great man's distinction, Jim picked up Alf's glass and swallowed the contents, only to discover the liquid therein was not ginger ale after all!

Another feature of Barbados cricket is the presence of pirate grandstands outside the ground. These certainly look the flimsiest of structures and I was not surprised to learn that past experience had taught the local hospital authorities to prepare beds for an emergency during important matches.

A low wall on one side of the ground gives boys the opportunity of watching the game standing on top of round poles whose diameter can be no more than four inches.

Apart from this being an outstanding feat of balance, no small endurance is required to stay on the poles any length of time. Moreover, in view of the intense competition for places, no boy dare relinquish his post for even a fleeting second.

One day, when the wind blew hard and strong, I was intrigued to see the boys maintaining their balance by pulling on thick string tied to the post lower down.

One of the charms of the West Indies and, indeed, something which provides a solid reason for their advance as a cricket power, is their unbridled enthusiasm.

Their players have no inhibitions, no hard and fast theories, and they are certainly not over-coached. A climate which gives them virtually a twelve-months' season, plumb wickets and a natural delight in hitting a ball enables them to overcome obstacles which most of their English counterparts would regard as impossible handicaps. Not all can afford equipment, so they make shift with bats carved from the branches of coconut trees.

This puts the coconut trees to better use than a notorious character of Barbados in the early 1800s, one Sam Lord. The players visited his "Castle" on the way to a delectable beach luncheon party at the Crane Hotel given to both Test teams by the Barbados Cricket Association.

Lord fixed lanterns on the topmost branches of the beach coconut trees. As they swayed in the breeze, these were mistaken by the masters of passing ships for the lights of other vessels riding at anchor in the bay. Assuming a safe anchorage to be there the unwary sea captains came nearer the shore only to be wrecked on the treacherous reefs.

Lord trained slaves to brave the heavy seas, which run against the reefs, and to plunder the stricken wrecks.

West Indies boys haunt cricket grounds and many are the M.C.C. batsmen who were given practice, and good practice, by bare-footed urchins. I have seen Hutton receive all types of spin, including the googly, from youngsters who would make many a strong London club side think twice.

Evidence of the knowledge they have of cricket and cricketers is available every day and really is an eye-opener. Nothing appears to escape them. I saw a group laughing heartily at photographs of M.C.C. players displayed in the window of a departmental store in Georgetown. Over Ken Suttle's name was a photograph of Peter Loader, the young Surrey bowler. Though Loader has only recently entered English county cricket the bystanders were able to tell me who he was and what type of ball he bowled.

Junior teams burn with ambition. John Goddard, who has done so much for West Indies cricket, told me of a side from the Leeward Islands which took the field at Kensington Oval in the manner of a squad of soldiers marching in military precision behind the captain.

As they reached the wicket, they peeled off to their fielding positions, standing alertly to attention until the first ball was delivered.

Umpires are equally enthusiastic. In one second-class fixture the

M.C.C., who were batting at the time, were much amused to see the action of the square-leg umpire when a stumping chance, offered by Len Hutton, was missed.

The umpire leaped high in the air and, when the ball was fumbled, he clenched his fist and jerked his arm in a gesture of acute disappointment.

In a junior game at Bridgetown the umpire, uncertain of his decision over a knotty point, held up the game, while he rushed off the field to consult a law book. Minutes later he raced back and, on arrival at the wicket, thrust up the index finger of his right hand to indicate that the batsman was out—for obstruction!

CHAPTER SEVEN

HUTTON and Co. did not take long to realize that a visit to
the far-flung islands of the West Indies was an unusual tour,
presenting unusual problems. As the weeks went by the M.C.C.
players grew accustomed to the scorching sun, the over-prepared
pitches, the noisy, restless and sometimes near-hysterical crowds
behind their high wire netting—even to the sight of the bulk of a
cinema audience remaining seated during the playing of the National
Anthem.

The M.C.C. party realized that lurking in the background was
the hidden but powerful hand of politics. In the open, for all to see,
and the outsider to wonder at, were the uncloaked inter-island
jealousies which, unless checked, threaten to become the Achilles
heel of West Indies cricket.

Added to everything was the vexed question of the standard of
West Indian umpiring which came to a head during the colony
match with British Guiana at Georgetown.

Before the next M.C.C. tour of the West Indies the matter of
umpiring is a subject which, for the sake of good relations between
the two cricketing powers, must be tackled fearlessly. Never again
must an M.C.C. captain be put in the awkward and ridiculous
position in which Hutton found himself at Georgetown.

The agreement for the tour was that the colony in which the Test
was played should provide the two umpires. Thus, in Jamaica the
umpires were Jamaicans; in Barbados two Barbadians officiated,
and so on—rather a throwback to the days when each English
county had its "own" umpire.

If he was not satisfied with the competence of the men standing
in the colony game which always preceded the Test, Hutton, as
England's captain, had the right to request replacements in the Test
Match. He did so at British Guiana. In his opinion neither Alwyn
Rollox nor Cecil Kippings gave evidence of being up to Test
standard. Hutton did not take the step without a great deal of
thought or without considering his action vital and necessary.
He further requested that either Burke and Ewart of Jamaica, or
Walcott and Jordan from Barbados, should be flown to British
Guiana for the third Test.

83

Hutton's objection to Rollox and Kippings was upheld but the British Guiana Board vetoed his suggestion of umpires from other colonies. Although they admitted the local standard allowed the minimum of choice, they insisted that British Guiana should provide the alternative officials.

Hutton was thus placed in the situation of (1) accepting the retention of the two men the Board had agreed were below the standard required, or (2) accepting two nominees only one of whom he knew. He was E. S. ("Wing") Gillette, a Chinese who had umpired in the corresponding Test of 1948 but had since retired.

Hutton was forced to take the word of the local officials that their other nominee, "Badge" Menzies, the fifty-seven-year-old Indian with the Scots name and groundsman at the Georgetown Cricket Club, the venue of the Test, was a good and competent umpire.

Because of his duties as groundsman, "Badge's" recent experience of first-class umpiring had been strictly limited. On the other hand he was an instructor to the local cricket umpires' association.

Hutton had to make a "blind" choice and he agreed to Menzies because, frankly, he saw no alternative. When the decision was reached Menzies was superintending the rolling of the Test wicket. Officially he was told that, while umpiring in the Test, he would be relieved of his tasks as groundsman but "Badge" would allow no one to take over his precious duties.

Throughout the game he supervised ground arrangements from seven o'clock in the morning until just before the start of play, when hurriedly he would don the umpire's white coat and "stand for" the five hours of cricket.

The decision to appoint Menzies and "Wing" Gillette was taken on the Sunday morning immediately following the colony game at Georgetown in which the umpiring had given little satisfaction.

While hundreds of guests fraternized at a pre-lunch cocktail party given in the Georgetown Cricket Club pavilion by the British Guiana Board, Hutton and manager Palmer sat in a corner of the room, discussing the situation with Stollmeyer and members of the West Indies Board.

The English captain and manager accepted the fact that time and distance made the flying out of Burke and Ewart from Jamaica impracticable but the arguments not to send for Walcott and Jordan really amounted to a confession that "we are afraid of political repercussions".

Many times over in British Guiana I was told, "We dare not bring other umpires here in case anything goes wrong." Who could deny the absence of such a possibility after the threats to umpire Perry Burke during the first Test at Kingston?

The West Indies plea of economy as grounds for appointing local umpires made no sense when players were sent long distances a week or so ahead merely "to be available for selection" and when those not chosen for the match remained as guests of the Board for the duration of the game.

Times have changed. The days when an English "second eleven" could be sent to the West Indies and be able to hold its own have disappeared. Unhappily new issues are at hand and, in the Tests, national prestige is fiercely at stake.

In future the M.C.C. should demand the appointment of a panel of the best umpires in the Caribbean, irrespective of colony or colour, from whom the Test officials should be chosen. Failing that, an English umpire should accompany the team.

Following complaints about the umpiring on a previous tour the late Joe Hardstaff, senior, accompanied the M.C.C. 1930 team to West Indies, as umpire and baggage man. M.C.C. could point to this as a precedent.

To ignore the issue will only store up trouble for future teams.

Hutton was clearly justified in asking for new umpires for the third Test. Since M.C.C. won by an innings and 98 runs—a convincing enough margin even if British Guiana are regarded as the weakest of the colony sides—his complaint could not be argued away as that of a peeved losing captain.

I do not wish to dwell on the controversies caused by the umpiring in the colony game, but a lot of private indignation was aroused by the refusal of almost every leg-before appeal and the action of the umpires in drawing stumps on the second day when two minutes remained for play and another over easily could have been started.

Unfortunately one decision, just before the close of play on the third day, was indirectly the cause of a scene. British Guiana had followed on 345 behind—Johnny Wardle having taken 6 for 77 in the first innings—with twenty minutes' batting time before the drawing of stumps. Trying to press home M.C.C.'s advantage, Hutton asked Trueman to make an all-out effort.

Freddie did so right away. Gibbs played back to his first ball which was well pitched up and apparently heading straight for the middle and off stumps. As soon as the ball hit the pad, Trueman and Dick Spooner, normally a very reticent appealer, roared their claim, which was refused. Spooner, trying hard to contain himself, walked round in circles, his cap pushed back well over his forehead.

Next ball Trueman was no-balled. He overstepped the crease again in the opening over and once more in the second. After calling the third no-ball Kippings, lanky and pith-helmeted, suddenly left the wicket and went down the pitch to Hutton, who was fielding in the gulley. On listening to what was obviously a complaint, Hutton changed places with Suttle at mid-on. The game proceeded without further incident until the close, but Hutton who left the field was white-faced and agitated.

Neither he nor Kippings would reveal exactly what took place. Hutton tried to cover up the episode with a lengthy explanation about Trueman's drag and the difficulties Freddie faced in seeing the line as he ran up to bowl, but it was only too clear that in the heat of the moment *l'enfant terrible* of English cricket had said something which he should not.

No matter how unjust or cruel it may seem at the moment, Trueman must realize that the umpire's decision is final. He must learn not to show his feelings either by word or gesticulation. Otherwise he may ruin what promised to be a golden future. As a friend—and I admire many things in this blunt Yorkshire lad—I urge him, with all my force, to make a serious and determined effort to keep himself in control.

In the colony match umpire Kippings refused to stand close to the stumps when asked by Tony Lock, who wanted to come from behind him, as he normally does when bowling round the wicket. Some overs afterwards Lock bowled one ball from directly behind the stumps and a yard away from them.

The rules of cricket stipulate a batsman is entitled to be notified of a bowler changing his style—from over to round the wicket or vice versa. Should not the bowler also have to advise the batsman before delivering the ball from behind the stumps? Lock's intention was to surprise the batsman. Had he succeeded it might have raised a fine point of cricket Law.

Years ago Wilfred Rhodes described the Georgetown pitch as the best in the world, and "Patsy" Hendren, whose name is never far away from any cricket conversation in the West Indies, declared that, as long as he concentrated, no batsman of class should be dismissed there.

Time has not changed the quality of the Georgetown pitch and when Hutton won the toss and batted first M.C.C. looked certain to amass a huge total.

They lost Hutton, May and Compton for only 51 runs but in the end made 607, the highest total of an M.C.C. side overseas since the war.

Hutton, who began the 1948 tour with a century at Georgetown, found the present pitch slower than most others in the West Indies and, playing a shade too soon, was caught in the covers for one of his rare "ducks".

On returning to the dressing-room Hutton said to his team-mates, "You'll never have a better pitch to bat on or meet a more moderate attack." May then went out, slashed at a short-pitched ball and was caught at the wicket. Back in the players' room he confirmed Hutton's opinion. Soon Compton then dragged an off-break well wide of his off stump into his wicket. He said precisely the same as Hutton and May.

The trio must have kicked themselves when they saw Willie Watson and Tom Graveney who, at number five, had given himself scant prospect of batting on the first day, crash club standard bowling all over the field. Both made double centuries and the highest scores of their careers and, had not Watson been first to follow the captain's instructions and get out after passing 200, the 55-year-old English record of 448 for the fourth wicket held by Bobby Abel and Tom Hayward, for Surrey against Yorkshire at The Oval, would have perished. As it was Watson and Graveney made 402 together.

One custom of the British Guiana crowd must be unique—it was new to me and nobody I have met can cap the experience. When a batsman is one short of either a half century or a century, say 49, 99, 149 or a similar score, the crowd at Georgetown break out into a steady handclap. They do so also when a partnership is within one or two runs of any corresponding landmark.

At first I thought this was a form of barracking. Then I discovered the crowd were trying to encourage the batsmen into obtaining the single needed for the immediate objective. The rhythm of the clap is different from normal handclapping. It gains in tempo as the bowler approaches the wicket. The last thought in the minds of the spectators is any attempt to distract the batsman, but I imagine it must be rather disturbing.

Georgetown Cricket Club has a special ladies' stand into which men may be invited but a similar courtesy is not extended to ladies in the men's pavilion. Women, being the more sensible and practical sex, have a standing rule forbidding "treating". They buy their own drinks and adhere strictly to the rules.

A tall flagmast by the pavilion serves as a reminder of the days when, as the Georgetown ground was not connected by telephone, a flag system was evolved to overcome the difficulties. Members, from quite long distances, were able to "read" the flags which, in the event of rain, saved them an unnecessary journey.

Rain in British Guiana often is so localized that a member, even within easy walking distance of the ground, cannot be sure whether conditions are fit or unfit for play. One night, on coming out of a cinema, I found hundreds from the audience blocking the gangway because of torrential rain which was forming into large pools by the roadway. The other side of the street, fifteen yards away, was bone dry.

Thus it may be appreciated how anyone not directly on the ground might not know whether rain was falling there or not. To spread the news as quickly as possible, in the days before the installation of a telephone, a red flag was raised on the mast when cricket was "off", and a blue flag flown if tennis had been washed out. When neither tennis nor cricket could be played both red and blue flags were hoisted.

The same ritual is observed today, as we saw when rain interfered with the Test Match. Bill Cooper, a member of the British Guiana Board of Control Committee and host at a very jolly evening party to the M.C.C., is one of the many who look through their bedroom windows each morning of a match to see if either or which flag is flying. Certainly that is one way of economizing on telephone bills!

Georgetown is also the home of the Sunday afternoon sport of goat racing, supervised by the British Guiana Goat Racing Association.

Out of sheer curiosity, I went to the British Guiana Cricket Club ground to see what this strange sport had to offer.

The goats, which looked to be extremely well cared for, and very keen to race, are piloted by jockeys, clad in multi- and gaily-coloured garb. The jockeys, holding on to their goats by string reins, run some two to three paces behind them. I did not know which to back—the goat or the jockey.

For my first wager I placed two West Indies dollars (8s. 4d.) on a much-fancied goat in the Len Hutton Stakes—never can one get entirely away from cricket in the West Indies—and the jockey clad in the blue and white hooped shirt as recently worn by the Queen's Park Rangers footballers. My pair won easily but my winnings amounted to the princely sum of eight cents—precisely fourpence!

I left the M.C.C. Stakes and the Jeff Stollmeyer Purse strictly alone, won 2s. 6d. in the W-Formation Handicap, only to lose all in the Fred Trueman Handicap.

Goat racing is just one of those things which, I am sure, could happen only in the West Indies.

The way M.C.C. disposed of British Guiana on Georgetown's notoriously lifeless pitch was not regarded as significant nor as a pointer to the possible course of the vital third Test which England had to win if they were to retain competitive interest in the series

After all, it could be asked, had not M.C.C. beaten the stronger
colony teams of Jamaica and Barbados and yet lost the Tests at
Kingston and Bridgetown?

To be honest, the hopes of the English supporters did not rise
noticeably after the victory over British Guiana. On the other hand,
to give an example of the unimpaired confidence of the West Indies,
I quote this published comment:

> "We (the West Indies) have got at least two teams who can
> give the present M.C.C. team a thorough hiding and teach its
> men the lesson they need to learn."

I still have not discovered what that lesson was supposed to be.

To many in British Guiana the result of the Test appeared to be
a foregone conclusion. One major question alone remained for
discussion—would Robert Christiani ("Sir Robert" to the crowd) be
included? Christiani, captain of British Guiana and undoubtedly a
fine player with a splendid Test record, enhanced his prospects with
scores of 75 and 82 against M.C.C. in the colony match.

These innings provided the inspiration the three Georgetown
papers and the public needed to back yet another campaign to get
the local hero into the Test eleven. Typical of the views expressed was
an open letter addressed to the Selectors and headed: "Our Robert
must play in third Test."

Another critic dismissed with disarming simplicity the big point
at issue—whom to drop for Christiani—with the words: "Christiani *must* find a place in the side. The question of 'who not to play'
is the selectors' funeral."

Certainly, in the colony game Christiani, a brilliant stroke-
player, treated the M.C.C. attack with scant respect, but it was an
open secret among the inner circle that at least one decision which
went in his favour early in his first innings was a factor in Hutton's
justifiable complaint about the standard of umpiring.

Little surprise arose when the Selectors, skipper Stollmeyer and
his first lieutenant, Frank Worrell, now joined by the local Board of
Control representative, an executive of the British Guiana club,
picked Christiani among the twelve players from whom the final
Test eleven was to be picked.

I could view this choice as only another instance of the insularity
which runs through all West Indies cricket. The awkward matter of
deciding whom to leave out was postponed, but the Selectors were
relieved of embarrassment, and perhaps another player was spared
injustice, by the withdrawal through injury of the other British
Guiana batsman, Bruce Pairaudeau.

The hand which Bruce damaged in the second Test had not responded to treatment as quickly as had been expected and he was a very disappointed man at having to stand down in his home town.

"If I had to choose to play in only one of the five Tests, I would plump for a game at Georgetown," he told me.

When the twelve names were announced (the team-sheet posted in the Georgetown Cricket Club pavilion listed M.C.C. and not England as the opponents) the crowd, which had waited patiently outside, cheered in warm approval. *Christiani was in.* Nothing else seemed to matter.

As the news spread to the centre of the town motorists, particularly when passing the M.C.C. hotel headquarters, pounded their horns with a gusto usually associated with events of great national importance—such as an armistice declaration. I preferred to look upon the affair rather as a complete surrender by the West Indies Selectors.

The outsider, like myself, could only wonder. At Kingston George Headley, the Jamaican veteran, and Frederick, another local star, had played in the one Test. Now Christiani was in the team in his native Georgetown. The inclusion of Denis Atkinson at Barbados, supported though it also was by strong local clamour, could hardly be entered in this category for Atkinson had earned his place on sheer skill and performance both as a batsman and as a general-purposes bowler.

Like Headley and Frederick before him Christiani failed in his one Test, scoring 25 and 11, and he was dropped when the "circus" moved on to the next stopping place, Trinidad.

Further, the case of Esmond Kentish could be cited. Kentish bowled out England in the second innings of the Kingston Test, and played a lion's share in the West Indies victory. Yet, for the second Test, at Barbados, he was displaced by Frank King (of Barbados). To be fair, King had been among the original selections for the Jamaican game but had to cry off on account of injury in a trial game there. King was left out of the third Test, but recalled for the fourth and fifth.

I simply cannot think what would happen in England if anything similar to the West Indies situation occurred over the choice of Test teams. Say, for instance, if the side for the first Test, at Nottingham, picked by Hutton (captain), Bailey (vice-captain), together with one Nottinghamshire selector, included Reg Simpson for the one game only; then, on a Middlesex selector taking over from the Nottinghamshire representative for the Lord's Test, if Jack Robertson came in for Simpson. And, if from there, the captain and vice captain moved on to Old Trafford where they would deliberate with the Lancashire representative, resulting in Cyril Washbrook replacing Robertson. Frank Lowson would become favourite to be Hutton's opening partner at Leeds, and David Fletcher at The Oval. It would be a queer business. It *is* a queer business in the West Indies.

CHAPTER EIGHT

UNBEKNOWN to Hutton a private dinner-party, called and
attended by his senior players, was held on the eve of the third
Test—the Test which few people in the West Indies believed could
finish with a decisive result, let alone in England's favour.

Already Charles Palmer, with a broad smile, had announced to
the correspondents that the one England change would be Wardle
for Palmer, and, though I would be the last to deny the ever-cheerful
Johnny had not richly deserved his promotion, I was left to regret
Palmer's one excursion into Test cricket had not produced the results
his ability warranted.

If Hutton wondered where and why his key men had disappeared during the hours of dinner I doubt whether it occurred to
him that they were scheming behind his back—scheming to organize
the maximum support for a captain carrying the responsibility of
probably the toughest-ever overseas assignment.

Compton, Bailey and Co. planned to mix even more freely
with the younger element and help disperse any lingering doubts
which the depressing experience of two successive Test defeats
might have produced. They agreed that everyone should be encouraged to do all in his power to avoid giving the captain the
slightest cause for worry. They knew that if they could "keep Len
happy" they would help to produce the maximum effort all round.

Several little pep talks were held during the course of the next
few days, and I think they had material effect in producing the
will-to-win spirit which swept through the side.

Another factor which played its part in completely uniting the
team was the bottle-throwing incident on the fourth day of the Test.
Little could the yob who started all the trouble have realized that
he was the unwitting instrument which spurred England to ever
greater efforts.

I doubt whether the real reason for the inglorious and disgrace
ful scene at Georgetown towards the close of play on Saturday
February 27, 1954, will be unearthed, or whether anyone can
prove either that it was spontaneous mob reaction to an unpopula

umpiring decision or an organized political anti-British demonstration.

Several local officials took the more serious view that it was a
staged and pre-arranged outburst. They pointed to the large number
of bottles, wooden and cardboard boxes and missiles which were
available at the one spot where the demonstration began.

Support to this theory was the fact that the Right Honourable
Alan Knight, the Archbishop of West Indies and Bishop of British
Guiana, telephoned both Bill Cooper, member of the British Guiana
Cricket Committee, and the Editor of the local *Argosy* newspaper a
week beforehand, reporting that he had heard from various sources
that trouble would be raised by the crowd during the Test. He
passed on the information so that suitable and necessary arrangements could be taken to deal with any disturbance.

In my opinion some of the trouble, apart from the cheapness of
rum and the Guianese love of betting, sprang from the crowd's
practice of clapping in anticipation of the completion of an individual
century or half century, or when a partnership was within striking
distance of a similar figure.

In this case here was the thrilling position of a local hero in
Clifford McWatt, the British Guiana wicketkeeper, and an injured
John Holt, batting with a runner because of a bad limp, stemming
a West Indies collapse, after seven wickets had fallen for 139 runs.

Excitement and near-hysteria, which inevitably must be associated with the West Indian crowds of 1954, mounted as McWatt and
Holt took the score nearer and nearer to the 286 needed to save the
follow-on.

By the time the stand had reached 98 the crowd were clapping
and cheering madly. Then McWatt struck a ball towards the leg
boundary and, either under-rating the fielding abilities of May or
caught up in the crowd's frenzy, he turned for a second run which
was never "on". When McWatt began to try and race back to his
original end May had the ball in his hand. Peter threw him out by
at least two yards. The distance by which McWatt failed to make his
ground was McWatt's own estimate—not mine. So the partnership
ended at 99.

A momentary lull followed, just as though the crowd had not
grasped the significance of the event. Then the first of hundreds of
bottles, tins and boxes streamed in the direction of umpire "Badge"
Menzies, who had given McWatt out, and Peter May, the nearest
English fieldsman to the unfortunate umpire.

One bottle fell at Peter's feet. He and Menzies quickly and
prudently scampered out of range.

As if in mob sympathy, a section of the crowd on the opposite side of the field, in the stand where the Press were accommodated, also pelted bottles and tins, and I am ashamed to say one bottle actually came from the Press box. The English correspondents insisted on a policeman being called. He came, looked and left with considerable speed, but without taking any positive action.

Meanwhile the mounted and foot police, who had been almost immobile at the height of the disturbance which threatened to become a dangerous riot, watched a man rush on to the field, speak to Ramadhin, the new batsman, and go back to his place in the crowd. Again they took no action.

By now some boys, with highly-developed commercial instincts, had gone on to the field to collect the bottles. Another missile narrowly missed the head of one of them. Immediately he picked up a bottle and returned it, with a strong left-arm action, right back into the thick of the stand from which most of them had been hurled. He followed up the attack strongly and then beat a gallant but hasty retreat.

For ten minutes not a ball was bowled. Players and umpires stood there surveying the growing mess. Then Denis Compton tossed a bottle back to the edge of the boundary and Johnny Wardle raised a laugh, at least from part of the crowd, by picking up another bottle, pretending to take a "swig" and feigning intoxication.

This eased the situation but Mr. W. S. Jones, President of the British Guiana Board of Control, acting on the advice of senior officials, then left the pavilion and went out to Hutton.

"This scene is becoming ugly," he said. "I think you and your team should come off the field."

To which Hutton made his magnificent reply: "No, we'll stay. We want another wicket or two this evening because we mean to win the match. These people are not going to get us off. That may be their idea but, if so, they are wrong."

The West Indies batsmen and the two umpires were far less anxious to remain than were Hutton and his team.

Meanwhile Mr. Ken Wishart, the Secretary of the British Guiana Board of Control and member of the West Indies Board of Control, who was commentating on the radio, hurriedly handed over the microphone to Crawford White of the *News Chronicle*, saying: "You'll have to take over, Crawford. I must go."

Wishart ran across to the pavilion and there telephoned police headquarters for them to send along the riot squad. Unlike the local writer who next day condemned the factual Reuter's report as approaching hysteria and asked people not to "make too much out of the incident" Ken Wishart took the most serious view possible of the disturbance.

When the game proceeded Jim Laker immediately obliged Hutton by bowling Ramadhin, but insufficient time remained for England to take the last West Indies wicket before the close of play.

No praise could be too high for Hutton, who had every excuse to lead his men off the field to the security of the pavilion, and there can be little doubt his decision prevented worse disorders.

The simple action of the dour strong-minded England captain in turning his back on the mob and concentrating on the job on hand was a symbol of English character and, as such, more eloquent than a thousand speeches, more forceful than a volley of bullets. I have never felt prouder of "our Len".

Lest any who were 4,000 or so miles from the scene thought that any of the correspondents reporting the tour were guilty of exaggeration I quote from the local Press. The first extract is from the *Sunday Chronicle*. Headed "Shame on You, British Guiana" it reads:

"The West Indies won Test Match recognition in the 20's by virtue of their prowess on the field. Not only that; they were acclaimed on all sides as jolly sporting fellows, who took defeat with a broad, white-toothed grin, and this helped greatly to their being admitted into the fold when their case came up in the councils of the M.C.C.

Now that we have attained to a position where we are handing out defeats to other sides, must we demonstrate to the world that we have not yet learnt to win? Never have I seen so disgraceful an exhibition of unsportsmanlike hooliganism as that with which the north-western section of yesterday's mammoth crowd sought to register their disapproval of an umpire's decision.

British Guiana has attained worldwide unwelcome notoriety in other fields of endeavour and that is bad enough as it is. Now the entire cricket world is to learn that it is unsafe for even our own umpires to give a decision against our players.

If ever I felt ashamed of fellow British Guianese it was yesterday evening at Bourda as the air grew thick with bottles, boxes, boos and imprecations. And what made the affair infinitely more shameful is the incredible fact that there were many of accredited superior intelligence ready to condone, even agree with the shameful display of uncouthness and lack of restraint. This was no fight or demonstration of one's inalienable rights but a vulgar expression of discontent and a shameful confession that we are poor losers.

I thank skipper Hutton for not leading his men off the field, as he had every right to do. It certainly did seem that the crowd had seen enough cricket for their money.

And now I can only hope that the report of this does not influence Australia to reconsider their decision to tour these parts next year. But perhaps that is what the demonstrators want; or do they?

No. The behaviour was unwarranted, unmannerly and indefensible and this newspaper would not be doing its duty if we did not in plain language condemn it.

Skipper Hutton and his fellow English players must understand that it is an expression of the sentiments of a very tiny section of the British Guiana public who, we claim, are in the main as appreciative of good cricket and what good sportsmanship means as any other community in the world."

The second extract is taken from the *Guiana Graphic*, under the heading "Cause for Anxiety".
It says:

"British Guiana is descending to lower and lower levels of behaviour in the eyes of the world, and this can do no good for the people of this country. What happened on the G.C.C. ground on Saturday last during the third Test Match between the M.C.C. and the West Indies was not a mere incident.

For some years now there have been foreign-trained propagandists in the Colony who have been concentrating on stirring up a spirit of disregard for other people's rights, a spirit of hostility to the old ideas of order and discipline, a spirit of contempt for religion and a very false idea that it savours of the spirit of independence for anyone to be as rough and as crude as possible in his deals with others.

It would appear to be a blessing in disguise that the Constitutional Commission is still in this Colony to witness for itself the pitch of lawlessness to which the masses of our people are being egged on, because they will be able to realize at first hand just what this country will be committed to if the ruling voice at present is deposited with people whose creed is mob law and who show no disposition to acknowledge the value of trying to control themselves.

What happened on Saturday was, as we have said, not an incident. It was of a piece with the spirit of lawlessness which caused spectators to mob the House of Assembly last year and cast its dignity and sanctity to the winds. And if a people cannot reverence their own caretaker Institutions then indeed their plight is a sorry one.

We are not concerned with whether the decision on the cricket field was right or not. What gives us anxiety is that even the field of sport is not now beyond the pale of the consequences coming from the venom which the subversive political propagandists have injected into the blood of our people.

We are not out to condemn the latter because we still believe that they can be capable of higher and better things as a whole, but we must point to the drift of events by which they are being taken, so to speak, right into the jaws of hell. If it be made possible for them to gain control of the affairs of this country before they learn to control themselves and pay proper consideration to such things as the rights of others and due observance of the decent obligations for living in a civilized community then we shall have nothing but ruin all around us.

When on top of this spirit of lawlessness there is being cultivated a spirit of disloyalty to the Throne to which we all owe Allegiance and without whose protection we could not defend ourselves against the attacks of any foreign enemies, then we foresee the time approaching when our misguided people will be lured into causing useless and serious shedding of blood. It is of no use shrinking from facing this reality; because if things are allowed to take, undisturbed, the course on which they are bent this will surely be."

The third is from the *Daily Argosy*, titled "Unseemly Behaviour At Bourda".

"This last-named incident (the run-out of McWatt)," says the *Argosy* writer, "seemed to be the touch-off.

Immediately the crowd in the public secondary school stand began to murmur dissent, then showed their feelings in a more practical form by hurling bottles on the field of play. The north-western stand was not long in joining in while the primary school children (also on the northern side of the ground) also got rid of bottles.

In a short while bottles and empty cartons were tossed on the field of play. Then a few from the rails, on the south-eastern side joined in, finally followed by the more eastern of the southern stands, an action that one would least have expected from this direction.

Whatever the reason, or reasons, however, there could be no justification for this flagrant breach of good manners. British

Guianese have ever been famed for their high sense of sportsmanship, and it is regrettable that such ill-behaviour should have been displayed, more so on such an occasion. Throughout the world, umpires' decisions are questioned and protested against, but when such actions as yesterday are employed, then it must be the duty of every well-thinking person to join in condemnation.

Another point is that the decisions were given by one of our own umpires, a British Guianese who for a number of years has been regarded as one of the most competent umpires in this Colony.

Never before has the fair play of this umpire been questioned; always has he been looked upon with esteem and with respect.

Thus, it is an even more disgraceful state of affairs that the umpire in question found it necessary to run off the field straight into the pavilion immediately play had ceased. Yet more disgusting is the sad fact that quite a few waited outside the ground, voicing threats—although the presence of a Police riot squad leaves the impression that these threats were empty ones.

The English players were alike astounded at the scene. There is nothing in the crowd's unseemly behaviour to amuse decent Guianese. Indeed, this is shocking behaviour. There is always a point beyond which one could go, and this was very much exceeded yesterday.

It can only be hoped now that during the remaining days of the tour this same crowd will strive its best in an effort to regain some lost decorum for this hospitable and friendly land of Guiana."

Shortly before the close of play square-leg umpire Gillette asked Godfrey Evans if he would be good enough to bring in the ball and the bails as he himself intended to hurry off the field.

Godfrey, who has never been known to be intimidated by any situation on or off the field of cricket, waited behind the stumps for the ball to be returned from the deep field, then nonchalantly picked off the bails and, with his friend, Denis Compton, coolly strolled towards the pavilion.

By this time umpires Menzies and Gillette, who had fled from the scene, were safely inside the West Indies dressing-room.

The moment the game finished some two or three score of English residents and other friends and well-wishers of the players hurried out to form an avenue of protection for the cricketers to walk through as they left the field. The gesture was greatly appreciated.

Behind them mounted and foot police held back the several thousands of the crowd who had swarmed on to the turf.

The police riot squad, complete with tin helmets, truncheons and tear gas bombs, arrived outside the ground and remained in their trucks in the road by the pavilion.

Menzies, still trembling twenty minutes after the close of play, would not leave the West Indies dressing-room for a long time.

Yet, in this strained and dangerous atmosphere, the M.C.C. players held their usual Saturday evening get-together in the England dressing-room. Not even riots could disturb that weekly function. The first toast, as usual, was "Wives and Sweethearts", then "Absent Friends"—and for the first time on the tour they added a third. It was "April 20th"—the day they were to arrive back in England.

Half an hour after the stumps had been drawn, Gerry Gomez and I stood on the pavilion steps surveying the bottles, broken glass, tumblers, cigarette and fruit-juice tins and big wooden cases which were scattered on the grass.

"They were just like the crowd at a bull-fight when the bull escapes the kill," remarked the unhappy Gerry Gomez.

Next to us was Ken Wishart, one of the men who give much time and energy to keeping first-class cricket alive in the colony. Ken, completely disgusted, told me he would have to support any proposal to take Tests away from Georgetown. This, as he told me, was not their first experience of serious crowd trouble.

During the Indian tour of West Indies the previous year rain seeped through the covers during the Georgetown Test and caused a wet patch. Captains Jeff Stollmeyer and Vijay Hazare agreed the pitch was not fit for play.

Such was the temper of the packed crowd who believed they might be cheated out of their money's worth, however, that the captains agreed to disagree and leave the matter in the hands of the umpires.

On their inspection of the pitch, the umpires confirmed the opinions of the two captains but, on returning to the pavilion, they were met by local officials who implored them to change their minds.

A lengthy conference then took place between officials, captains and umpires, as a result of which the captains reluctantly agreed to make a delayed start, merely to appease the crowd.

If Test captains are to be at the mercy of the crowd, International cricket, or any class of cricket for that matter, becomes farcical. Cricket cannot, and must not, be dominated by *mob rule*, for it is no other.

I firmly believe that the large amount of betting which takes place on many of the cricket grounds of the West Indies is responsible for much of the unhappy and unhealthy atmosphere in which the game is played.

To bet on an uncertain game such as cricket is simply crazy but the urge to wager is much too strong for many West Indians to resist, and they will bet on the most ridiculous and fantastic things, such as the number of runs scored from any ball, or from any over, where the ball will be played and even which hand a fieldsman will use to pick up the ball.

In the M.C.C. colony game with British Guiana, Trevor Bailey came to sit next to me in the Press box. Scarcely had he taken his seat when two excited men ran up and asked him whether a ball which had been grounded earlier in the day was a catch or a bump ball. When the verdict was given as a catch two dollars changed hands.

After play one evening in the same match a terrific fight developed between two men in front of the pavilion. Their quarrel started over the manner of Hutton's dismissal in the second innings of the second Test at Lord's in 1950. One of the contestants pulled a knife, and the situation looked really ugly, but police intervened in time. Both men finished in a Black Maria.

Then Denis Compton, fielding on the edge of the boundary on the last day of the Test, was challenged to bet £50 England would not win by more than eight wickets. The spectator said he would call at the England dressing-room half an hour after the end of the match, one way or the other. Denis merely smiled back. England won by nine wickets but the would-be gambler did not appear. I wondered whether he would have turned up to collect his supposed winnings if England had lost another wicket, as indeed they might, Willie Watson being missed at cover by Alf Valentine before making the winning hit for six from a half volley bowled by Everton Weekes.

I heard also of a wager laid and accepted for 50 dollars without odds (the West Indies dollar is worth 4s. 2d.) that Hutton, then 72, would not reach 75. Hutton did so from the very next ball and a sum which must have amounted to a fortnight's wages passed over on the spot.

All day long this sort of nonsense goes on. When, in the mind of the crowd, any element of doubt exists about a dismissal, an argument is almost certain to start. Often these lead to fights.

I am not criticizing either and it is impossible to be dogmatic on the point but the action of two West Indies batsmen in staying at the wicket to await an umpire's decision against them earlier in the day unwittingly might have been the first spark which caused the demonstrators to work up a vendetta against umpire Menzies. Each time he was the man who had to give the batsman out.

First, despite Watson's signal that he had taken the ball cleanly, Christiani waited after Willie, at mid-wicket, had dived forward and held an excellent falling catch.

Then Weekes, with more apparent justification, remained after Lock had clipped his off bail with a very good ball which utterly beat him.

Weekes explained afterwards that he simply did not know what had happened. That being so, he was entitled to be reassured that the ball had not bounced back from gloves or pads or wicketkeeper Evans. Weekes had covered up immediately and "Wing" Gillette, whose view had been obscured by the batsman's pad, was right to go across to umpire Menzies to confirm that the batsman had been bowled.

At the next interval Everton apologized to Hutton for not walking out straight away, but Charles Palmer, the M.C.C. manager, assured Weekes that, had he been the batsman, he too would have waited for the umpire's verdict.

Poor Menzies, the diminutive Indian groundsman, first had the thankless task of giving out Christiani, whom the crowd idolized; then to decide against Weekes, upon whom so much rested; finally he had to lift his finger on the run-out appeal against British Guianian McWatt.

For the rest of the match a four-man police guard was stationed outside Menzies' house which, as groundsman, was next to the club pavilion, and inside the ground. Hutton went out of his way to tell Menzies that, no matter what measures had to be taken, he would guarantee that both he and Gillette would come to no harm.

There was abundant common-sense in an observation made by "Long-On" in the *Sunday Graphic*, Georgetown. He wrote:

> "It is putting it mildly to say that umpiring in this country, especially in inter-colonial and international matches, leaves much to be desired, *and it should not be left to unpleasant occurrences to force a complete overhaul of this very important link in the chain of cricket control.*"

The main difficulty in British Guiana is to persuade suitable candidates to take up the hazardous and always tricky task of umpiring. As one prominent ex-cricketer of the West Indies expressed himself to me with brutal frankness, "How would you care to face the prospect of being hit on the head with a hammer?"

Former players, who would make ideal umpires and help to

raise the standard of cricket in the colony, fight shy of taking on such an unthankful job. Automatically therefore many of those who do officiate are young men suffering from the indisputable handicap of little or no practical experience of the game.

Unfortunately for Menzies he failed to give Holt out in the second innings, caught behind the wicket, when all the England players were certain he had touched the ball. "He hit it for six" one of the England team told me. Holt seemed to be a specialist in avoiding this type of dismissal. It had happened before on the famous occasion in the second colony match against Jamaica at Melbourne Park when he was 47. Holt went on to score a century, as a result of which he won a place in the Test team.

It occurred again in the first innings of the third Test. Now came the third but not the last umpiring error.

On all three occasions the fieldsmen declared there could not have been the slightest doubt that Holt had touched the ball.

At the time of Holt's second escape in the British Guiana Test the crowd were particularly noisy—in such din fieldsmen often found themselves quite unable to hear the spoken instructions of their captain—and Menzies might have been excused for not hearing the snick so audible to those closer to the wicket and also to Brian Statham, the bowler.

Apparently the deviation of the ball's flight also escaped him. If he neither heard nor saw anything Menzies was perfectly correct to ignore the instinctive action of Holt who, as soon as he made the stroke, began to walk from the crease. Denis Atkinson, his runner, took off his gloves and also turned to start for the pavilion.

Fortunately for England Holt was out soon afterwards, but the affair might well have been much more costly than it was.

This, however, was the first and apparently only error made by Menzies and I imagine that most umpires would be grateful to get a Test Match "clearance" of no more than one mistake! To my mind the strictures and suggestions made by some that "Badge" was influenced by the bottle-throwing and the generally hostile attitude of the crowd were most unfair to him.

Afterwards Menzies told Hutton that he probably had made a mistake over Holt but, as Walcott's leg-before decision in the second innings raised some doubts among the West Indies players over the height of the ball when it hit the pad, the teams broke about even in the game over real or alleged umpiring blunders.

My view was that on the whole both Menzies and Gillette proved very good officials. Neither was paid a cent for what must have been the most thankless voluntary occupation yet devised by the wit of man.

The devotion to duty of "Badge" Menzies to his work as groundsman and "spare-time" umpire involved him in hours of toil which
no self-respecting union would ever permit.

Not only did he umpire for five hours a day, a period which
in tropical heat Messrs. Frank Chester, Frank Lee and Co. would
consider more than sufficient, but he continued to supervise the
preparation of the ground each day.

During lunch on the first day of the Test, rain began to fall
suddenly. Jumping from the table, an alarmed Menzies saw that
no covers had been placed on the pitch. His deputy had gone to
lunch and no one had given orders to the ground staff to act. Menzies
raced out to organize the necessary labour. Only seven minutes
were lost at the resumption but, had he not acted so promptly, the
delay might have been much longer and the pitch made dangerous.

Following the downpour on Friday, the third day, no play was
possible from lunch onwards after England, or rather Statham,
had shot out Stollmeyer, Worrell and Walcott for 31 runs. The
skies had become black during the interval and Menzies, ever
watchful, made sure the covers were in position before the heavens
opened.

During a temporary halt in the torrential rain that afternoon
Menzies and his staff spent their time digging holes just off the
square to allow the pools of water to drain away and when one man
marched out to the middle in military fashion and saluted the
wicket he should have saluted Menzies as well. Soon afterwards
the rain began again and washed out any lingering hopes for the day.

At nine o'clock that evening Hutton went to the ground and saw
the water still on top of the covers. He told me, "If none of it seeps
through I shall have raincoats made out of the material for the
whole of my family!"

None did get through. The ground staff stayed throughout the
night and every time the rain eased they used spades and buckets
to remove the water from the tarpaulin covers.

Thinking they might have the advantage of bowling at the
West Indies on a difficult pitch, the England players sought
immediate information on the state of the pitch when they entered
the ground next morning.

The gateman, whose habit it was to examine tickets with one
hand and grasp a hockey stick with the other, told them the pitch
was bone hard and dry. They felt in no position to query his pro-
nouncement but soon they found he had not exaggerated. Not a
drop had seeped through anywhere. Play resumed promptly to time.

After the bottle-throwing, immediate and serious discussions
began in the pavilion and continued at a cocktail-party given by the

East Indian club later in the evening. Many and various were the
suggestions put forward to prevent a repetition of the hooliganism
on the Monday. (Perhaps the Sunday intervening and so providing
time for hot tempers to cool off and runaway tongues to be silenced
was a blessing.)

One idea was to raise the entrance fee to the ground to fifteen
dollars minimum and for any balance, which the West Indies
Board of Control might think their due, to be made up from sub-
scriptions from members of the Georgetown and other local cricket
clubs.

I did not think this was a good idea because I could picture a
thwarted and howling mob gathering in the road outside the pavilion
and stoning the building.

The second and more serious suggestion was to ask the First
Battalion of the Argyle and Sutherland Highlanders, garrisoned
in the colony, to patrol the ground. Manager Palmer discussed the
idea with Major Troop, the Commanding Officer, but the Major
was reluctant to take the step without the direct order of the
Governor, Sir Alfred Savage, who, with Lady Savage, had been a
witness of the trouble.

Actually in that dangerous period the nearest the M.C.C. came
to being identified with the Argyle and Sutherlands was when Jim
Laker donned the Regimental Sergeant-Major's kilt and tunic for
the Carnival dance held in the hotel the same night as the bottle-
throwing party.

Later it was generally agreed among the various officials that the
presence of the "Jocks" might incite rather than prevent trouble.
As upholders of law and order they were already unpopular enough
among the disorderly elements in Georgetown and it was felt that
to ask them to assume another difficult role might be inviting
further trouble in an already delicate situation. The soldiers might
have been the unwitting cause of touching off another incident.

A third suggestion was the practical one of placing hose-pipes
at strategic positions inside the ground, to dampen the spirits of the
over-enthusiastic. How near cricket in the West Indies is approaching
the South American version of controlling football crowds!

Already in the Caribbean a section of the ground is enclosed
behind ten-feet-high wire netting which prevents spectators from
encroaching on to the pitch. Is the encircling moat the next
precaution?

Early on the Sunday morning manager Palmer tumbled from
beneath his mosquito net and telephoned a request to police headquarters for foot and mounted police strength at the ground to be
doubled and for the riot squad to stand by all day.

"I am not an alarmist," he told me, "but I am responsible for the safety of the players under my charge. I cannot take any chances of a repetition of Saturday, or even worse."

Although the sole incident on Monday was the mild one of a spectator who had left his seat to return the ball from the boundary being set upon by the police and forcibly removed back to the ringside, the precautions were wise and necessary.

Not everybody, however, welcomed the sight of extra mounted police. "Fairplay" wrote an indignant letter to the Editor of the *Daily Chronicle* in which he said:

"I was unable to see anything of the cricket as two mounted policemen came and stood right in front of me, blocking my view. They were asked to shift aside a bit but remained, and to top it all the horses began swishing their tails right in my face. I paid to see cricket, not to be nearly blinded by the flicking of horses' tails."

"Fairplay" was not the only one to feel indignant. The wife of the Chief Justice of British Guiana, sitting next to the Governor and his wife in the box for V.I.P.s, had the contents of her handbag stolen from under her seat.

Apparently the thief opened the bag, took out the valuables, and closed the bag again without being overheard or seen—which goes to support the argument that cricket is an absorbing game.

By this period of the tour my colleague Reg Hayter of Reuters was nearly driven to despair. On the basis of the 1948 M.C.C. tour of West Indies, when news stories were scarce, he was pre-budgeted 60,000 words for the whole tour, with instructions not to exceed the number. By the first Test he had written 34,000 words, by the second 46,000 and by the third nearly 55,000. All the time he was receiving frantic cables to keep down his wordage. For all his good intentions to do so, how could he ignore the stories which daily hit the front pages of the English national newspapers? He reckoned the task of squeezing a quart into a pint pot was infinitely easier than his.

And while all this was happening news came through that the 40,000 dollar stand at the Queen's Park Oval, Trinidad, the scene of the fourth Test, had been razed to the ground in a mysterious fire which began at five o'clock on the same Saturday morning!

The ugly word arson was not ruled out. Trinidad people told me that until a few weeks before a number of loafers regularly slept in the Queen's Park Stand, until the secretary of the club turned them out and gave strict instructions that no unauthorized person was to be allowed in after dark.

The suggestion was that the loafers got even with the club secretary by clambering over the fence and burning down his stand. This, of course, was mere hypothesis at the time, but the police began investigations. No one thought that the incendiarism, if such it was, had been directed against M.C.C.

Almost as soon as the fire was put out, the club committee called an emergency meeting and plans were proposed and carried to set to work to erect a temporary stand in time for the M.C.C. visit less than a fortnight ahead.

Work could not be started for two days, however. Trinidad was in the middle of "Carnival". Nothing could be allowed to interfere with that wild reckless jamboree. A new stand went up with miraculous speed thanks to the supervision of Mr. Ed. Watson, an Englishman.

CHAPTER NINE

Reasons for victory—And for defeat—Statham's great spell—Best fast ball since the
war—Psychology on Walcott—A modern blueprint for Tests—Valentine's
hundredth at twenty-three—New "Find the Lady" trick—Palmer films his
first wicket—Bailey's help—Advice to Peter May—Hutton the victor—Cable
from M.C.C.—A notable triumph.

IN the dressing-room after England's tonic Test victory at
Georgetown Hutton gave me these reasons for his team's success:
  (1) Winning the toss.
  (2) The splendid team spirit, which was evident even among
the players not included in the team. They helped in the dressing-
room and elsewhere, busying themselves for the good of the side in
many and various ways.
  (3) The brilliant bowling of Brian Statham in breaking the
back of the West Indies batting in the first innings, and some
fine bowling by everybody in the second innings.
  (4) Exceptionally good fielding all round, and some first-rate
slip catching by Tom Graveney who had never fielded slip until
going to the West Indies.
  Hutton might well have added something about his own score
of 169, his 18th Test century, which had laid the foundations for
victory.
  Jeff Stollmeyer, the West Indies captain, freely acknowledged
that England were the better team and deserved to win. "How
they fought," he said to me. "My goodness, how they did fight!"
  Stollmeyer added that England had enjoyed whatever luck
was going and he noted three factors.
  First were the injuries to himself—he fell heavily on his left
shoulder in trying to catch Willie Watson on the first day and,
despite treatment, he was handicapped for the rest of the match—
and John Holt. Holt strained a muscle in his left leg while fielding.
  Secondly there was Worrell's loss of form. Frank had toured India
with the Commonwealth team until December and he looked stale
and obviously out of touch. Public reaction was unkind and the
slogan "Why worry with Worrell?" was properly ignored by his
fellow selectors, though England would have given the campaign to
drop him full and unstinted support!
  Third, that Statham was helped by an extremely fast wicket in
the first innings, the fastest, claimed the West Indies, they had
encountered during the whole series.
  The wickets in Jamaica and Barbados were easy-paced, and

Stollmeyer argued that his team were placed at a disadvantage in facing Statham on a fast pitch.

I can imagine Brian, who had bowled with extreme hostility, pace and accurate direction but seldom with any luck in every previous Test innings, claiming that *he* had faced a disadvantage in having to bowl against the West Indies batsmen on the easy-paced pitches of Kingston and Bridgetown.

I think Stollmeyer and his men found themselves in a similar position to Hutton's team in the first two Tests by having to practise mainly on soft pitches. Fast or not, the Georgetown pitch was perfection and Statham's opening spell was the finest from an English fast bowler—classifying Alec Bedser as medium-fast—since the war.

Strangely enough, Statham opened with a wide to Worrell, who had gone in first instead of the injured Holt, but the next ball was an outswinger which Worrell followed and touched to Godfrey Evans. As Peter Bayley, the former West Indies cricketer, said on the Demarara radio, it was a new version of the three W's —Wide, Worrell, Wicket.

In the second innings Statham dismissed Worrell third ball, so in four Test innings Brian's record against the West Indies vice-captain was to get him second ball twice and third ball once.

At Barbados the perceptive Brian, who knew his Worrell, predicted Frank would try to begin with a single to mid-wicket. So Brian bowled him an inswinger pitched on the middle and off. Worrell made to push him to the on, as Statham had forecast, and missed his stroke. Away went the middle stump.

Stollmeyer was unfortunate in receiving what the players described as the best fast ball bowled for England since Alec Bedser dismissed Sir Donald Bradman at Adelaide in 1947. The difference, according to Hutton and Evans, who saw both deliveries, was that Brian's was nearly twice as fast.

In a way this wonder ball was part accidental. In the moment of delivery Brian felt his fingers cross the seam with the result that his inswinger, which pitched on the leg stump, turned into a leg-cutter which took the top of the off stump. I doubt whether any batsman on earth could have stopped the ball. Stollmeyer told me that after the ball hit the ground he knew nothing about it.

Brian's third victim was Clyde Walcott. Clyde arrived on the scene with the air of a confident and genial heavyweight boxer who had just seen two lightweights felled by half-power punches in the preliminary bouts.

Knowing Clyde's dislike for being crowded, Hutton placed Compton and Bailey at silly mid-off as near as they dared go to such

M.C.C. Touring Team to West Indies and British Guiana, 1953-54

Standing: K. Suttle, G. A. Lock, B. Statham, T. Graveney, A. Moss, P. May, F. Trueman, T. G. Evans, R. Spooner. *Sitting:* W. Watson, J. Laker, T. Bailey, Len Hutton (captain), D. Compton, C. Palmer (Manager), J. Wardle

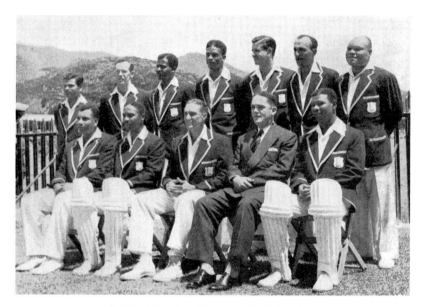

West Indies Team at Trinidad

Back row (left to right): S. Ramadhin, B. Pairaudeau, J. Holt, F. King, D. Atkinson, C. McWatt, W. Ferguson. *Front row (left to right):* C. Walcott, F. Worrell, J. B. Stollmeyer (Captain), E. Burnett (Manager), E. Weekes

Denis takes strike, Peter May slip, Reg Hayter
(Reuters) wicket-keeping

Evans on Police horse at British Guiana. Lock, Trueman
(Calypso shirt) and policeman look on

Headley's (*right*) Test farewell at Jamaica.
With him is Walcott

Graveney and Watson after England's British Guiana victory.
Photographer: Tony Lock

Umpire Walcott no-balls Lock for throwing (Barbados)

Leg-bye winners, Trueman and Moss, at Barbados

Jumps of joy when Compton plays on (British Guiana)

Start of Georgetown's bottle-throwing. McWatt run out

The bottles and boxes begin (Georgetown 1954)

"We want wickets" Hutton told President Jones, Georgetown

Holt was walking—but Umpire Menzies said "Not out". Note runner taking off his gloves
(British Guiana Test)

Great Compton catch, off Stollmeyer

Spooner and Lock unsuccessfully appeal for catch off Weekes (43) in Fourth Test. This decision caused controversy

a powerful driver. Walcott's instinct and design was to make the place unhealthy for them to remain so close. He accepted Hutton's challenge and immediately bisected Denis and Trevor with a cover-drive which scorched the earth as it whistled through to the boundary.

Compton and Bailey stayed put, like obstinate bystanders asked to move on.

Next ball Statham again pitched an inswinger well up to the bat. Once more Walcott opened his mighty shoulders to attempt another punishing cover-drive at the two daredevils. This time he misjudged the ball, which touched the inside edge of his bat. Walcott turned round to see his stumps at crazy angles. He was not very wise in trying to slay the bowling before he had played himself in.

At lunch West Indies were 31 for three in reply to England's 435. Then came the tropical downpours which finished any hopes of further cricket for the day.

"Bad luck, England" was the sentiment on everybody's lips. It did appear that, after all, Hutton might regret the snail-like pace of England's batting on the first day when only 153 runs were scored for the loss of the wickets of Peter May and Willie Watson.

This, the slowest start of the series, was only partly explained away by the steadiness of the West Indies bowling, particularly by Ramadhin and Atkinson, and the expert field-placings of Stollmeyer.

In the positioning of his fielders, Jeffrey must be the most meticulous captain playing, but the results seem to justify his care in planning his field forces. Hutton and Compton, who eventually shared a partnership of 150, and to a lesser degree May, all made handsome strokes bearing the stamp of a boundary but which went straight to or close enough to be stopped by one of the agile West Indies fielders.

With local knowledge of their grounds and conditions the West Indies, all of whom were superb natural athletes without an awkward movement or jerkiness among them, positioned themselves better than England both to save the one and prevent the four.

The slowest start previous to Georgetown was at Kingston where West Indies made 168 for two on the opening day, but there England bowled only 79 overs. The inclusion of four fast bowlers in the team, all taking long runs, meant that the number of overs which could be bowled during the day was bound to be comparatively few. At Georgetown England scored their 153 for two from 106 overs.

Even so, that was an improvement on the Barbados sloth of 128 runs and seven wickets lost from 114 overs.

Unquestionably, the knowledge that he carried the main burden of England's batting was a main reason for Hutton's slowness. Past experience had left him in no doubt of the probable happenings if he failed.

When England pushed the score along the next day, however, Hutton had an even more effective answer to the charge of lack of batting enterprise. He could say that the end had justified the means.

Hutton merely followed the modern blueprint for Test cricket: (1) to win the toss and avoid all risk while any moisture remaining from preparation was left in the pitch; (2) dig in for the remainder of the first day; (3) consolidate the position on the second.

Whether the policy is right or wrong is a matter of opinion. Personally I believe a more positive approach from the start would be just as profitable.

Anyway, all went well on the second day until just before lunch when, in pushing for one, Denis Compton fell to a catch at forward short-leg.

During the interval the tiring Hutton, who had then batted for six hours and a half, told Johnny Wardle to follow Tom Graveney, who had gone in on Compton's dismissal, in the order.

Hutton thought the time had come to push the score along and that Johnny was the man to play an attacking game such as he hoped Graveney would now produce while he himself kept the other end shut.

Directly after lunch Tom Graveney was beaten by a leg-break from Ramadhin—the previous balls to him had not turned at all, but this fairly whipped across.

In came Wardle whose first-class aggregate before the Test was a princely eight. Furthermore, on account of indisposition, he had been unable to practise in the nets on the two days before the Test.

Johnny's luck was in. When six he gave what looked to be a fairly simple chance to Stollmeyer at mid-on. This dropped, he settled down and helped Hutton to add 50 in 50 minutes and 79 in all. The stand put England back on top.

Before the innings closed Jim Laker provided Alf Valentine with his hundredth Test wicket. Jim's previous strokes from him that over had been two, four, six.

Valentine's feat was celebrated with congratulations all round a great ovation from the crowd and the presentation to him after wards of the ball, appropriately mounted, with which he had reached the target.

Little did I imagine when I was introduced to Valentine in 1950, with only two first-class matches behind him, that less than four full years later I would see him take his hundredth Test wicket. At twenty-three, Valentine became the youngest player to perform the feat in Test cricket.

Even more meritorious was the fact he did so in four series, a record by itself, and that many of his matches were played on wickets, in Australia and the West Indies, which were said to be all in favour of batsmen.

Valentine, who had remained at the tantalizing figure of 99 for almost two whole innings, was born at Kingston, Jamaica, on April 28, 1930, three days before Sonny Ramadhin, his spin "twin", first saw the light of day in Trinidad.

Here is Valentine's record up to his hundredth Test wicket:

	Overs	Maidens	Runs	Wickets	Average
1950 v. England	422·3	197	674	33	20·42
1951–52 v. Australia	218	39	691	24	28·79
1952 v. New Zealand	113·4	55	153	8	19·12
1952–53 v. India (Home)	427	177	828	28	29·57
1954 v. England (Home)	185·5	80	357	7	51·00
Total	1,365	548	2,703	100	27·03

Well done, Val!

Going into the ground at Georgetown, I noted that Valentine and Ramadhin figured in a peculiarly West Indian version of the three-card trick in which punters are invited to "find the lady"— but seldom do!

The "proprietor" of the stall outside the Bourda gates proffered the backs of three cards, on the picture side of which one carried the photograph of Valentine, another of Ramadhin, and the third nothing at all. After the usual show and swift criss-cross of hands customers were invited to gamble on picking Valentine or Ramadhin, whichever they chose. They were rarely right.

Foot and mounted police watched the proceedings, and the interchange of money, with casual interest. Nor did they attempt to interfere with the activities of the many who scaled the dozens of trees surrounding the ground in order to obtain a free sight of the game from the comfort of the high branches. To provide easy foothold thick nails had been driven into the tree-trunks every yard or so up from the ground.

Jim Laker showed himself to be such a good prophet that he might have done well had he tried to pick the Val or Ram card outside the ground. Before the West Indies began batting he

correctly forecast to me they would lose a wicket in Brian Statham's
first over and next day that seven would be out by tea-time. In the
latter prediction he would have miscalculated had Denis Compton
not dropped Clifford McWatt at slip when the West Indies wicketkeeper was only five. Visions of "another Jamaica", where McWatt
was missed five times, began to loom ahead.

When Denis went into the slips Graveney, who had fielded
there all day, told him at that time of the afternoon and at that
end he found difficulty in following the ball from the bat, on account
of the dark background of the crowd and the trees.

Perhaps Denis was unfortunate to be given a chance so soon
after moving to slip. The ball came slower than he expected and,
in grabbing for it, he shut his left hand too soon. The ball hit the
end of a finger and dropped to the ground—England's only lapse in
the field throughout the match.

Graveney took two first-class catches and Lock one from his
own bowling which dismissed a surprised Atkinson. Lock, who
made a welcome return to bowling as well as catching form, jumped
high and wide to his left, and held a hard return when Atkinson,
desperate at being tied down 25 minutes without scoring, lashed
out at a good-length ball.

Except for Lock, nobody was more pleased than Charles Palmer
who, for the first time since he had operated his ciné camera, filmed
the fall of a wicket.

Previously Palmer had taken 30,000 feet of film on M.C.C.
tours to South Africa and the West Indies without having the luck to
record the taking of a wicket. Yet, on the same day, Major Troop,
of the Argyle and Sutherlands, captured three wickets in less than
half an hour.

When they smelt the scent of victory England, in the field,
were scarcely recognizable as the same set of hard-working but
uninspiring fielders who had laboriously toiled in the second Test.
Their speed in covering the ground, energy and agility, picking
up on the run and the accuracy of their fast returns to the
ubiquitous Evans, were revelations.

Two West Indies batsmen, McWatt and Valentine (with 100
wickets and 75 runs in Test cricket, Valentine would probably
smile at such elevation to batting rank) were run out at moments
of importance in the first innings, and May, Graveney, Bailey
Lock and Watson were always outstanding in an outstanding
side.

Team spirit, carefully guided by Hutton, largely enabled
England to take the long final pull after West Indies had been
forced to follow on.

In the West Indies second innings England produced a collective piece of bowling as fine as could be imagined.

One point of interest was that, bowling at medium pace, Bailey took the valuable wickets of Weekes, with an outswinger, and Christiani, with an inswinger. I am sure Bailey does his best work with the ball when he does not try to bowl too fast.

West Indies began the last morning 21 runs ahead with four wickets to fall. Hutton knew if he could separate the two not-out batsmen, Gomez and Atkinson, England virtually only had to take one more wicket, because Valentine and Ramadhin belonged to rabbit class.

For an hour, Gomez and Atkinson played with concentration and care, resisting every bowler from speed to spin. England faces began to look anxious. The pitch was giving bowlers no help, although in the last hour on the fifth day the ball had turned and sometimes lifted.

Hutton took Wardle aside before the start of an over and said to him, "Bowl Atkinson a Chinaman"—the left-hander's off-break to the right-hander.

Wardle did as he was instructed, pitched it perfectly. Atkinson, beaten in the flight, swung through with his stroke in desperation but failed to connect and was bowled. In the next thirty minutes the last three wickets went down and England required no more than 73 to win with three hours and a half left.

Hutton sent in May and Graveney in the hope that they would win back some of their big-match confidence. In two overs they punished Worrell and Atkinson for nine apiece and both produced a number of lovely strokes.

Then May received a squatter from Atkinson about which he knew absolutely nothing. The ball could not have risen more than two inches from the ground. For the second time in the match, May was out for twelve.

He could not be blamed for missing the ball which got him in the second innings but, remembering Peter's other dismissals, at the end of the match Denis Compton took him on one side. "For your own sake, Peter, you must try to ignore the spectators out here. Otherwise they will affect your cricket terribly," said Denis. Certainly in other Test innings Peter had looked to become fidgety whenever the crowd raised voice.

This was typical of the way the experienced Compton took interest in the welfare of the up-and-coming players in the team.

England ran into no further trouble and, with Graveney and Watson using all their strokes, the runs took only 63 minutes. At the finish Hutton and his colleagues, winners by nine wickets, had 147 minutes to spare.

Considering that they had lost 217 minutes through rain and ten minutes during the bottle-throwing this was quite an achievement. In fairness to the crowd, I must say that at the end England received a fine ovation.

Perhaps the hooligans were away thinking up some trouble elsewhere!

I returned to the hotel with Hutton who, although well contented, was feeling the strain of the six previous days. For two nights he had been unable to sleep, so much was he turning over in his mind the hundred and one events of the cricket. How many people realize the strain placed upon the top men in big cricket?

Outside the ground, as Len and I entered the taxi, the usual crowd waited. As soon as they saw him they shouted, "Hutton the Victor."

And Victor he was! He was inundated with messages of congratulation. The one which pleased him most came from Lord's. It read:

Best congratulations to you all on well deserved victory and to you on personal contribution and fine example in difficult circumstances. M.C.C.

It was a notable triumph indeed!

THE THIRD TEST

Played at Georgetown, British Guiana, February 24, 25, 26, 27, and March 1, 2. England won by nine wickets.

ENGLAND

First Innings

W. Watson b Ramadhin	12
L. Hutton c Worrell b Ramadhin	169
P. May lbw b Atkinson	12
D. Compton c Stollmeyer b Atkinson	64
T. Graveney b Ramadhin	0
J. Wardle b Ramadhin	38
T. Bailey c Weekes b Ramadhin	49
T. G. Evans lbw b Atkinson	19
J. Laker b Valentine	27
G. A. Lock b Ramadhin	13
B. Statham not out	10
Extras (b 20, nb 2)	22
Total	435

BOWLING ANALYSIS

			O.	M.	R.	W.
G. Gomez	..	..	32	6	75	0
F. Worrell	..	..	16	5	33	0
S. Ramadhin	..	..	67	34	113	6
A. Valentine	..	..	44	17	109	1
D. Atkinson	..	..	58	27	78	3
J. Stollmeyer	..	..	2	1	3	0
C. Walcott	..	..	2	0	2	0

WEST INDIES

FIRST INNINGS

F. Worrell c Evans b Statham	0
J. Stollmeyer b Statham	2
E. Weekes b Lock	94
C. Walcott b Statham	4
R. J. Christiani c Watson b Laker	25
G. Gomez b Statham	8
D. Atkinson c and b Lock	0
C. McWatt run out	54
J. Holt not out	48
S. Ramadhin b Laker	0
A. Valentine run out	0
Extras (b 8, lb 7, w 1)	16
Total	251

BOWLING ANALYSIS

			O.	M.	R.	W.
B. Statham	..	..	26	6	64	4
T. Bailey	..	..	5	0	13	0
J. Laker	..	..	21	11	32	2
J. Wardle	..	..	22	4	60	0
D. Compton	..	..	3	1	6	0
G. A. Lock	..	..	27·5	7	60	2

The West Indies followed on,

WEST INDIES

Second Innings

J. K. Holt b Lock	..	..	..	..	64
J. Stollmeyer c Compton b Laker		..	..	..	44
F. Worrell c Evans b Statham		..	..	..	2
E. Weekes c Graveney b Bailey		..	..	..	38
C. Walcott lbw b Laker	..	..	..	..	26
R. Christiani b Bailey ..	..	..	..	..	11
G. Gomez c Graveney b Wardle		..	..	..	35
D. Atkinson b Wardle	..	..	..	..	18
C. McWatt not out	..	..	..	..	9
S. Ramadhin b Statham	..	..	..	..	1
A. Valentine b Wardle	..	..	..	..	0
Extras (b 2, lb 4, nb 2) ..		..	..	..	8
Total ..	..	..	..	..	256

Bowling Analysis

			O.	M.	R.	W.
B. Statham	..	..	22	3	86	2
T. Bailey ..	..	..	22	9	41	2
G. A. Lock	..	..	25	11	41	1
J. Laker ..	..	..	36	18	56	2
J. Wardle	..	..	12·3	4	24	3

ENGLAND

Second Innings

T. Graveney not out	..	..	..	..	33
P. May b Atkinson	..	..	..	..	12
W. Watson not out	..	..	..	..	27
Extras (b 3)	..	..	..	..	3
Total (for 1 wicket) ..		..	..	..	75

Bowling Analysis

			O.	M.	R.	W.
G. Gomez	..	..	5	1	15	0
D. Atkinson	..	..	7	0	34	1
S. Ramadhin	..	..	4	0	7	0
C. Walcott	..	..	2	0	6	0
E. Weekes	..	..	2·1	0	8	0
R. Christiani	..	..	1	0	2	0

CHAPTER TEN

Conforming to rule—Coal black—Trouble for Evans—Double vision—The Nelson touch—Sprightly at eighty—A "W. G." memory—Amazed—House stoned—Sleeping tablets for Hutton—Looking ahead—"Toughen up, Peter"—Experiment—And failure—Bailey to open—M.C.C. record feat—Trueman hits Fergie—The Gladiator—"Unsportsmanlike" charge—Contrite Freddie—Chapter of accidents—The Ministerial way.

BETWEEN the third Test and the colony fixture with Trinidad, who had not been beaten in a colony match at Queen's Park Oval since 1905, M.C.C. played a two-day game at St. George's, a quaint little town built by the French on the pleasing slopes of the breezy island of Grenada.

After sampling the bathing from the silver sandy Gran Ance beach, the cricketers were prepared to agree that Grenada was one of the better discoveries of Christopher Columbus.

Two men, Dick Spooner, whose right eye was cut in two places by a piece of wire, while he was helping Willie Watson to pack a suitcase at Georgetown, and Brian Statham, suffering from sore feet, remained behind at Port of Spain, which is fifty minutes' flying time from Grenada.

From there they sent the following telegram to the M.C.C. Saturday night club: *Transport difficulties prevent us attending tonight's meeting but good luck. Signed Whippet and Nelson.* Statham had been known as Whippet from the start. Spooner had recently acquired a nickname which he kept for the rest of the tour.

In their hotel bedroom at Port of Spain, Trinidad, Dick and Brian held their own Saturday evening party at which they drank the usual toasts. On Monday when, by rule of the club, all members had to wear the M.C.C. touring tie at breakfast or pay a heavy fine which went to the club funds, they decided to eat in bed.

To conform with club rules, Brian and Dick donned their shirts, fixed the M.C.C. touring tie in their collars and, propped against the pillows, settled down to their eggs and bacon, marmalade and coffee.

The team spirit of Dick Spooner, always a grand reserve and tourist, showed itself in many ways before Trinidad and it was to do so again then.

During the third Test, for instance, Spooner had given rival wicketkeeper Godfrey Evans a piece of coal for luck. As the hot days wore on and Godfrey perspired, a black mark appeared on the hip pocket of his trousers—where Godfrey had put the coal!

Then, at Trinidad, although unable to see properly out of his right eye, Spooner insisted on playing in the colony match because he knew that Evans was unfit and in any case badly in need of a rest.

Godfrey, who was laid low by a carbuncle in Jamaica and troubled by a boil on his hand in British Guiana, had also been affected by suppurating fingers caused by his hands sweating inside his wicketkeeping gauntlets.

Now, he arrived from Grenada with a boil on his left instep. He would have been in anguish had he tried to play because the boil quickly grew worse and Godfrey had to take to his bed, his left foot badly swollen and inflamed as far as the ankle.

Ordinary medical treatment was prescribed but the foot remained an angry sight and Godfrey suffered intense pain whenever he tried to put his foot to the floor.

Soon the question arose whether he would be fit to play in the Test. None was more concerned about Evans than deputy Dick Spooner, and when, visiting the local Fire Brigade Chief and his wife, he heard of a specialist who had successfully cured their daughter's foot of similar trouble within a matter of three days, he hurried back to the hotel to tell manager Palmer and captain Hutton.

Next day the specialist was called in. He began new and intensive treatment and twenty-four hours later a smiling Godfrey walked down to lunch—the first time out of his room for four days.

Dick Spooner, who had dined with Godfrey in his room the previous evening, sat with him at lunch, rejoicing in his friend's recovery.

Frequent injections of penicillin and the taking of extra large doses of medicine in the desperate race against time, however, left Godfrey feeling low and weak. On the Monday and Tuesday morning preceding the Test which began on the Wednesday Evans practised in the Trinidad nets, but in the end he had to admit that he would not be able to play.

So Dick Spooner was to keep wicket after all. Actually Godfrey's foot ailment would have been allowed to run its natural course had there not been some considerable doubts about Spooner's ability to see properly after his eye accident.

Fortunately the change of wicketkeeper was made easier by Dick's brilliance, despite double vision, in the colony match.

He made three spectacular leg-side catches off Alan Moss, a smart stumping from Johnny Wardle and, by swift thinking and action, he ran out Tang Choon from mid-wicket.

No wonder the rest of the team jokingly told Dick that if he kept wicket so well with one eye he should put a patch over the other for the rest of the tour!

Before the events at Trinidad M.C.C. had fulfilled their two-day engagement at Grenada where, as at Antigua, the Governor, Mr. Betham Beetham, who had travelled on the *Stirling Castle* with the M.C.C. team returning from South Africa in 1949, had declared a public holiday.

On the cricket-cum-racetrack ground, with its matting wicket and set in an amphitheatre of hills, the pick of the Windward Islands cricketers held the touring team to an honourable draw.

Not for 52 years had an English side visited the Island—among the 1902 party was the famous B. J. T. Bosanquet, then a fast bowler with apparently no thought of the googly with which his name has ever since been associated. Many cricketers refer to the googly as the "Bosie" ball.

Ian Neverson (eighteen) who had just entered a St. Vincent lawyer's office as a junior clerk, gained immortal local fame by carrying his bat through the Windward Islands innings for 90 runs.

For four and a half hours he showed a disciplined concentration and an organized defence which suggested the makings of a fine batsman. His strokes were limited on the off side but the way he glanced and hooked proved his confidence and speed and certainty of eye.

In fact the only occasion I can recall Neverson being genuinely puzzled was when Johnny Wardle, always the star of a picnic game, and later to clout four tremendous sixes in five balls—and to be no-balled for the first time in his life!—hid Neverson's bat under the matting during the mid-afternoon stoppage for drinks.

After Neverson's innings the hat was passed round a large and enthusiastic crowd, which cheered even his defensive strokes, and he was presented with £52 in a wicker basket—no small compensation for narrowly missing the distinction of scoring a century against an international combination.

Moreover, Jimmy Crozier of the *Voice*, St. Lucia, contacted Trinidad business friends in an effort to find Neverson a business post which could also further his cricket career. Being the Windward's wicketkeeper as well, Neverson was on the field for every ball bowled.

Another eighteen-year-old lad, Evelyn Gresham, also showed promise as a right-handed batsman and a slow orthodox spinner, with a smooth, high action. Trevor Bailey was caught off his first ball.

Watching the game was Mr. W. H. Mignon, a sprightly eighty-year-old and one of the two survivors of the first West Indies team to tour England in 1900. After the Grenada match he flew across to Trinidad where he was made an honorary member of the Queen's Park Club for the duration of M.C.C.'s visit. At the Queen's Park Oval he also met L. S. "Tommy" D'Ade, the only other living member of the 1900 team which visited England. They sat together to watch the colony and Test matches.

One of their memories concerned the cartoon about the team which appeared in the *Star*, London, carrying the caption "We have come to learn, Sah!"

No Tests were played on that tour, but the "learners" could point to a commendable record against the counties, including victory over Surrey.

Mr. Mignon rather shocked Hutton by asking him if he had ever seen Doctor Grace in action—"W. G." died several years before Len was born—and later, when I asked him to compare Hutton with Grace, he said:

"I watched Hutton bat and he is undoubtedly a great player. Yet the Doctor had to play on inferior pitches, and he did something which neither Bradman nor Hutton attempted—he bowled the others out after making a big score himself."

Another link in Grenada with "W. G." was Dr. W. S. Mitchell, whose son, Richard, was twelfth man for Oxford University in 1936. While a student at St. Mary's Hospital, London, Dr. Mitchell, a slow left-arm bowler of considerable skill, played several years for Ealing. He showed me letters from Grace inviting him to turn out in county matches.

Once, in 1905, while bowling for Ealing against London County, Dr. Mitchell almost caught Doctor Grace off his own bowling—at square-leg! As soon as he delivered the ball he anticipated the stroke would go towards square-leg and, running like a hare, reached it and only just failed to hold it.

Doctor Grace thoughtfully stroked his beard before his voice boomed out: "How the blazes did you get there, young man? I'll see you don't pull anything like that on me again."

The "Old Man" was as good as his word; he finished with a score of 84 not out.

When we were returning to the Grenada airport, en route to Trinidad, the taxi-drive passed a bus carrying the name "Amazed" All buses in Grenada have names of some kind or other but behind the choice of this was an odd story. Apparently the owner originally bought a broken-down car for 70 dollars, raffled it and made 200 dollars. This sum he invested in a lottery in which he won a large prize, large enough to enable him to buy a single-decker bus.

Hence, Amazed. So would I have been!

I hope the day will never come when touring teams cannot find a place in their itinerary for "up country" matches, as they are known in Australia.

These are played in a "homely" atmosphere not found in the bigger centres—the tea, with cakes baked by the wives of the committee-men, is typical of the arrangements—and the welcome to the visiting team contains a genuine warmth which is more than appreciated.

Yet, with six-day Tests and colony matches spread over five days, and air travel now eliminating the once-relaxing voyages between the islands, the players find less and less time to themselves and, understandably, they acquire even less inclination than normal to take all but the big matches seriously.

The trouble is that the second-class teams contain a number of fine cricketers, some of whom are rightly ambitious. They hope to gain recognition and possible entry into a stronger side and they know their performance against the touring eleven is the surest stepping-stone for doing so.

As a result they take the matches against M.C.C., or whoever the visitors might be, with the utmost sternness and determination.

While the players are practising hard to be at their peak for the visit of the touring team, local interest often reaches extreme and ridiculous heights. At Antigua, for example, the captain's house was stoned because the local fast bowler had not been included in the team, on account of an injured leg. The explanation of unfitness was not held to be good enough. On the day before the game a demonstration march was held through the town, banners being flown, demanding a boycott of the match. Happily, good sense prevailed among the vast majority of the population.

In their "missionary" work, teams like M.C.C. do a power of good, but I am afraid that sometimes the very last people to be considered are the visiting players.

At a time when they were beginning to feel the effects of a strenuous tour the M.C.C. went to Grenada, played the two-day match there, returned to Port of Spain the next afternoon, arriving at 6 p.m., and on the morrow tackled Trinidad without even the opportunity of a net practice on the mat.

Then, only one day's interval had been provided between the finish of the five-day colony match and the start of the six-day fourth Test.

When passing through Port of Spain on the way to Grenada, Charlie Palmer had half-jokingly suggested to Cyril Merry, Secretary of the West Indies Board of Control, that the fixture with Trinidad should be restricted to four days instead of five.

Merry made enquiries on the possibility of curtailing the game but, on their return from Grenada, M.C.C. were told that as tickets had been sold for the last day nothing could be done about it. So the non-stop cricketing programme continued.

The day after the fourth Test finished M.C.C. flew to Jamaica, had one day off, played a two-day game at Montego Bay, enjoyed another free day, then went straight into the fifth and final six-day Test. The morning after that was over they boarded the ship to take them home to England.

The chances of a touring team in the West Indies winning time off by completing matches inside the scheduled time of five or six days are remote. Mainly in the interests of finance, the perfect pitches of the Caribbean are completely covered throughout the game.

Besides which a glance at the names of the players forming the opposition in the colony teams gives some indication of their all-round strength.

One distinct advantage in Grenada was that Len Hutton had thinking time to take stock of the tour. Len had not slept well for some weeks and at Georgetown even sleeping tablets could not ease him from the mental strain of re-playing his big innings all over again, re-analysing his own and the side's tactics, and working out how to extract the best from his players, especially the youngsters.

Ever since the M.C.C. landed at Bermuda, Hutton had been conscious of the urgent need to hasten the advance, if there was to be an advance, of such batsmen as Graveney and May, and such bowlers as Trueman and Lock.

Never far from his thoughts was the moulding of the team for Australia. Time and again he told the young men under him:

"How England fare in Australia next year largely depends on how quickly you boys can develop. You cannot expect the same few to carry the side all the time, especially as they are getting older. The future is in your hands and you have a golden chance in front of you. Remember that I am here to help you. If you want to know anything come and ask me. I will do all I can for you."

At the Santa Maria Hotel, overlooking the beautiful bay of St. George's, Grenada, Hutton sat in one of his frequent contemplative moods. Earlier in the day he watched Peter May show unmistakably that he did not relish the pace bowling which, on the matting, reared dangerously and flew round his ears. On returning to the dressing-room, Peter had said this was the most fiery fast bowling he had ever faced.

In the evening Len invited Peter to join him in a private drink. In the old days the Yorkshire team, whether they had played well or badly, always held an "inquest" on the events of the day. Over a glass of ale and with the air thick with tobacco smoke and the dialect of the dales, they assessed with northern clarity their achievements and errors, like a balance-sheet indicating profit and loss. They were as free and blunt with their criticisms of each other as they were with their praise.

Hutton, then a fledgling, had usually been the listener, but he has never lost the habit of retracing the day's cricket and very little happens that he does not see and weigh up in his shrewd business-like Yorkshire manner.

That Saturday evening at Grenada, his first words to May were: "Peter, I think you are going to be an England captain in the very near future and I want you to be one, but you are now twenty-three and, as a potentially great batsman, you should be producing big scores regularly.

"Lad, you must toughen up. If you are to make a success of being an international batsman your motto must always be 'They get me out only over my dead body'.

"If the situation is strange to you, Peter, or the bowler ties you in knots, you must only grit your teeth harder and fight your way out of your problems. Only you can do that.

"By all means come and ask me for advice. That is what I am here for. Accept or reject my advice, as you wish, but ask, think, and learn from your mistakes, and live cricket night and day."

For three hours Len talked to Peter in this vein, much the same way, I imagine, as his own mentor, Herbert Sutcliffe, must have talked to him in his younger days.

On the Sunday Hutton tackled Tom Graveney, who put off a golf match purposely to listen to his captain.

During their conversation Len ascertained from Peter that he welcomed the chance of going in first, instead of at number three as he had been accustomed.

This encouraged Len to continue the experiment he began in the second innings of the third Test, carried on in Grenada, where Peter scored 93 not out, and against Trinidad with less happy results.

Not only was Hutton trying to find a reliable opening batsman to play against Australia the following winter, but he felt that at first wicket down May was rather on edge.

The strain of waiting to go in at number three, thought Hutton, might have been adversely affecting Peter's form. Hutton argued that any batsman successful at first wicket down should find no difficulty in going in first—in fact he thought a real batsman should be able to go in at any position and do well.

To the realistic Hutton, May's dismissal in the colony match with Trinidad to the first ball of the innings from Oliver Demming was a big disappointment. A snorter of a ball pitched outside the leg stump and hit the middle and off, but Len was indignant when an outsider tried to convince Peter that the policy of trying to help him regain his form by sending him in first was wrong.

Whether he was right or wrong, Len felt the team tactics and strategy should be left in the hands of the captain without interference from outside.

In point of fact May welcomed the chance to open the innings and he was consoled by Hutton telling him that Demming's ball might easily have disposed of Jack Hobbs in his prime.

With the fourth Test so near, however, Hutton thought it best to restore May to number three for the time being, although still of the opinion that eventually Peter might find his proper place as an opening batsman.

Back at first wicket down for the second innings of the colony match, Peter still groped to regain his form. After making four runs he padded up to a medium-pace ball which was only a shade outside the wicket. The ball came back off the seam, flicked Peter's pad and knocked back the off stump. He had not padded up far enough.

The Hutton plan to convert May into an opener for the two last crucial Tests at Port of Spain and Kingston was upset by Peter's loss of form. In nine first-class innings since the opening Test May had made only 163 runs.

Yet, paradoxically, I think Watson's ability as an attacking batsman, so brilliantly demonstrated against Trinidad, rather than May's failure, was the reason for Hutton's final decision to change his own opening partner.

Since he had not been provided with an accredited number two for the tour, Hutton had been obliged to give a full trial in the position to Watson—the man Headquarters had nominated for the job. In the colony matches Watson had often been peerless, but the fact remained that his Test average was a modest 32, mainly the result of his 116 at Jamaica.

As Hutton watched his county colleague compile a magnificent century against the useful Trinidad attack—an innings which ended with a hotly debated leg-before decision—the skipper must have been more than ever convinced that here was a player eminently suited to the more aggressive role at number five.

Accordingly, on the Sunday of the colony match Len, not playing in the game but holding a captain's watching brief, asked acting-captain Trevor Bailey to open the second M.C.C. innings with Ken Suttle, to put Peter May at three, Denis Compton at four, and Willie Watson at five.

With the exception of himself for Suttle, he could see that as England's probable batting order in the Test.

With the rapid dismissal of the last two Trinidad batsmen, M.C.C. wanted 231 runs to win in four hours and a quarter and, by an innings of 90, the last 64 of which came in the double quick time of 75 minutes, Trevor accomplished the dual feat of playing the major part in Trinidad's first home defeat since beaten by M.C.C. in 1931 and confirming Hutton's hopes that he would make a suitable opener. The second half of Bailey's innings was an eye-opener to those who had looked upon him as a stodgy player with practically no strokes except the cut, the dab and the glide, and Hutton had no hesitation in telling his vice-captain they would open together in the Test.

By beating each colony in turn—Jamaica and British Guiana by an innings, Barbados by one wicket and Trinidad by seven wickets—M.C.C. had created another cricket record for a touring team. Theirs was a splendid achievement.

Ever since the team had arrived in Jamaica and the prospects of the tour were discussed, time and time again the pessimists declared that to win any type of game on the jute matting pitch of Trinidad was impossible.

West Indians had, in fact, become so accustomed to colony and visiting teams failing to overcome Trinidad on the mat that the question of defeat never entered their minds.

The last occasion when Trinidad were beaten at the Queen's Park Oval by a rival colony—Barbados—was as far back as 1905. In the long period since only the M.C.C. side of 1931, who won by a mere 32 runs, could claim to have lowered their colours.

On the first day, when rain interfered with play, Trinidad ran up a score of 166 for two. Their eventual defeat did not then appear likely. Next morning, however, captain Jeff Stollmeyer, celebrating his thirty-third birthday, had his off stump removed by a good-length ball from Trueman which came back a lot from the off. Stollmeyer missed a century by 11 runs whereas Gerry Gomez, who played a fighting knock, did so by only nine.

Both Alan Moss and Fred Trueman produced spells of exceptionally good pace bowling at the right time for M.C.C. and in doing so ripped apart the middle of the Trinidad batting.

To recall the famous words of Middlesex and England slow bowler Jim Sims, the batsmen, while not afraid, looked decidedly apprehensive. Trueman repeated his form in the second innings and as a result regained his place in the Test eleven. He also took three difficult catches.

Unfortunately much of the merit of Trueman's performance evaporated in the minds of the crowd through an incident which involved the ever-popular Wilfred Ferguson, affectionately known as "the ugliest cricketer in the world".

"Fergie" has a face like a full moon which, more often than not, is beaming with cordial geniality.

Shortly before the close of play on the Saturday "Fergie" was helping Gomez to stem the Trinidad rot when he received two successive bumpers from Trueman. The first he avoided by ducking. As he rose to his feet, he raised a laugh from the crowd by making an imaginary pass with his bat.

The second, however, was a no-ball. Ferguson went into his wicket to hook, missed his stroke and was struck in the face. He fell to the ground and all the fielding side, with one exception, rushed to his aid.

Trueman, the exception, strode back to his bowling mark, stopped there and rolled up his sleeves even higher as he surveyed the scene, leaving a sad but unmistakable impression that he saw himself as the victorious gladiator.

Not until Charles Palmer, acting on skipper Trevor Bailey's suggestion, went to him did Trueman walk down the pitch to sympathize with the stricken batsman now being attended by first-aid men, who were applying an ice-pack to the bump high on his cheek.

Ferguson recovered, but was bowled the next ball by as lightning a full toss as could ever have been delivered. As Ferguson, the right side of his face growing still larger, passed him on his way back to the pavilion, Trueman shook him by the hand and patted him consolingly on the back.

Still, the damage had been done. Trueman had created a bad impression and when, at the end of the day's play, he raced off the field, ignoring the time-honoured courtesy of waiting at the gate for the batsmen to pass through first, the club members received him in stony silence. Next minute they broke into hearty applause for the batsmen and the other ten M.C.C. players.

The *Trinidad Guardian* described Trueman's action as "frightfully unsportsmanlike" and the *Evening News* of Trinidad, in an attack on Trueman and no-balls, regretted that Trueman did not have the "common decency" to apologize.

The writer continued: "No batsman in the Trinidad team, or the West Indies team for that matter, is seeking sympathy from the British. The day when the British handed out pretty beads to the natives are long past."

I have little sympathy for those who bewail the bumper which, on the matting, remains one of the few offensive measures left to the bowler. Probably if Ferguson had not heard the shout of the umpire calling a no-ball he would not have attempted a hit. But he did and was struck in the face. No excuse could be found for Trueman in not showing some concern.

That evening Trueman was upset, sorry and contrite, and genuinely concerned lest Ferguson, who could not be X-rayed until the Monday, had been seriously hurt. Fortunately Ferguson was not, but Trueman had not added to his reputation.

On the credit side, Freddie did try to get in touch with Ferguson on the Saturday evening, and he was man enough to recognize he had done wrong.

One of the features of the match was a first innings partnership of 198 between Watson and Palmer in three hours which began at a time when M.C.C. were in an unhappy position, Suttle, May and Compton having been dismissed cheaply.

Mr. Frank King, the Leicestershire County Cricket Club chairman, could not have arrived at a more opportune time to see his county captain play his finest innings of the tour. I always thought the M.C.C. made a mistake in emphasizing the managerial rather than the playing aspect of Palmer's duties.

Another new arrival was Mrs. Valerie Compton who, watching her husband bat for the first time since she had landed in the West Indies a fortnight earlier, saw him make a superb and undefeated 90 with all the old Compton sparkle and genius.

When Denis was in the 80's his partner, Willie Watson, suggested that, as ample time remained to get the runs, he should bat quietly to enable Denis to hit his first century of the tour.

"I'll close up so that you can make your hundred," said Willie.

"No thanks, Willie, let's both get on and win the game," replied Denis, which they did.

Sitting in the stand with Mrs. Compton for over two hours that afternoon was much-maligned Fred Trueman. So many had found him hard to handle but afterwards Mrs. Compton told her husband that to her Freddie behaved in every way like a perfect gentleman. "His manners and consideration could not have been improved upon by anyone," said Valerie, with a soft spot in her heart for fighting Fred.

During the colony game the accidents to Trinidad players amounted to four. Apart from Ferguson's injury, Nyson Asgarali was knocked off his motor-cycle by a boy who flew over the handle-bars of his bicycle and whose elbow crashed into his nose and eye; Tang Choon was in a car smash in which he received cuts and bruises; and Gerry Gomez pulled a leg muscle in making a second innings stroke against Johnny Wardle.

When Gerry arrived at hospital on the last morning of the match he found his three team-mates already in the waiting room.

With only two days left before the fourth Test, Gerry, one of the original selections, was desperately anxious to get fit if at all possible and, after heat and ray treatment at hospital, he drove to the Trinidad Government offices, where he sought audience with the Hon. Ajodhasingh, Minister of Works and Communications.

Leaving his ministerial duties for the time being, the Hon. Ajodhasingh, whose knowledge of muscle formation and structure was said to be unsurpassed in the island, ran his fingers deftly over Gerry's leg and began to manipulate.

Next morning Gerry visited him again and, after more swift manipulation, was passed as fit to play in the Test. In the meantime, however, the West Indies Selectors had left Gerry out of the team and brought in our old friend "Fergie", taker of 26 wickets against G. O. Allen's Test team, more than any bowler on either side. The Selectors were not prepared to risk Gerry going into a six-day Test so soon after injury.

The Trinidad Minister of Works and Communications is certainly a remarkable man. For the sheer love of helping others, he opens his office doors on Sunday morning to all who wish him to treat them for muscle trouble and he told me that his "patients" number between 800 and 1,000 a month! He charges not a penny piece.

CHAPTER ELEVEN

More umpiring squabbles—Graveney's disgust—Rumour and counter-rumour
—Charmed life—"Conscience is clear"—Protest to Hutton—No more inter-
views—Ears buzzing—Open letter to Len—Guilty plea on two counts—A
case against M.C.C.—Nut between crackers—Persecution—Attack on Press
—"Just retaliation"—Not cricket—Fourth-rate country.

THE fourth Test was barely three hours old when the English
players were smarting under the belief that they were again
the victims of umpiring injustices.

Unfortunately the bitterness reached new levels, and the high
hopes that at the pleasant Queen's Park Oval, Trinidad, the wounds
from British Guiana would soon be healed were quickly buried. To
the English protests the West Indies counter-attacked with blistering
and indignant references to the conduct of some of the English
players.

In no time, all the appearances of a first-class row had developed,
with an open letter to Len Hutton in the *Trinidad Guardian*, an
interview giving the umpires' versions of events, and a private
conference by Hutton and Palmer on the course of the whole
matter.

At the time anyone mixing with the English party could not
fail to sense their sickness of heart and it was impossible to enter the
Queen's Park Oval Pavilion without hearing pungent comments
on the standard of English sportsmanship. As usual, the English
Press were roundly condemned.

I give the facts of the case as I see them uncoloured, I believe,
by any personal feelings or prejudices. Most people agreed that in
the Trinidad Test umpires Ellis Achong, a former West Indies
Test player, and Ken Woods had each committed a serious blunder,
one of which had an important bearing on the West Indies
innings, and possibly on the whole game.

The first incident happened through the last ball before lunch
on the opening day. With the first delivery of the over Denis
Compton, the bowler, had caught and bowled Jeffrey Stollmeyer,
who looked to be well on the way to making his first century against
England.

Everton Weekes then got off the mark with a single, so bringing
John Holt, who has never impressed against Compton, to face the
bowling. Holt made a defensive push at Denis, and the ball finished
in the hands of Tom Graveney at slip. To my mind there could
have been no possible doubt that a fair and straightforward catch

had been taken from a ball rising from the upper edge of the bat.

The incident occurred at the lower end, nearest to the pavilion, and the members sitting in the pavilion and occupants of the Press box nearby could obtain a good and unimpaired view of the proceedings.

Holt, who is a former Lancashire League professional, turned to leave, hesitated, then stopped as if not sure what had happened. At once Compton, who obviously thought an appeal quite unnecessary, asked umpire Achong, at the bowler's end, for a decision. When Achong said "Not out" most firmly, the English team, who had been congratulating Denis on what they automatically looked upon as his capture of a second wicket, were stunned into surprised silence. So were those in the crowd who had watched closely.

Then Compton began gesticulating and to wave his arms. Graveney, who had been holding the ball, hurled it to the ground as if it had suddenly become white hot or diseased.

Slowly the England players realized that lunch time had arrived and they trooped off the field slowly and thoughtfully with, as one critic put it, their faces red from causes other than the sun.

Graveney, a quiet man who is normally so slow to anger, was booed by a section of the members nearest to the England dressing-room. On arrival in the changing room Hutton, apparently the first to recover from the shock, grinned out from behind the wire netting across the windows. The grin contained more than a trace of amazed bewilderment.

The lunch interval of forty minutes passed amidst a confusion of ideas and discussions. First the umpire Achong was said to have stated that it had been a bump ball. Weekes, the batsman at the other end, was supposed to have told friends that he had no doubt at all that Holt had touched the ball cleanly to slip. Then Achong was reported to have declared that Holt did not touch the ball at all and the second version of the opinion of batsman Weekes was a reversal of the first.

So it went on, rumour and counter-rumour. All were equally unconvincing. Possibly Holt did not feel the touch of the ball on the edge of the bat, but for the fourth time on the tour he had become the centre of an umpiring dispute.

At Melbourne Park, Jamaica, Holt was 47 when he gave what was conceded generally as a clear catch at the wicket. There Evans, after tossing the ball in the air in triumphant announcement and appeal combined, turned to talk to the slips. The umpire said "Not out" and Holt went on to make 152, so ensuring his place in the Test team, something he might not have done had he been given out to Godfrey's appeal.

Twice more, with Evans as wicketkeeper, Holt appeared to give catches—one in each innings of the third Test. On the second occasion Holt began to leave the wicket and Denis Atkinson, his runner, actually started taking off his batting gloves as he too walked away. I am not suggesting the batsman is at fault if the umpire does not agree with an appeal against him, even if the whole crowd hears a distinct snick. No one, however, could deny that Holt bore a very charmed life.

Fortunately for England at Trinidad Holt did not survive long after lunch, but undoubtedly an atmosphere of suspicion had been created.

The second scene, and as it turned out, the more serious, came when the score was 168 and Everton Weekes 43. Everton slashed at a ball from Trevor Bailey, and Dick Spooner, standing up to the wicket, seemed to take a snick.

The unanimous England appeal was promptly turned down by umpire Woods. Everton, one of the best sportsmen in cricket, turned to Spooner and said "Bad luck, Dick."

Weekes then settled down to a score of 206 and he shared with Frankie Worrell in a stand of 338 which was not only a third wicket record for the West Indies but passed the 264 hit by Hammond and Hutton at The Oval in 1939 as the best in the series between England and the West Indies.

I am not going to pretend I *know* for absolute certainty that Weekes was out, but no doubt existed in the minds of the Englishmen nearest the scene, and so best qualified to judge, that the decision of umpire Woods was wrong.

Of course it may be said that fieldsmen on the spot are likely to be biased. I know from experience what can happen over a hair's-breadth decision. On many occasions, trying to seek out the truth in Test and county games, I have approached umpire, wicketkeeper, bowler and batsman and the different versions about a single delivery that sometimes they provide in all honesty and sincerity is really staggering.

I must, however, place on record that among cricketers Dick Spooner enjoys a reputation for honesty which is second to none and I know he confirms what I thought—that Weekes gave him a clean catch.

Afterwards I spoke to umpire Woods, who told me that, although he heard a snick, he did not see the ball deviate in its flight. I suggest that for an umpire to see positively and clearly the ball deviate from the inside edge of the bat into wicketkeeping gauntlets a matter of inches away, from a medium-pace bowler, is next to impossible.

Still, "My conscience is clear" Woods assured me, and I has-
tened to tell him that not for one moment was I suggesting he was
anything but honest.

Woods, a young official, is so keen on umpiring cricket that he
retires to bed at seven o'clock in the evening before each day's
play and he drinks nothing but coffee to keep his head clear for the
job entrusted to him.

A few minutes after Woods had allowed Weekes to continue
batting umpire Achong, from square-leg, began the walk to Hutton,
an umpiring act which was now becoming a familiar sight. Achong
complained to the England captain that, by actions as well as
words, some of the fieldsmen were showing their strong disapproval
of the decision.

Regrettably, I must mention that at the end of the day, both
umpires were seen surrounded by members on the pavilion steps
and heard to be giving an account of what had happened on the
field.

The next morning the following account of the incident appeared
in the *Trinidad Guardian*:

> "One player asked Woods 'Are you deaf?—didn't you *hear*
> the tip?' Woods is said to have replied that he did not know
> he has to *hear* a tip to give a decision.
>
> 'I know I have to *see* a tip, and I did not see one here.' This
> same player asked Woods if he had wax in his ears.
>
> Another England fieldsman enquired by signals whether
> Woods was hard of hearing. Achong and Woods in their protest
> to Hutton pointed out that if they are supposed to control the
> game they should have better conduct from the English players."

Quite properly Achong and Woods were told by home officials
to keep their views and news to themselves and Hutton and Palmer
deliberated whether they should take any official action. They
decided not to do so.

The important point is that the English players completely
deny the umpires' version. An English player, for instance, never
uses the word "tip". He would say "snick".

That, however, is a minor matter. While walking down the
wicket at the end of the over Tom Graveney and Dick Spooner
did talk about the decision and they suggested to one another that
Woods might not have heard the snick on account of the noise
from the crowd.

Spooner touched an ear as he said to Graveney: "I'm not
surprised if he didn't hear it, Tom, with all that noise going on

I find it very hard to hear things out here in the middle with all the babble from the crowd. Often my ears are buzzing."

To those who are prepared to accept the umpire's account and condemn out of hand the English cricketers I would ask some indulgence for several reasons.

As the ever-unpopular English correspondents pointed out in their despatches home the two incidents climaxed a series of equally provocative happenings in the Tests, and over a friendly drink representatives of both sides agreed that by far the majority of disputed decisions had gone against England.

As Crawford White, of the *News Chronicle*, wrote at the time:

"I have never known any company of cricketers as incensed by gross injustices and flagrant decisions as this English side. I cannot condone demonstrations, scenes or quibbles on the field but when these things go on and on, and mistakes seem to build up and up, one must sympathize as well as condemn."

The next morning J. S. Barker wrote an open letter to Len Hutton which ran:

"Dear Len Hutton,
        We in the West Indies are becoming increasingly distressed by the undercurrents of hostility and suspicion which began with your arrival in the West Indies and have been growing in strength ever since.

'We in the West Indies' means *your* admirers and supporters, not that small minority for whom the West Indies can do no wrong. It means, also, many hundreds of your fellow country-men (and even your fellow Yorkshiremen!) whose anticipatory delight in your tour is slowly turning to dismay and embarrassment.

The Charges

The charges against us are:

1. The West Indies umpiring falls below the standards of English umpiring.

2. West Indies umpiring is not only incompetent but dishonest.

3. A hostility bordering on intimidation has been directed at your team since the Tests began.

To charge No. 1 we modestly plead guilty. Charge No. 2 we reject with the contempt it deserves. To charge No. 3 whilst emphatically dissociating Trinidad from it, we must also plead guilty.

Nevertheless, we submit that the astonishing departures from all canons of good taste and good sportsmanship made by certain members of your team are at once more painful to bear and easier to remedy than any of these charges—even if they were all true.

STRANGE CONDUCT

The criticizing of umpires' decisions, whatever your private opinions, the public arguments with, and even the brow-beating of these much-tried gentlemen, is not the conduct to which we are accustomed, or which we expect from men dignified by the colours of the M.C.C.

May I suggest that you yourself cast the first stone by seeing to it that the pleasure we find in your tour is not marred by other 'incidents'.

That England should lose a well-deserved reputation for good sportsmanship is a far more serious matter than the loss of a cricket match, even a Test Match, and will be remembered much longer than and in far more important fields of life than the cricket field.

Yours sincerely,

J. S. Barker."

The open letter—one of journalism's oldest ideas—gives the writer added licence and liberty, and freedom to be provocative, and in this case the recipient was gagged and forbidden by contract to reply had he wished to do so.

The letter was quoted in length, so we were told, in most newspapers throughout the Commonwealth. I was having breakfast with Len Hutton when he read it.

Having spent the previous evening with him also, I knew him to be a very depressed and worried captain. Everything was taking a wrong turning.

He had lost the toss for the third time in the series, two decisions had gone against England, with all the attendant fuss and controversy, and furthermore early in the game Brian Statham had severely strained rib muscles, an injury which not only deprived England of their spearhead for the remainder of the Test but created serious doubts whether he would be fit for the fifth and final Test at Jamaica.

Hutton's reaction to the letter was merely to ask who, in point

No. 2, raised by Mr. Barker, had charged the West Indian umpires with being not only incompetent but dishonest? Certainly neither Hutton, Palmer, nor vice-captain Bailey had done so.

Earlier on the tour Hutton had been present in the England dressing-room when a former West Indies captain had come in and apologized over a vital decision, saying, "Len, I am ashamed of that."

Whatever other opinions had been expressed, however, no suggestion that the umpiring was anything but honest had been made.

In fact, at Jamaica, Barbados and again at British Guiana, Hutton had publicly praised and thanked the umpires. He knew they did their job voluntarily and, unlike English officials, were not professional umpires, with six days a week in which to improve their standards.

The answer to Mr. Barker centred on his admission in point No. 3 that "a hostility bordering on intimidation has been directed against your team since the Tests began"—he pleaded that, Trinidad apart, the West Indies could be found guilty of this charge.

I hope that point will be digested thoroughly by those who would be the sternest critics of the England cricketers.

Also, on his own admission, Mr. Barker was witnessing his first Test of the series. I wondered if his opinion would have changed had he watched the previous Tests and, above all, suffered the painful sight—and it was painful to all who love the game of cricket—of the bottle-throwing at British Guiana.

On purely ethical grounds a case can be made against some members of the English team. No doubt the bluff, tough and outspoken Freddie Trueman let himself down when he failed to go to the aid of the fallen Ferguson in the Trinidad game preceding the Test; that the kindly Tom Graveney, with the soft west-country accent, should not have thrown the ball on the ground to register his disgust on Holt being given not out in the Trinidad Test; that Denis Compton, with all his experience on the cricket and soccer fields before vast crowds, should not have given way to his pent-up feelings and waved his arms in protest about the same umpiring decisions.

Any deterioration of standards of sportsmanship by an England team is to be deplored, but I guarantee no touring side has been under so much stress as was Hutton's side.

Ever since they had used Bermuda as a stepping-stone to the West Indies, the politics of the islands and their special problems had followed the M.C.C. cricketers around like a detective shadowing a suspect. They felt that they were the nut between the crackers.

The crowds, at times friendly, made things harder to bear through their continuous shrieking and screaming and other noise.

On some islands the English fraternity made a bee-line for the Englishmen with something like a prayer for them to succeed. If they lost then the rumours about off-the-field misbehaviour began to fly. I did not envy them their lot.

Rightly or wrongly, too, the M.C.C. felt that some of the decisions gave them a raw deal. This was the straw which did so much to break the camel's back.

The actions of Compton and Graveney were not so much on account of Holt being given "not out" to what everyone thought was a clear catch but a culmination of what Mr. Barker so rightly declared as "a hostility bordering on intimidation" since the Tests started.

Nor were the Trinidadians prepared to allow the matter to die a natural death and I could not escape the impression that to be still reminded of faults and misdeeds in print some three days after the event savoured of persecution.

So, to my mind, did an article from British Guiana giving the opinion of a newspaper writer there—one who occupied the same Press box from which a bottle was thrown—that Hutton's team were the worst-behaved ever to leave Britain's shores.

Ross Hall (*Daily Mirror*) declared:

"English tempers have not been improved by attacks in the local newspapers on their sportsmanship. There was enough trouble when India were here a year ago. Nothing was done Now that exactly the same thing has happened again the West Indians are accusing the Englishmen of being squealers. What nonsense."

As always the incidents became exaggerated and distorted out of all proportion and as early as 7 a.m. the morning following the first day's squabble the telephone in manager Palmer's room began to ring with complaints about the team.

I gather Palmer, in his most diplomatic manner, was not inclined to agree with many of his callers.

From the first days all could see that the tour would be as much a test of character as of cricket skill, and so many of the players emerged with the utmost credit in the most trying circumstances that for one or two incidents to blind the public to the general tone of the party, which I insist was exemplary, was real tragedy.

Not unnaturally, a large measure of resentment was aroused s that the basic cause of the disputes came to be forgotten in the general allegations of misconduct. A good many of the team felt like a man kicked in the teeth and then forced to make a public apology for protesting that he had been hurt.

Next target for attack were the eight correspondents travelling with the team: Charles Bray (*Daily Herald*), Crawford White (*News Chronicle*), Frank Rostron (*Daily Express*), Reg Hayter (Reuters), Ross Hall (*Daily Mirror*), E. W. Swanton (*Daily Telegraph*), Peter Ditton (Express Syndications) and myself.

Each day extracts from our cabled stories were sent back to the West Indies and, taken out of context as they were, they did not always provide a fair and reliable guide to the general tone of the reports. Naturally only the more sensational passages were used and published in the island papers and, though others might think it a case of people in glass houses daring to throw stones, some of the West Indians charged us with being misleading.

Now for one thing I would emphasize that the use of the term Press as a collective noun in grouping together so many factions of the newspaper profession cannot be justified. On the tour were eight journalists representing different types of newspapers, and all required by their organizations to offer opinions.

As trained and experienced observers the things they wrote were their honest convictions. If the truth sometimes was hard to bear the blame should not have been levelled at the correspondents.

A writer from Georgetown, who saw only one Test, claimed the reports sent to England were most misleading and he called on the West Indies Cricket Board of Control to make a firm protest and a condemnation of the travelling correspondents.

In a letter of extraordinary length (by English standards) a correspondent charged the English Press with

> "despicable and deliberate distortion of facts, insinuations and bogus alibis which have again and again been cabled to England by these pharasitical pundits since the arrival of the M.C.C. in Jamaica".

Then we come to this interesting passage:

> ". . . Len Hutton undoubtedly had a good case in British Guiana where obviously incompetent umpiring presented a grave problem which must be tackled in a practical and businesslike manner by the B.G. Board of Control. Local prestige and face-saving must not be allowed to blacken the good name of the West Indies. It is a fact that the standard of umpiring in the

Colony has not measured up to the exacting demands of International cricket either in 1948, during the Indian tour 1952,
and again during the recent tour. But maybe such happenings
are merely a just form of retaliation for equally bad and ques-
tionable decisions perpetrated against visiting sides to England
during the post-war years.

Many Australian, Indian, South African, New Zealand and
West Indian cricketers can bear testimony to the biased
judgments exercised by English umpires in county games and
Test Matches during this period."

Note the phrase *just form of retaliation*.

After reading that I felt that *The Times* had more than a little
justification for commenting editorially that the expression "It's
not cricket" may have had its day!

Cricket correspondents cannot expect to please everybody and,
speaking personally, I have received a fair share of critical letters,
but I wondered at the reasoning of the man who wrote to young
Peter Ditton, whose reports for the Express Syndications were
prominently displayed in many leading West Indian papers, in the
following strain:

"I have come to the conclusion that the Englishman has
lost completely the idea of 'playing the game'. There are fourth-
rate sportsmen in the various fields of sport in England, and the
Englishman bluntly refuses to realize this fact, rather he prefers
to abuse and insult his opponents publicly.

Poor Englishman! One day you may again be able to sing
'Britannia rules the waves'. But gone for ever are the relationships
which for so long the English tried to maintain, of master,
servant, teacher, pupil, etc.

Face it, Mr. Ditton. Your country is only fourth rate now
and let us not hear or read so much prejudiced poppycock
when cricket is being taught and shown you by those superior
to you in that field."

CHAPTER TWELVE

Bouncer battle—Accident to Laker—Brainless bowling—King *v.* Trueman—Put
to sleep—Wife's illness—The wicked mat—Turf experiments—A wet patch
—Worrell and May reply—Bradman tip—Wives on tour?—Will Weekes
retire?—Fancy caps—Roller-boy—Buffoonery—"Fergie" keeps wicket—
Evans in the wars again—Two for none—Barracudas and sharks—Statham
breaks down—World Championship?—The next six days.

HAVING produced almost every possible controversial issue
involved in the once-innocent pastime of cricket—umpiring
disputes, defensive time-wasting leg-theory, team selection differences
and so on—it was in keeping with the nature of the stormy series
for the fourth Test of the rubber to produce the one bitter angle left,
a battle of bouncers.

The leading contestants were Fred Trueman and Frank King.
Withdrawing from the bout after nine overs was Brian Statham
(through injury) but in support of the main rivals came Trevor Bailey
on the one side and once, by accident, Sonny Ramadhin on the other.

Trueman and King are as far apart in personality as the two
poles. While Freddie is by no means averse to giving his views on
any debatable subject to any assembly from one upwards, King's
longest recorded speech is "How's that?"

King, a groundsman (or ground superintendent as he styled
himself) in his native Barbados, surprised even his colleagues with
his pace and hostility at Trinidad.

By common vote he surpassed Freddie in the number of bouncers
he bowled. The aggregate was far in advance of any number I
have ever seen in any match anywhere.

In defence of the bumper fast bowlers argue that it is the only
weapon left to them when they are committed to try to dismiss
batsmen of international class on a jute matting.

I have every sympathy for these arguments but far too many
bouncers were bowled in the Trinidad Test and they culminated
in a nasty accident to Jim Laker.

Earlier in the match, after being on the receiving end of two in
succession from Trueman, Stollmeyer had looked enquiringly in the
direction of the umpire as if to say, "How many more do I have to
take before you declare this form of attack to be intimidation?"

Later, when fielding, the West Indies captain went from his
mid-on fielding position to give what were obviously cautionary
words of advice to King, who in one over-zealous period sent down
four bouncers in five balls.

Just how many can be bowled before the umpire steps in and declares the point of·"persistent and systematic" bowling of short-pitched bumpers as having been reached? Surely when the law was framed the legislators could not have envisaged a bowler getting away with four an over, as was the case in the first colony match in Jamaica. Realizing the position was getting out of hand the two captains sought the advice of the umpires for the fifth Test. They settled on a maximum of two an over.

I have every feeling for the bowler called upon to work on matting where the stakes are so heavily set against him, and I believe the bumper, used sparingly and fairly, remains a legitimate weapon. A totally different situation arises, however, when as many as three or more an over are bowled.

To my mind to exorcise the bumper from cricket altogether is neither desirable nor possible but to attempt to limit them to so many an over by legislation is an extremely difficult matter. In any case the fewer laws and regulations the better. The spirit of the game is failing, not the legislation.

I believe the only solution to be a tacit arrangement between the captains, an unwritten law, that bumpers are to be kept within limits and must not be bowled at the lower order batsmen who are not gifted with the same reflex actions, the speed of footwork or the timing of the accredited batsmen either to duck out of the way or to hit them.

During the early stages of the Trinidad Test the injured Gerry Gomez, for once a spectator and not a performer, deplored the over-use of the bouncer in an interview with Roy Lawrence of Radio Jamaica. When Roy pointed out to him that nobody had come to harm through the excessive use of bumpers, Gomez predicted that someone would one day. Unhappily he was to prove right within a very short time.

Asked what he thought of King's bowling Gerry used one pointed word—brainless. He said also that to bowl bumpers to tail-enders was "completely outside the spirit of cricket".

If somebody had to be hurt by a bumper in the West Indies Test series, perhaps providentially it was an Englishman, and I know that Jim Laker, the victim, will appreciate what I mean. Everybody was sorry for Jim, who was equally popular with both sides and the last man to stoop to any low practices on the cricket field.

Late on the fifth day the last slender chance (and it was mighty thin) of the West Indies snatching a victory rested in their ability to make England follow on.

Tony Lock, seventh wicket down, did not long survive the new ball. He became Worrell's second victim of the series in three Tests and, when Trueman went in at number ten to join Laker, twenty-one runs were still needed with two wickets in hand to make the West Indies bat again and virtually banish any competitive interest from the game.

Worrell, who had taken over the captaincy from Stollmeyer (split finger) gave specific instructions to King to bowl at the wicket. "Cut out the bumpers," he said in effect, "and aim at the stumps and see if you can bowl them out."

The crowd, however, always roused to excitement at the appearance of Trueman, at once envisaged a situation charged with drama—that of "Mr. Bumper Man" being bumped! Before Trueman had reached the wicket sections of the crowd were calling out to Frank King to "Give him a bumper, King."

At first Trueman faced Worrell and the opening ball he received he cracked through the covers like a Hutton or a Walcott.

Then came the contest King v. Trueman. Each ball was accompanied by shrieks of excitement. The first was wide of the leg stump; the second passed over the top of the bails from just short of a length, and the third produced a single to the covers.

The bouncer which the crowd (and probably Trueman himself) thought would be directed at him was, however, unleashed at Laker. Moving in the air and pitching on the off stump it flew straight at Laker, who could not resist the temptation to hook.

He had never missed a bumper before, but, as he afterwards told me, this was easily the fastest he had ever received—and he had taken his share from Lindwall, Miller and others.

In the fleeting second after he had missed the ball, Laker instinctively realized that he was going to be hit. The ball struck him in his right eye and split the skin above and below the eye.

Jim fell to his knees and, immediately he felt blood oozing from the area of the eye, instinct made him struggle to his feet and move towards the dressing-room. He had barely covered the twenty-two yards of the pitch before he started to stumble.

Denis Atkinson rushed to his aid, to be joined by King and first-aid men running in from the crowd, and the little group made its erratic way to the pavilion watched in silence by a hushed and stilled crowd.

On Saturday Peter May had come as close to being the first victim of a bouncer in the match as he ever will. He felt a lightning bumper whizz just past his face.

Although cricket does not provide any physical contact between the participants it is not a game without physical danger, as illustrated by some of the events of recent years.

Only a few months earlier Tony Lock, batting on a bad wicket at The Oval against Charlie Grove, the Warwickshire opening bowler, had been hit sharply on the side of the head. He went down like a log and spent the next week in hospital.

When Cuan McCarthy, the South African fast bowler, was at Cambridge he bowled a fast ball which pole-axed James Langridge so completely that for a moment players as well as spectators thought that the batsman had been fatally injured.

In 1948 a Lindwall special smashed into the face of Jack Robertson of Middlesex and broke his jaw and on the same tour Sid Barnes, the Australian, had been carried off the Test field at Manchester after stopping a full-blooded pull from Dick Pollard in his ribs.

The cut above Laker's eye had to be stitched, and when he returned from hospital the eye was blackened and closed and as bad as one I saw in Bruce Woodcock's dressing-room on the notable occasion at Harringay in 1946 after being hit by the gallant Freddie Mills, who lost the fight on points.

Jim, sharing a room with Alan Moss next to mine at the comfortable Queen's Park Hotel, insisted on going down to dinner, but he found he was not so strong as he had imagined and he returned to his room. Given some sleeping tablets by Mrs. Denis Compton, he slept soundly and awoke to find cables of sympathy from many parts of the world awaiting him.

Laker was more worried about his wife's reaction to the news than about himself, because at the time she was not well and had spent some time with friends in Ireland.

Earlier Jim had applied to the West Indies Board of Control for permission to fly home instead of returning by ship which would mean a difference to him of a fortnight.

As the attendances for the colony match and the fourth Test were large (116,289 paying 124,563 dollars) and by now the expenses of the tour (216,000 dollars) had been covered Jim was granted the requested change in travel arrangements.

Amid his discomfort and disappointment that the injury had put him out of the match, however, Jim found time to smile. "Only one man is to blame for the accident—Everton Weekes," he cracked in reference to his being dropped by Everton at slip off Ferguson when he had scored only a single.

Mainly through a swashbuckling effort by Trueman, England managed to save the follow on and, for all the purpose of the sixth and last day, the match might well have ended there—twenty minutes from time on the fifth day.

Almost five complete days had been taken to decide the issue

of the first innings and, on that basis, about ten to twelve days
would have been needed to complete the game. In all 1,528 runs
were scored for 24 wickets, one of which was a run out, and others
were frittered away during the last light-hearted hour when nothing
counted for much at all.

Of the five centuries hit, Everton Weekes made the highest
individual score with 206, single hundreds came from Worrell,
Walcott, May and Compton, and Tom Graveney missed recording
a sixth by a matter of eight runs.

England's Selectors had known what would be in store on the
mat and the bowling position before the match afforded a very
interesting guide to the speed of wicket-taking by the individual
members of the side.

To then, Statham had averaged a wicket in 51 balls, Moss just
over 53, Wardle 61, Trueman roughly 67, Bailey 83, Laker 85 and
Lock 97.

The one thing Hutton and his co-Selectors might well have
borne in mind was the horrifying history of spin-bowlers on the
Trinidad mat. In two Tests Valentine (who was kept out of the
final two against England because of a bad finger) had taken
five for 306, Sonny Ramadhin four for 273, Vinoo Mankad, the
Indian left-arm slow bowler, one for 208, and Jim Laker two for
108, in 1948.

On figures the only spinners with even a reasonable chance on
the mat are the genuine leg-break and googly bowlers, with wrist
action and finger spin, and their left-armed equivalents—those who
bowl "Chinamen", the left-hander's off-break to the right-hand
batsman, and googlies.

Support for this theory comes from the bowling of Gupte, the
Indian leg-break and googly bowler whom the West Indians declare
firmly must be the best of his type in the world today. In the previous
West Indies season he took 13 wickets for 290 in the Trinidad Test,
whereas Valentine, Ramadhin, a finger-spinner with a straight
wrist, and Mankad were being hit all over the Queen's Park Oval.

The main hope of getting out the opposition for a reasonable
score at Trinidad would seem to be a combination, in cricket
parlance, of seamers and tweakers.

The choice of Lock for Wardle, who bowls the "Chinaman"
well as he demonstrated in the third Test, was illogical to me, and
that opinion became strengthened by the success of Denis Compton
in his all-too-restricted spells.

In his first bowl, just before lunch on the opening day, Denis
gained the important prize of Stollmeyer's wicket, thus breaking
dangerous first-wicket stand, and nothing will convince me that

Holt was not clearly taken off him by Graveney at slip a few balls later.

Despite this, throughout the second day Denis did not bowl one ball and, being used again towards the end, he emerged with easily the best figures of the seven bowlers used by Hutton.

Holt especially has never given the impression that he knows how to pick Compton's googly from his "chinaman" and I feel sure Hutton's reluctance to give Compton more bowling was a mistake.

Lock nearly spun his fingers to the bone and, although his figures were far from impressive, his achievement in closing one end by sheer accuracy at a period when the scoring threatened to get entirely out of hand deserved more recognition than it received.

Whether Wardle would have done better is, of course, hypothetical, but in my view Wardle, with his chinamen and googlies, would have been more suited to the jute surface.

On the other hand Wilfred Ferguson, who bowled a genuine leg-spinner but not the googly, conceded 155 runs in 47 overs for only one wicket, that of Trevor Bailey.

A second would have been his had Weekes taken the slip chance offered by Laker, but two for 155 could hardly have been claimed as successful.

Clyde Walcott actually improved on his already-superior average to Ramadhin on the mat by the simple virtues, so often ignored, of length and direction and "doing a bit".

Considering the conditions he returned the exceptional figures of three for 52 and, curiously, the only really bad ball he bowled out of 204 cost Watson his wicket. Watson hit a long hop firmly but rather too high on the bat. The stroke looked good enough for a four any day but that splendid all-round athlete Denis Atkinson leaped high to his left at square-leg and clutched the hurtling ball for the catch of his life.

For all that, frankly, the status of the bowler, whatever his type, on the mat is absurd. None know that better than the players and officials of the Queen's Park Oval. Their latest efforts to provide a turf wicket were represented by two long strips of green on either side of the matting.

The new wicket was due for a trial in April, and groundsman-umpire Mr. "Badge" Menzies, from British Guiana, was engaged to lend his practical skill. Should the turf stand up to match play this time Trinidad is prepared for wickets as perfect as that at Georgetown, which have the reputation of being the best in the Caribbean, but anything is an improvement on the matting which gives the bowler no chance at all. In this case it is a bad substitute

In the past the chief difficulty had been to counteract the ravages of the mole cricket which destroyed the tender young grass roots.

Each morning at seven all the indentations made by the ball during the previous day's play on the base under the matting, a base made of a mixture of clay and sand, have to be filled in. The whole is then rolled and watered. When the ground is sufficiently dry the mat is fixed down. Pegging the matting, which must not be too tight or too loose, is an art in itself.

On the Saturday morning Hutton, who had lost his wicket the previous evening to a ball which flew unexpectedly from a fair length, found a wet patch near the leg stump. In his follow-through fast bowler King had made the patch which had to be repaired and was still damp when Hutton made his inspection.

Hutton rightly said he could not agree to a prompt resumption. The spot could easily have assisted Ferguson's leg-breaks. Exposed to the sun the patch gradually dried out, but Stollmeyer, having had a long experience of the mat, was concerned lest the mat should be left off too long.

To overbake the clay-sand base was reckoned just as dangerous as leaving it wet because if the ground became too dry the ball would fly alarmingly. Knowing this Stollmeyer and the West Indies Board of Control Secretary, Cyril Merry, were most anxious that Hutton should not have the laying of the mat delayed too long. With everything else that had gone before in the series they were concerned at possible events if England were trapped on a "flier".

Hutton agreed to a restart forty-three minutes late and a small section of the crowd, probably tired of waiting, mildly booed Bailey and May as they went to the wicket. Otherwise I was impressed by the crowd in general who were a model of patience, good temper and understanding at the unusual delay.

Within a few overs of the resumption Bailey was back in the pavilion, having followed a leg-break from Ferguson and given a catch to Weekes at slip. Nothing in the matting wicket was responsible for his dismissal and happily the mat played just as well from the start as it did throughout the other days of the match.

The next West Indies success did not arrive until after tea when Peter May, having completed 135, made a tired stroke and was caught in the covers by Pairaudeau. As in the case of Frank Worrell, some minor agitation had been made to leave out May after a run of low scores. As it happened, both Worrell and May made centuries, the most effective reply of all to their critics.

May had not scored a hundred in Tests since his maiden appearance for England at Headingley in 1951 against South Africa. By a coincidence Compton, who had last hit a Test century at Trent Bridge, Nottingham, in the same series, followed suit on the Monday morning, after being 81 not out over the week-end.

Whereas this was May's second century for England, it was Compton's fifteenth. I would like to be able to peep into the future to know whether May, now twenty-three, will have as many hundreds to his name as Denis when he is Compton's thirty-five. How many Denis would have scored but for the war years and subsequently serious knee trouble provides an interesting speculation.

Neither May nor Compton made the semblance of a mistake in a partnership of 164 which really killed the West Indies' hopes of forcing a victory. Compared with the 338 by Weekes and Worrell, a stand of 164 seems small but it came at a vital stage and when the opposition had all the psychological advantage of being on top and in a position to experiment with bowling and buy wickets at a heavy price.

Perhaps Denis's Test hundred was the least exciting and spectacular of his fifteen, but the very nature of his mission precluded him from stroke-making. He had to be content with the role of staying at the wicket as long as he could. For all the perfection of the wicket England had to make 532 runs to be sure of not batting again—a task which on any type of pitch is tall enough to upset most sides.

After England had lost the toss again, and been deprived of the bowling of Brian Statham, their key seamer, with only nine overs bowled by him in the match, to save the follow-on was by no means an unsatisfactory feat, taking other factors into consideration as well. The spirit of the side which had been largely discovered at British Guiana was in no way impaired by the depressing experiences.

May began his innings on the Friday evening and, after dinner that night, Hutton once again took him to one side and offered him some shrewd advice to which May listened intently and carried out most effectively next day.

Part of the England captain's instruction was not to waste needless energy in hitting the ball hard when the stroke was purely defensive, and not to try to force the ball to the on side but to play with the left shoulder pointing to the opposite wicket.

Hutton asked May if he knew precisely all the positions of the fielders at all times. Peter had to confess that he did not. Hutton then told him he should try and cultivate the habit of making sure of the exact location of each fielder. Hutton went on to tell Peter that when Bradman batted he looked round the field before each ball was bowled, one of the important reasons why Bradman's placing of the ball was so uncannily accurate.

May is the type of cricketer who assimilates quickly and does not forget what he learns. Much will come to him with more experience.

On Saturday evening Compton was hit on the instep by Walcott and he spent two hours on Sunday evening, at his wife's insistence, with his feet in salt water as hot as he could bear. Which can be used as another argument in favour of a player being allowed to have his wife with him on tour.

Normally the M.C.C., like other cricketing bodies, frown in disapproval of wives accompanying the team. This is a human problem which M.C.C. should tackle, with the accent on the heart rather than the head. More than one married player on tour in the West Indies told me he would not agree to go on another tour, if invited, without his wife, and as the celebrities of cricket nowadays are globe-trotters theirs is not an unreasonable case.

These are the men who bring in the gate-money on which cricket lives. The magic and power of the name of Hutton, for instance, makes a difference of thousands to the attendances—at least acute disappointment is felt if he is rested from any match.

Cricketers receive no extra emoluments for being the stars of television recordings of the big matches in which they play, they are sometimes used without consent for advertising and publicity stunts. Their wives are inclined to become lonely and weary of being alone in the house for months at a time.

Since the war Hutton and Evans, for example, have toured Australasia twice, the West Indies twice and South Africa once and both face the prospect of going to Australia and New Zealand again in September, 1954, taking them away until April, 1955. Before that, however, as soon as they returned from the West Indies they had to start off again on the county cricket circuit.

Immediately they come back from Australasia in 1955, taking the obvious assumption that they go, they will again have to start on the county round. By comparison commercial travellers are stay-at-homes.

The problem was far less serious before the war when a cricketer might go abroad only two or three times in his career, and then with two or three or even more years' interval between tours.

Nowadays cricket is not a normal occupation for the few men who fill the top places and, as a consequence, are always first on the list for the cricket tours. I suggest it would not be asking too much of the authorities to pay the passage money of as many wives as are able and want to accompany their husbands on tour.

There the expense to cricket could end, for my experience of the hospitable nature of the Australians, South Africans and all members of the cricketing community is such that many would gladly open their homes to their guests.

For the wives to go around with the team all the time would not be practicable or desirable but much heartburning and loneliness would be saved if they could stay in one centre, such as Sydney or Melbourne, or Cape Town or Johannesburg. A point to think about also is that the form of some cricketers does seem to be affected by long separations.

Certainly Denis Compton was a far happier man when his wife arrived in the West Indies. The next time he played he scored 90, his highest innings to that point, and in the following innings he made his Trinidad Test century.

To return to that Test. For the first time against England the three W's, Weekes, Worrell and Walcott, scored centuries in the same innings, a feat they had accomplished previously against India in the last series in the West Indies, at Sabina Park, Kingston, Jamaica.

All three had come from the small island of Barbados and they are still to the West Indies what Bradman individually represented to Australia, Hobbs to Surrey and Hutton to Yorkshire. All three, in my opinion, would be automatic selections for any World XI. Definitely no opposition would be certain of winning until they had seen the backs of them all.

The performances of Everton Weekes have been all the more remarkable because, at the age of twenty-nine, he suffers from torn fibres of the thigh muscles which have caused a visible ridge and depression and made him well below 100 per cent fit.

In Australia Weekes was carefully nursed, but was unable to do himself justice. What might be expected from him had he the physique of Walcott, for instance, can only be imagined but, unhappily, at the time of writing his future in Test cricket is uncertain.

If Weekes has to confine his future between the Lancashire League at Bacup, where he is the professional with a sports business in the town, and a newly acquired coaching appointment a Trinidad and its neighbouring island of Tobago, international cricket will suffer a grievous loss and be deprived of one of it main drawing cards. His batting is sheer uninhibited genius.

In world ranking Weekes must come directly after Hutton, wh leads through his technical perfection on all types of pitches. He i more brilliant in his stroke-play than Hutton, as was Compton i his vintage, injury-free years—or should I say that Hutton purposel disciplines his range of versatility much more than either?

To what dizzy heights of batting achievement Hutton woul have climbed but for his war-time accident in the gymnasium a

Catterick Camp, which left him with his guiding left arm one and
a half inches shorter than his right, and his left wrist one inch
thinner than the other, can be only a matter of speculation. Equally
who can say what would have been his achievements had he lived
in an era of stronger English batting?

A distinct measure of responsibility has always weighed heavily
on Hutton, who was also taught very early in his career for Yorkshire
to eliminate all but the safest scoring strokes. In his first game for
his county, for example, Hutton made a perfect square-cut, the
type of stroke which Everton Weekes or Sidney Barnes, of Australia,
the two best exponents of the square-cut in modern cricket, could
not have excelled.

Instead of offering the expected praise to the proud youngster,
Hutton's seasoned Yorkshire partner came half-way down the pitch
to him and told him in no uncertain terms that he wasn't a Saturday-
afternoon fancy-cap cricketer!

Like the other two W's, Weekes is superbly equipped by a
generous Nature with perfect balance, speed of eye and footwork,
supple and iron wrists and forearms, and a firm decision, by which
I mean that if he thinks the ball is hittable he makes no suggestion
of anything but a full-blooded stroke. How to dismiss this superb
player on a good wicket—all West Indies implicitly trust their
pitches and most noticeably very few plant the left foot to the pitch
of the ball when driving—or set a field to him when he is set is a
real problem to any captain no matter how experienced and versed
in tactics.

However, an analysis of the dismissals of Weekes in his six
innings up to the last Test—he did not play in the second on account
of injury—suggests that, like Stollmeyer, he is more vulnerable to
the ball pitched on or just outside the off stump than to any other.

In the first Test his off stump was knocked back when he
attempted to cut Alan Moss after being tied down for a long stretch
by the nagging accuracy of Lock. At Georgetown Lock clipped his
off bail and, in the second innings, Bailey had him caught in the
slips from an outswinger.

The much-disputed decision at Trinidad when he was 43 was
for a catch at the wicket just outside the off stump. For all the
punishment he can and does mete out to them, bowlers prefer
bowling to Weekes than they do, say, to Walcott. They say that,
however many runs he scores, he is always giving them a chance
because on and around the off stump he is, in their vernacular,
something of a "flasher". That is not said in any uncomplimentary
sense.

Like many of the leading West Indian players, Weekes received precious little coaching and the mechanics of the game came to him through the school of experience and profiting from his own mistakes.

He began as a ground boy at Barbados, pulling the roller and cutting the grass and bowling at the nets—he still takes wickets in the League—and did not link up with Worrell and Walcott, who knew each other while at school, until after his discharge from the Army.

All three were good enough footballers to have represented Barbados. Worrell, a forward, and Walcott, a full-back with a prodigious kick, as one might expect from such a massive man, played Soccer for Barbados, and Weekes was chosen to do so but was already committed to go on a cricket tour. In the West Indies cricket is played for seven months of the year and Soccer for three months, with a month's gap at each end of the seasons, and, by one of those freakish happenings which seems specially arranged by fate, football was the indirect cause of Worrell turning from a slow left-arm bowler to a batsman.

With Clyde Walcott, Frank Worrell went training at the crack of dawn and, scorning the customary method of entrance to the ground by the gate, they regularly climbed over the wall. At the top of the fence was some broken glass and once Worrell cut his left hand so badly that in the next match he was unable to bowl. Thus, in his own words, "batting was rather forced on me".

He started at number ten for Barbados, one higher than Denis Compton for Middlesex, and when he concentrated on the art of batsmanship, so rapid was his progress and promotion that he was soon scoring centuries.

Worrell is more closely linked with the orthodox school of batting and is more technically correct in defence and attack than either Weekes or Walcott.

Not until the series was well advanced did he approach anything like his true form—and even then he was hardly the real Worrell, the Worrell who pulverized England at Trent Bridge in 1950 and fought through to score the century at The Oval which laid the foundation for a West Indies victory.

Perhaps his nomadic career made him travel-weary and cricket stale. After he had finished playing with Radcliffe in the Central Lancashire League in the summer of 1953, Worrell went to India with the Commonwealth side and was back in Jamaica for the start of the M.C.C. tour. An injury sustained in India took longer to mend than expected and kept him out of the first Test, and though he figured in a near-record stand with Holt in the second innings of the second Test, he was still searching for his touch.

The first time the three W's came together in the series the West Indies suffered defeat but not until the second day of the fourth Test when the score was 430 for three and Walcott emerged from the pavilion did the English players realize the full implication of the presence together of the three W's.

For the sorely-pressed bowlers and fielders, to see Walcott walking towards the "wicked" Mat, as Neville Cardus once described it, could not have been the most encouraging sight of the tour.

Like Charlie Barnett of Gloucestershire, in 1947, when Edrich and Compton were the "Terrible twins" smashing records, Walcott had sat with his pads on waiting and waiting for his turn to go in to bat in a Test.

To walk to the wicket when a huge total is on the board and at the end of a big stand is not so simple as it would appear to the non-cricketer.

The duty of the incoming batsman is to capitalize the situation with fast scoring and he is expected to begin right away without the formalities of getting set. The bowlers think they have a chance of getting him before he has settled down and they summon up fresh energy and heart. An attacking field is set for him.

By his confidence and easy approach, however, Walcott, who hits his strength and whose back-play is brilliant, might have been Worrell returning to the crease after a rest of two minutes.

Up and up the score rose, and on and on went the innings. A collection had been made for Weekes and Worrell in recognition of their record stand of 338, and, when Walcott completed his century, the pair invited him to share the 1,020 dollars which had been poured into empty cricket bags and suitcases for them.

In Jamaica, where he was anything but the most popular of captains, Stollmeyer was criticized for delaying his declaration in the Trinidad Test. His critics asked why he did not apply the closure at a score in the region of 500.

The answer is that two points were uppermost in Stollmeyer's mind. First, he knew that England could not win the rubber if the match was drawn, and on this perfect wicket his only chance of snatching a victory was to enforce the follow-on. Therefore he wanted as many runs "to play with" as he could obtain, and he tried to ram home his moral advantage by keeping England out in the sun and in the field for as long as was expedient. A side kept in the field for almost three days is sure to be tired, and when he declared Stollmeyer left himself just over 18 hours in which to try to dismiss England twice.

The first innings issue was not decided until late on the fifth day, at which rate of progress ten to twelve days would have been required to finish a match which I heard described in turn as a farce, a travesty, a prostitution of cricket and so on.

The sixth and, mercifully, the last day, arrived with each side two short—Holt was in hospital receiving oxygen to relieve an attack of asthma, Stollmeyer had a split finger. Statham was undergoing daily treatment for his strain and rib muscles, and Laker's eye was closed and blackened. Yet any suggestion of a definite finish to the game already had been abandoned. The match, which had begun on a dangerous note of tension, finished in a meaningless and light-hearted atmosphere of buffoonery.

Stollmeyer made a token second innings declaration at tea, leaving England the impossible and purely statistical target of 357 runs to win in 90 minutes.

To the delight of the crowd chunky Wilfred Ferguson, last man out of the dressing-room on purpose, wore the wicketkeeper's pads and gauntlets. "Fergie", who had kept wicket at school, took two catches, standing up close, from Watson and Spooner, which showed that without any doubt he was capable at the job.

Having also been promoted to open the innings and having scored 44, "Fergie" had the ironic satisfaction of succeeding in all but the part he was originally selected for—that of a leg-break bowler!

Hutton had used six bowlers, including himself. The last occasion he had bowled for England was in the ill-fated adventure at Leeds in 1948.

In England's second innings wicketkeeper McWatt went on to bowl and took a wicket, and Pairaudeau, one of the few West Indian cricketers who does not bat and bowl, was persuaded to take an over. He politely refused a second.

So the Test was drawn and the M.C.C., in their charter plane, left for beautiful Montego Bay, millionaire's paradise and rich man's holiday resort, touching down at the busy and modern airport of Caracas (Venezuela) and Willemstad, a Dutch possession—and as Charles Palmer said, the second visit to Jamaica would provide the opportunity "of closing whatever breaches there may have been".

First to greet Len Hutton when he stepped off the 'plane at Montego Bay was his wife Dorothy who had travelled from England a fortnight before with Mrs. Godfrey Evans to join their husbands for the final stages of the tour.

The England captain's cheery smile at seeing his wife again soon dropped when, turning, he found Godfrey Evans with the fourth finger of his left hand in splints.

When Godfrey, kept out of the fourth Test by the worst of a series of boils, had been granted permission to go off to Jamaica to spend few days' rest and recuperation there with his wife Jean, who was due to arrive a day or so afterwards, he had no knowledge of any dislocation to the finger which he hurt in the two-day match in Grenada. The finger had been a trifle sore ever since and, having time to spare in Kingston, he visited the local hospital for examination. An X-ray revealed a small dislocation but Godfrey was told he stood an even chance of being fit for the final Test.

Another Hutton worry was in the slow recovery being made by Brian Statham from the severe strain to his rib muscles in the fourth Test. Statham received deep massage daily and, on medical advice, took long spells of sea bathing in the hope of being available for Jamaica. In both cases no decision was to be taken until the injured players tested themselves at the Sabina Park nets on the morning before the match.

Unfortunately for the enthusiastic local inhabitants, and the many American tourists who were anxious to obtain their first glimpse of what, from hearsay, they reckoned must be a very strange game, rain prevented play on the first of the two days allotted for the fixture with the Country Colts XI, and when the local captain put M.C.C. in after winning the toss next day the possibility of more casualties to the visiting cricketers became immediately obvious.

Some of Friday's rain had penetrated the covers and the pitch was a flier such as would have gladdened the heart of any fast bowler.

Trevor Bailey, captaining the side in the absence of Hutton, who took one of his few but well-earned rests, went in first with Ken Suttle. The opening three balls of the match flew from a good length high over Bailey's head.

At the other end Suttle was shaken by one which sailed past his ear, then struck hard on the elbow by the next. He asked captain Bailey whether he had permission to advance down the pitch and take a crack at the bowling from there.

Told that he could do so if he wished, Suttle sallied forth, struck, and was clean bowled, for his fourth duck on the tour. Peter May came next and he, too, was "castled" by fast bowler Pryce. M.C.C. were no runs for two wickets—in a one-day game!

Bailey, batting as sensibly as usual, and Willie Watson held out till lunch, after which the pitch became a good deal easier.

Suddenly, however, one ball rose nastily from a still-damp patch and Watson, not prepared for a now unusual occurrence, mishit it into his eye. He put his hand up, and his glove was covered with blood.

Visions of another Laker injury loomed up but fortunately for Watson his cut was slightly higher on the forehead. The eye itself was undamaged and not discoloured but, even so, six stitches had to be inserted.

The news went quickly back to Hutton as he lay sunning himself on the Montego Bay Beach, along with his wife, Mr. and Mrs. Compton and Mr. and Mrs. Evans.

Evans doubtful, Laker doubtful, and now Watson injured three days before the vital fifth Test was due to start. Hutton had every reason to wonder whether the fates were ganging up on him again.

While the M.C.C. cricketers enjoyed the four days of luxury at the Montego Bay hotels, many of them wondered how long they would have been able to afford staying in them had they themselves had to foot the bills.

The general rate was £12 a day on the all-in American fashion, and one of the hotels charged as much as £17 a day. The prices of everything seemed to be correspondingly high with a gin and tonic costing 6s. 6d. and a 100-yard taxi-ride—requested by one of the ladies whose shoes were pinching badly—no less than five shillings!

Some of the correspondents staying there with the team also wondered what reception would be given to their expense accounts by their firms' accountants.

For the players, however, the interlude was most enjoyable. Some went deep-sea fishing, and helped in the catching of a four-foot barracuda, a small shark, and many red schnapper, others took tours in the glass-bottomed rowing boats peering down into the depths of the crystal-clear ocean at the masses of beautiful coral formations beneath, in and out of which swam hundreds of brightly coloured tropical fish, most took full advantage of bathing in the still sea which was never below 82 degrees, and, inevitably, the golfers found their way to the first tee.

All good things have to come to an end and on the Sunday morning the party rather reluctantly said farewell to Montego Bay, to set out on the long, winding road journey to Kingston, nearly 100 miles away.

On the way they made two stops. Mr. Stanhope Joel, the millionaire who had arrived from Bermuda on a special visit to see the last Test, entertained them to a sumptuous lunch at the famous Jamaica Inn, where they again bathed in the soft, inviting waters of the blue Caribbean, and 30 miles on they were the guests at tea of an Englishman who, going to Jamaica only three years before on account of his health, had, in that short space of time, built up one of the most flourishing banana plantations in the West Indies.

Next day Hutton and his men went along to Sabina Park for the important practice. First in the net to bat was Jim Laker, his right eye still three-quarter covered by plaster.

Knowing that Jim was rather apprehensive about seeing the ball properly, Trevor Bailey took him into a separate net and bowled slow half volleys to him. The first time he dropped one short, however, Jim was all at sea and received a tap—not a really hard blow—on the hand. Obviously he could not focus properly. Still his services were needed badly and the Selectors agreed to defer a decision about him till just before the start of the match, in the hope that another day's rest would help his recovery.

Godfrey Evans was soon in action with the wicketkeeping gloves, taking fierce throws-in from less than twenty yards away, and when he had batted only a few minutes he announced happily that he would be all right if wanted.

The problems were sorting themselves out but the last, and probably most important, was to come. Brian Statham had been to the masseur for more treatment and he arrived at the ground just as the others had finished their practice.

With his ribs red from massage and strapped tightly to provide him with support, Brian went to the nets. He measured his run, ran to the wicket at full pace, lifted his arm—and groaned.

"No good," said Brian disconsolately. He was right. With all the will in the world, it was just "no good". He was out of the Test.

First on the Test wicket, then in the dressing-room, Hutton, Bailey, Palmer and Compton deliberated on the composition of the side.

Their only concrete decisions were to play Godfrey Evans again and to bring in Wardle for the injured Statham. On the question of an alternative choice to Laker they agreed to either Moss or Suttle.

To have both a bowler and batsman in mind as deputy for a bowler may sound strange but the Selectors were worried about their fielding problems, because Alan Moss, never the best of fieldsmen, had thrown his arm out some weeks ago and simply could not throw in from the deep which was the only place for him. Close to the wicket, Alan is too heavy and slow to snap up the fast catches which come there.

Over in the West Indies camp Stollmeyer and Co. announced that as Alfred Valentine was still suffering from a septic spinning finger, a place in the side would be given to seventeen-year-old Garfield Sobers, from Barbados, who had left school only a month or two earlier. Sobers bowled his left-arm slows reasonably well and showed some promise with the bat when M.C.C. played in Barbados but he was a long way below Valentine both in class and in experience.

Compared with the Trinidad Test, the West Indies left out Ferguson and Pairaudeau, their places being taken by Gomez, who had recovered from his pulled leg muscle, and the boy Sobers.

Thus all was set for the match that would decide whether the West Indies supporters would be entitled to claim them as the 'Cricket Champions of the World", as so many of them proudly proclaimed they were already.

South Africa might well have a claim for this distinction as they had held Australia to a drawn series and outclassed New Zealand who proved, by their performances against the Australian State sides on their way home, that they were more than a useful side.

England, having lost the first two Tests, won the third and drawn the fourth, stood a chance of drawing level in the rubber but not winning it. Even to draw level, however, after such a shocking start as losing the first two Tests heavily would be a wonderful achievement in West Indies' conditions.

So we went to Sabina Park on Tuesday, March 30, prepared for a tremendous battle, the West Indies flat out to hold what they had and England equally determined to salvage a series which had begun so disastrously.

What were the next six days to hold in store?

THE FOURTH TEST

Played at Trinidad, March 17, 18, 19, 20, 22, 23.
Match drawn.

WEST INDIES

FIRST INNINGS

J. Holt c Compton b Trueman	40
J. Stollmeyer c and b Compton	41
E. Weekes c Bailey b Lock	206
F. Worrell b Lock	167
C. Walcott c sub b Laker	124
B. Pairaudeau run out	0
D. Atkinson c Graveney b Compton	74
C. McWatt b Laker	4
W. Ferguson not out	8
Extras (b 6, lb 4, w 4, nb 3)	17
Total (eight wickets dec.)	681

BOWLING ANALYSIS

	O.	M.	R.	W.
Statham	9	0	31	0
Trueman	33	3	131	1
Bailey	32	7	104	0
Laker	47	8	154	2
Lock	59	14	178	2
Compton	9·4	1	40	2
Graveney	3	0	26	0

ENGLAND

First Innings

L. Hutton c Ferguson b King	..	.. ..	44
T. Bailey c Weekes b Ferguson	..	.. ..	46
P. May c Pairaudeau b King	..	.. ..	135
D. Compton c and b Ramadhin	..	.. ..	133
W. Watson c Atkinson b Walcott	..	.. ..	4
T. Graveney c and b Walcott	..	.. ..	92
R. Spooner b Walcott ..	.. ..	.. ..	19
J. Laker retired hurt ..	.. ..	.. ..	7
G. A. Lock lbw b Worrell	.. ..	.. ..	10
F. Trueman lbw b King	.. ..	.. ..	19
B. Statham not out ..	.. ..	.. ..	6
Extras (b 10, lb 5, w 7) ..	..	.. ..	22
Total ..	.. ..	.. .. ..	537

Bowling Analysis

			O.	M.	R.	W.
King	..	.. ..	48	16	97	3
Worrell	..	.. ..	20	2	58	1
Ramadhin	..	..	34	13	74	1
Atkinson	..	..	32	12	60	0
Ferguson	..	..	47	17	155	1
Stollmeyer	..	..	6	2	19	0
Walcott	..	..	34	18	52	3

WEST INDIES

Second Innings

B. Pairaudeau hit wicket b Bailey	..	.. ..	5
W. Ferguson b Bailey ..	..	.. ..	44
E. Weekes c sub b Trueman ..	..	.. ..	1
F. Worrell c sub b Lock	..	.. ..	56
C. Walcott not out ..	..	.. ..	51
D. Atkinson not out ..	..	.. ..	53
Extras (lb 2) ..	..	.. ..	2
Total (four wickets dec.)	..	.. ..	212

BOWLING ANALYSIS

			O.	M.	R.	W.
Trueman ..	..	..	15	5	23	1
Bailey ..	..	..	12	2	20	2
Compton ..	..	..	7	0	51	0
Hutton ..	..	..	6	0	43	0
Lock ..	..	..	10	2	40	1
Graveney	..	..	5	0	33	0

ENGLAND

SECOND INNINGS

W. Watson c Ferguson b Worrell	32
R. Spooner c Ferguson b Ramadhin	16
P. May c Worrell b McWatt	16
L. Hutton not out	30
T. Graveney not out	0
Extras (lb 4)	4
Total (three wickets)	98

BOWLING ANALYSIS

			O.	M.	R.	W.
Weekes ..	..	..	5	1	28	0
Atkinson ..	..	..	4	0	12	0
Ramadhin	..	..	7	4	6	1
Worrell ..	..	..	9	1	29	1
McWatt ..	..	..	4	1	16	1
Pairaudeau	..	..	1	0	3	0

CHAPTER THIRTEEN

The vital Test.

FIRST DAY

ON almost any ground in the West Indies the discerning spectator, anxious to know which side has won the toss, does not wait for a formal announcement but concentrates his attention on the ground-staff boys who hover as near as they dare to the captains.

A momentary hush envelops the ground as the coin is flipped through the air, but the moment it touches the ground—or so it seems—and certainly before the victor has had time to commiserate with the loser, there are whoops of joy and much arm-waving.

"We have won the toss." No news travels faster.

To the last Hutton remained faithful to his call of "tails" though, if a popular vote had been taken in the English dressing-room, his call would have been "heads".

Hutton's unlucky calling, the least successful feature of his captaincy, meant that England had to field first in four of the five Tests in the West Indies, while his personal record since assuming the England captaincy was three wins and eleven losses. Nine of the losses were in the last ten Tests against Australia and the West Indies.

Stollmeyer did not hesitate to bat first for the pitch looked perfect. To English eyes it was not unlike a cold marble slab on which crazy paving tracings had been made, but the groundsman told me the patches which looked like brown patches of scrub on the top were grass.

There seemed no reason why the West Indies should not make a substantial total, and the only chance given England was the flimsy one of snatching a wicket or two in the first hour when the pitch was expected to be at its liveliest.

In the pre-match discussions Hutton and Bailey planned to make the maximum use of the new ball, particularly as Brian Statham was absent. So important, in fact, was its use that even the matter of six balls was considered important and Bailey, the more accurate of the two fast bowlers, opened in preference to Trueman.

The strategy produced immediate results. Holt, who is susceptible to the ball swinging in to him, turned the fifth of Bailey's first over low to short square-leg, where Lock, falling forward, took a catch with both hands before rolling over.

To the surprise of those who have become accustomed to the

sight of Test cricketers indulging in mass celebration at the early fall of a wicket, the England players gathered slowly in small discussion groups as if no more thrilled than if a wicket had fallen in a charity match. There was a reason behind it. Hutton had laid down a deliberate policy and a few minutes before the team took the field he said in effect: "We must do everything possible to avoid giving the slightest offence. I do not want anyone to appeal unless he is absolutely convinced it is a certain wicket. And to all of you, no matter what happens, I say keep your feelings to yourself."

Perhaps an even better test of control came fifteen minutes later when Everton Weekes, who had striven hard to get off the mark, was completely beaten by the fifth ball of Bailey's third over, another inswinger, which flicked his pads before knocking the off stump out of the ground.

The only two runs on the board had been scored by Stollmeyer off Trueman with a stroke which went perilously close to Bailey at forward short-leg, and when Hutton immediately brought up another leg slip Stollmeyer almost did the same thing again.

In half an hour only seven runs were squeezed from the reluctant attack, all to Stollmeyer, and the first run off Bailey did not arrive until his fifth over, Worrell pushing between Wardle at mid-wicket and Hutton at mid-on.

A two by Stollmeyer through the covers followed, and then, from the last ball of the over, Stollmeyer attempting to drive, snicked a catch so hard to Evans, the wicketkeeper, that it was audible even from the boundary. At last an England bowler had been sensible enough to attack Stollmeyer's off stump. On the leg side he has few peers in the world.

Worse was to come for the now sorely pressed West Indies, who had made by far their worst start in the series—even worse than at Barbados. The first ball of Trueman's fifth over was a bumper to which Worrell ducked hurriedly.

The next pitched just short of a length and rose towards his chest. Understandingly he stabbed apprehensively in a gesture of self-protection. The ball found the splice of the bat and cocked up towards the leg slips where Lock made a despairing effort to reach it. Fortunately for England, Wardle, Lock's companion in the position, with fine judgment and splendid covering, raced behind Lock and took what was really an awkward catch comfortably with both hands.

In 45 minutes England had captured the wickets of Holt, Stollmeyer, Weekes and Worrell, who normally are worth a packet of runs, for a paltry 13, a wonderful performance indeed. The wickets went: 1—0, 2—2, 3—13, 4—13.

Only one fielding mistake was made in the innings, and if Graveney had held on to a catch offered by Atkinson, when he was 7 with the score at 29, the West Indies plight would have considerably worsened. Atkinson, cutting at Wardle who had been a first change, replacing Trueman, should have been easily caught. Graveney saw the ball leave the bat's edge, but lost it in flight and the next thing he knew was it touching the outstretched fingers of his right hand.

Walcott and Atkinson, however, were equal to all Hutton's manœuvres to separate them before lunch, although Atkinson, chopping down late on Trueman, all but played on. The ball missed the off stump by inches.

Still Hutton was more than a happy man at the interval with four of the best of West Indies batsmen back in the pavilion for 38 runs. Before the innings started he would gladly have settled for one wicket for 50 runs or so in the morning period.

The question remained whether the pitch would retain its life and for some time afterwards when the ball rarely beat the bat everything pointed to a West Indies recovery.

Walcott, who scorched the earth with the power of his driving and hooked with almost brutal force, raised the 50 with a glorious back-foot shot off Lock. After a few overs by Trueman, Hutton recalled the inevitable Bailey to bowl at the end opposite to which he had used during the morning. The intention was to try and utilize the cross wind for his outswingers. And once again the move worked. In Bailey's second over Atkinson walked right into a perfectly straight ball, and in the next over from the same end Gomez, after opening with a neat glided four to the fine-leg boundary, failed to off drive one which left him a little. Watson at third slip took as easy a catch as can be expected there.

Bailey's figures were then: O. 12·5, M. 6, R. 25, W. 5. The position for the West Indies was fast deteriorating into a desperate one.

In came McWatt and, with past experiences in mind, the England team never breathed freely until they had seen the back of the left-hander. Walcott with a vicious hook reached a magnificent half-century in 127 minutes and for skill and courage he deserved the highest praise. But the first really bad stroke he made cost him his wicket. Trying to force a short ball from Lock, which normally he would have gratefully smacked to any part of Sabina Park with safety and certainty, he sent it, by what might be termed a happy accident for the fielders, straight to Laker at mid-on. There were not a few English hearts missing a beat as the ball went in the direction of Laker, who had confessed earlier he still had some difficulty in focusing the ball. But he coolly watched it and took the catch without any trouble.

Seven out for 110—and young Garfield Sobers, not yet eighteen, could not have faced a less promising position in his first Test innings. England were by now right on top and thirsting to polish off the tail-enders. The light was dim and rain clouds threatened overhead. Hutton drew in his field for the slim, shy youngster, but Sobers is clearly gifted with a cricketer's temperament and he accepted the challenge and presented a full blade to every ball. When rain stopped play 15 minutes before tea Sobers had still not scored but he had not made a mistake. It is always an unnerving experience to bat for the first time in a Test, and particularly so when the side is struggling hard to recover, more particularly so when a second start has to be made. The rain caused a delay of 20 minutes but it had left the outfield wet enough to make the bowlers dry the ball after almost every delivery.

Sobers, having to begin all over again, made a beautiful wristy cut to the boundary off Laker for his first scoring shot. In Barbados I had noticed Sobers' most profitable stroke was the cut and I wondered why Hutton did not plug the gap. Maybe Hutton wanted the boy to go on cutting; to feed his strong point in the hope of his making a mistake.

McWatt was also square cutting well, but he was the victim of a great catch by Lock backward of square-leg. McWatt swung at a ball from Bailey outside the leg stump, hitting it cleanly and on the rise. At the moment of connecting he must have booked himself a boundary. Lock, however, leapt his full height and with left arm outstretched took the ball still going up and at a fast pace—a magnificent catch and the equal of Atkinson's effort to dismiss Watson which was the talk of the Trinidad Test.

Enter King to face Trueman. Some of the melancholy which had settled over the crowd disappeared as both King and Sobers hit 11 runs from the over. Trueman temporarily lost his direction and was too often outside the leg stump. He was still worried by the wet ball.

Next over King walked too far across his wicket to Bailey and lost his leg stump. Trueman, who had given Bailey admirable support and was hostile and accurate except for the last erratic spell, gained a second and belated reward by collecting Ramadhin's wicket.

The West Indies, recognized as one of the, if not the, most powerful batting combinations in the world, were thus routed in 221 minutes for 139 runs, their lowest total against England since 1935 when they made 102 on a rain-affected pitch at Barbados. The different conditions made the feat of Hutton's men far more meritorious. Apart from the early suggestion of pace and liveliness the Kingston pitch could not be held responsible for one of the worst collapses in West Indian history.

Bailey, whose dogged defence so often has served England well in the past, brilliantly seized his opportunity to play the more spectacular role of the attacking bowler. His 7 for 34 in 16 overs was easily his best performance in Tests. For once fortune had favoured England. Often bowling equally good goes rewardless —when the batsman plays at the ball and misses—or the vital catch is grounded. Bailey covered himself with glory and he was splendidly supported all round. Throughout England's fielding remained at a top level of efficiency, apart from the one mistake, and was almost as good as the high water-mark performance of the tour at Georgetown.

There was cold comfort for the West Indies. Much of their batting was irresolute and indifferent, the only real fight coming from Walcott, Atkinson, McWatt and the youthful Sobers.

Compared with their aggregate of approaching 500 at Trinidad the three W's contributed 54 runs between them—with 50 from Walcott! Take away the scores of Walcott, Atkinson, McWatt and Sobers and the remaining seven, aided by two extras, made 46 between them. And that needs a good deal of explaining away, particularly when Worrell received the one vicious ball.

But that is cricket, in all glory and uncertainty. Even the best batting in the world may fail unaccountably on a true wicket. The West Indies could scarcely credit what had happened to them. They offered no excuses for, as McWatt said to me later, "That's cricket —you just can't explain it."

As if Bailey had not done enough for one day he opened with Hutton when England had 35 minutes' batting. They stayed together until the close, surviving a series of extra fast bouncers from King who, knowing he had to bowl only a few overs, could afford to let himself go flat out. Bailey, with his customary imperturbability, went right back on his stumps and killed the bouncers dead at his feet, or, if they were short enough, calmly ducked out of the way. Sometimes Hutton ducked too. At other times he played a one-handed defensive stroke which looked risky but which was safe and under control.

England indeed achieved a notable triumph. The individual honours belonged to Bailey with Walcott in second place. At the end of the important first day England were in the promising position of being 122 behind with all their wickets in hand and a wonderful opportunity seemed to be in their grasp. They needed a substantial lead.

SECOND DAY

A grim but intensely interesting day passed with the West Indies, if not succeeding in their primary aim, at least achieving their secondary objective of not permitting England to settle down and amass a big lead. To those who are content only when wickets are flying and boundaries are being flogged the phase might have been dull. But there was hardly a period without some significance. Any side without the defensive shield provided by the skill of Hutton and the courage of Bailey might well have completely surrendered the advantage they had won on the first day.

The West Indies counter-attack was spirited and hostile and full of courage.

During the four hours 45 minutes of cricket—play started 15 minutes late through rain—England made only 177 runs and lost five wickets. Yet in conditions which were similar, with the ball liable to fly off a length, the West Indies had four out in 45 minutes for 13.

Every run England scored had to be squeezed from a reluctant opposition. Hutton's caution was regarded as excessive by Jamaicans accustomed to faster scoring. "If any of the W's had been there as long as Hutton double the number of runs would have been scored" was the common argument. This was a poor compliment to their own bowlers, especially Frank King, magnificent in his sustained aggression even if, in my opinion, he bowled too many bumpers, and Denis Atkinson, who was spot on a length and was always liable to make the ball turn sharply into the batsman. King's ability to make the ball rise from a length made attacking strokes almost impossible—and it also needed no small degree of courage to face a ball bowled at a fast pace and rearing towards the head.

Once Bailey was struck on the point of the jaw but fortunately a glove softened the blow otherwise he might have known the fate of many a heavyweight and been knocked out. He staggered, shook his head and continued with a graze as evidence of the spot where the ball had hit him. Later Compton, hurriedly attempting to dodge a bumper, dislodged a bail with his foot and was correctly given out through the unsympathetic law of hit wicket.

They were the extent of the day's injuries until King, who had responded gallantly to his captain's plea for pace and more pace, had to retire with a strained thigh muscle. He had done a great job.

The sternest duel came in the first hour when the pitch, having sweated under the covers, was again pacy. The weather had been cold during the night and a heavy dew had settled, but I doubt whether the shower had made any difference to the turf.

Stollmeyer wanted an early wicket, and the stubborn Hutton and Bailey were equally determined he should not have one. Hutton took a single to fine leg in the first over and the next scoring stroke did not come until the twelfth over when Hutton drove Atkinson through the covers for three. From the first to the twelfth over neither King nor Atkinson bowled a single ball which was hittable without serious risk. That was how good the bowling was. Bailey took the King onslaught and Hutton presented a padlocked defence to the medium-pace swing and nip off the pitch of Atkinson.

The field placed for King, who bowls only the outswinger, was the menacing ring of two slips, a gully, two leg slips, a forward short-leg and a silly mid-off. With such a setting, the intentions of the bowler to drop the ball short became obvious and ball after ball went thudding through at head height to McWatt, the wicket-keeper, standing well back. I think Stollmeyer would have preferred Hutton to have been at the receiving end of the King onslaught for in the West Indies they believe his only technical flaw might be to the short riser on the leg stump. King should have presented Bailey, who had taken squatter's right at his end, a single to test the theory. But when the run famine was at last broken and King bounced three in four balls to Hutton he remained unshaken to the point of seeming indifference as they whistled overhead.

In the first hour from 19 overs only 13 were added to the 17 scored overnight, but the important thing for England was that the opening pair were still there.

Bailey had one escape. He dangerously cut against the off spin of Gomez and Weekes, thrusting out his left hand, touched, but could not hold a ball going fast enough to reach the boundary. There was a Hutton cover drive and by lunch the score was 41. Not many had been scored—actually 24 came in the 90 minutes' pre-lunch period—but England had good cause to be satisfied.

It is strange that such an otherwise disciplined player like Bailey should permit himself the indiscretion of cutting—when he shouldn't cut—and this stroke brought about his dismissal just after lunch. Garfield Sobers, the seventeen-year-old slow left-arm bowler, had been given his baptism of Test bowling. His first over produced a single from Hutton and, with the first ball of his second, he trapped Bailey with a faster ball. Bailey tried to cut one just short of a length, inches outside the off stump, and snicked hard into the wicketkeeper's gloves.

Sobers takes only a few steps to the wicket and has a smooth, high action. In pace he is a shade faster than the usual bowler of his type and in my view he would be more than useful on English wickets—as would King.

Peter May helped to raise the 50 in 127 minutes, but something was wrong with his timing. He took six lucky runs in one over from Walcott, who varies his pace cleverly.

Suddenly Hutton slashed Sobers over Stollmeyer's head at mid-off and May, although he did not get hold of the shot perfectly, cleared the sight screen. Sobers kept his head. Then Walcott, stopping a fierce drive from May off his own bowling, had to go off for repairs. And while he was away his substitute, Bruce Pairaudeau, took an excellent catch low down in the covers to dismiss May. Ramadhin, the bowler, sent the ball well wide of the off stump.

By now Hutton had completed his 50 in 179 minutes with seven boundaries and his disinclination to hasten drew from a section of the crowd the slow hand-clap—surely the silliest invention of modern sports crowds.

The loss of May's wicket seemed compensated by the brightness of Compton's beginning. I had to go back to his palmiest days to recall him starting an innings as if he was in the middle of it. Gone was the hesitancy which unhappily marked the struggling beginning of almost every innings at the start of the tour. He hooked risers and thumped the over-pitched ball through the covers as if he had been batting for an hour or more. When he was 25, however, Walcott largely by virtue of his inches made the sort of brilliant diving stop which are wrongly classed as chances. He saved four runs rather than was guilty of missing a catch, even though he remained on the ground in reflective silence!

Such was the rich promise of Compton's form that the ending of his innings was all the more disappointing and unsatisfactory to both sides.

King, who had taken the new ball at 130 and was making another concentrated effort, bowled Compton a terrific bouncer. In the greatest possible haste Compton careered out of harm's way in the direction of point. In doing so he turned, overbalanced, his feet became locked and as he went down his foot grazed the off stump, dislodging the bail. His head hit the hard ground with a thump and he rose holding it. In his semi-dazed condition Compton was convinced he had been struck by the ball. Still nursing his head in confusion, Compton was told he had been given out "hit wicket"—a decision hotly debated but which was without question right.

Law 38 reads: "The striker is out hit wicket if, in playing at the ball, he hit down his wicket with his bat or any part of his person." The operative words are "in playing at the ball".

It is an unlucky way of getting out and it was the second time I had seen Compton as the victim. At Trent Bridge, Nottingham, in

1948, while ducking to a bumper from Miller, he tumbled into his stumps.

While the ground buzzed with debate Watson, a prolific scorer in colony matches, added to his dismal Test record by touching a slower ball from King which sailed through to McWatt, and soon Graveney was leg-before to Atkinson. In the opinion of McWatt, who was in the best possible position to judge, this ball which came back sharply was one of the two best bowled during the day. The other Hutton stopped. Graveney had looked to be settling down after an uncertain start, which included an opening stroke which went through the slips at catchable height to the boundary. He was the third to go for only 27 runs, and, once again, Hutton, going steadily towards his century, must have reflected on the brittleness of England's batting. But in the last important 20 minutes he found a staunch partner in Evans who, in 1947 at Adelaide, in support of Denis Compton had kept his end up for 90 minutes without scoring.

King limped off holding his thigh, and Hutton's last act was to square-cut Atkinson with a stroke which left the fielders standing in powerless admiration—without doubt the shot of the day.

England finished with a lead of 55 and Hutton needing 7 for his 19th Test century, but the West Indies felt they were still very much in the game.

THIRD DAY

England's task of gathering runs was considerably lightened by the absence of King. The plan was simple: first to try and consolidate and then to attack. In the morning session defence and a broad bat was the order with 50 runs scored of which Evans contributed 10, and in the two hours from lunch to tea the score rose from 244 to 390—and Hutton was 205. Evans stayed long enough for the sixth wicket to add 108 and Wardle helped to put on 105 for the seventh wicket.

At the end of the day some of the West Indians discussing the genius of Hutton came to the conclusion the two most remarkable of his gifts were: (1) his powers of concentration over a long period; (2) his uncanny instinct of selection—that is knowing which ball to hit and which ball to stop or the ball to leave alone. In theory this sounds delightfully simple.

Physically Hutton would not be classed as a robust man and as he went on for hour after hour under the fierce Caribbean sun, a human scoring machine seemingly incapable of making a mistake, or committing the simplest error of judgment, one wondered where the stamina and endurance came from.

I think it springs from a completely disciplined mind and a dedication to the task at hand. Every so often, in the manner of a boxer, he allows himself a "coasting" period when he takes things a little easier. Then he will return and indulge in a flurry of scoring.

Off the field he believes in getting as much rest as he possibly can. He argues he needs all the energy and strength he can conserve for his cricket. An astonishing man is Leonard Hutton.

In terms of arithmetic this is how his innings was built:

> 50 in 179 minutes with seven 4's.
> 100 in 340 minutes with eleven 4's.
> 150 in 432 minutes with sixteen 4's.
> 200 in 504 minutes with one 6 and twenty-two 4's.

If any captain deserved to be the architect of his side's victory Hutton did, and when he was out in the first over he faced after tea, caught at the wicket off Walcott, he had taken England's score to 392, giving them a lead of 253. His was a marathon effort quite beyond praise.

What I found so astonishing is that in 532 minutes against a fine and varied and always-keen attack, cleverly handled, and which never wilted under pressure, Hutton did not give one direct chance. He might have played on to his stumps once, and when he was 103 he permitted himself an uppish drive off Ramadhin which went perilously close to Gomez at deep mid-on.

Only those spoiled by the recent efforts of Atkinson and Lock, however, would ever dare to pretend it was a catch in the sense of a mistake by Gomez. The next ball was directed to precisely the same spot on the boundary but along the ground, strictly according to the coaching manual, and in the manner of a professor demonstrating exactly how it should have been done.

I remember also a pull which sizzled to the square-leg boundary from a Gomez ball which pitched outside the off stump; another fierce pull to mid-wicket off Stollmeyer and, in answer to a tree-top spectator, loud and persistent in his demands for a big hit, Hutton sent a soaring six over the brick, whitewashed sightscreen and out of the ground. The carry was fully 80 yards and, perhaps purely by accident, the ball went straight in the direction of the Voice.

When Stollmeyer took the new ball—which had been available for seven overs—Hutton promptly banged it against the sightscreen a stroke which certainly did not improve the shine!

Evans is, by natural instinct, an aggressive batsman, but, when the situation demands, he can be an excellent defender. For the first time on the trip he was fully fit. All the zest and energy returned to his wicketkeeping, and he clearly enjoyed his fight to preserve

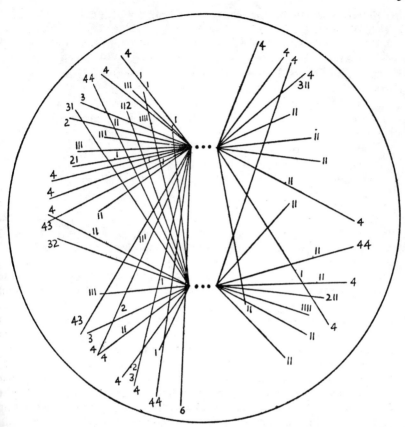

Chart of Hutton's innings of 205 runs

his wicket. In the last overs before lunch Stollmeyer brought up for
Sobers a circle of six around the bat, all near enough to pick the
batsman's pocket, but they had scant chance of collecting a catch
for every ball was played plumb in the middle with the perfect
dead-bat technique.

After lunch Hutton gave Evans permission to open up and he was
getting into second gear when he stopped in his drive and presented
Worrell at mid-off with a comfortable catch. He had helped Hutton
to add 108 in 142 minutes.

Johnny Wardle is one of those batsmen who drive bowlers to
exasperated fury. He is liable to play at and miss two balls and
hit the third with a perfect shot. Always a powerful driver, particularly straight, he cuts crisply and firmly. In fact if he tightened

his defence he would make a fine bat, but I think he enjoys his batting too much to make a serious job of it.

Twice in the series he did exactly the right job for England. At British Guiana he averted what might have been a crisis and at Kingston he pushed the score rapidly on when aggression was the policy.

Ramadhin was clouted to square-leg, straight, and finally over the sightscreen for six by the Yorkshire left-hander who reached his 50 in only 78 minutes.

Walcott then dropped him off a skier at mid-wicket.

England's score went from 250 to 300 in 37 minutes, and from 300 to 350 in 35 minutes, which must have been fast enough for those who complained the rate was too slow! The 100 for the partnership came in 81 minutes.

When Hutton left after tea Wardle was caught at deep long on from Sobers, who also bowled Lock, cutting on the off stump, and Laker trying to hit him out of the ground.

West Indies were left 30 minutes to bat out. Stollmeyer and Holt did so successfully but not without adventure. Bailey and Trueman, with attacking fields, each bowled four overs at top speed and Holt was hit over the heart but apparently unhurt by Trueman. When he had made six he was nearly caught at backward short leg off Trueman by the acrobatic Lock, who reached the ball but could not hold it. It was a grand attempt. The West Indies collected 20 and Stollmeyer and Holt a few bruises, and a lively day ended with the home team 255 behind and with all their wickets intact, but still facing a hard, uphill fight.

Fourth Day

England planned for four wickets and hoped for six. They obtained their four—a satisfactory performance considering that they included two of the three W's, Weekes and Worrell. The wicket, though still quick, had retained none of the moisture which made it fast at the beginning of the game; and England were deprived of Trueman's shock attack after tea, when it was needed most in an attempt to snatch a further wicket. Trueman felt a pain between the ribs and left the field to be strapped up. He bowled one more over but was so clearly distressed that Hutton spared him any other effort.

Earlier in the day Trueman was the mainspring of the attack taking three of the four wickets which fell, and not since he had helped to shatter Jamaica on the same ground had he worked up such a fast and hostile pace. Locals, who had dubbed him "Feeble Freddie", had to eat their own words. An obtrusive, but important part was played by the spinners who conceded few runs during their spells between the fast onslaughts. Laker, the best, completed the day with these figures: O. 29, M. 19, R. 32, W. 0.

Trueman's fastest stretch was at the start when England pressed hungrily for a quick wicket. For twenty minutes Trueman and Bailey hurled their whole strength and skill into every ball, and the fielders, clustered around the wicket, crouched tense and alert for the possible catch which would be so important. Then Holt failed to keep the ball down when forcing Trueman off his toes, and Lock, in the leg trap, greedily accepted a sharp catch—a blow for the West Indies. A second was to follow soon.

Everton Weekes, with a first innings failure to wipe out, was only one when he cut Laker to Graveney, who all but brought off what would have been a great slip catch. To a man the crowd asked, "What is that going to cost England?" The answer was surprisingly soon supplied. Two runs! Weekes, cutting at the fifth ball of Wardle's first over after he had replaced Lock, got only an inside edge and dragged the ball on to his wicket—once again a victim of cutting.

Two down for 38, the West Indies were now in a difficult position, but slowly Stollmeyer, once beaten by a "Chinaman" from Wardle which jumped over the middle stump, and Worrell slowly settled down. They were still together at lunch and also when the new ball was taken at 99.

Suddenly the game leapt into life. In his second over Trueman bowled three successive bumpers at Worrell, the second of which was taken in the back. Worrell, being human, did not like it, nor did the crowd, and Trueman walked back to his bowling mark with a wide grin on his face.

In the next Trueman over Worrell was hit on the glove, and obviously he thought the following ball would be a bouncer or at least going to rise. Half withdrawing, he discovered too late the ball was of normal height. He tried to get his bat out of the way, but the ball struck the shoulder and lobbed in a high gentle arc into the waiting hands of Graveney at slip. With Holt, Weekes and Worrell out for 102, England were now very much on top.

Trueman rolled up his sleeves even higher and delivered a lightning bouncer at Walcott, who, instead of retreating, hooked it high for two in the direction of the vacated mid-wicket. Big men are not usually the best of hookers, but Walcott, full of courage and skill with a wonderful eye, is an exception. Two hooks flashed to the boundary and another big hit fell short of May, who was looking straight into the sun. A terrific over was crammed with excitement and, for the first time, the crowd roused to a high pitch of excitement.

Three balls after tea, however, Stollmeyer's elegant defiance of four hours' duration was ended by a straight ball from Trueman to which he was leg-before. More and more the West Indies hopes of saving the match weighed on the broad shoulders of Clyde Walcott.

Hutton dearly would have liked another wicket before the close, but, without Trueman, the England attack lost much of its sting and penetration. Gerry Gomez provided a sound and reliable partner to Walcott. In one over by Bailey he scored three excellent boundaries —a glance to fine leg, an off drive and a neat late cut.

Walcott went along smoothly and less spectacularly to his 50. And on that note of individual success the day ended, West Indies being 184 for four.

FIFTH DAY

West Indies started the fifth day, which was to prove the last, 91 runs behind with six wickets left—and one of the wickets was Walcott's. Rightly they thought that as long as Walcott stayed they had a chance, however slim, of saving the match. The pitch remained good, and England realized they could not expect much help from it. Although his ribs still hurt, Trueman declared himself fit to bowl, and Hutton used him sparingly. However, he managed to unleash an early bouncer at Walcott who, accepting the challenge as usual, missed his hook and came within an ace of treading on his stumps.

Laker went on and decided as a variation, rather than because he thought he could get something out of the pitch, to bowl round the wicket. Immediately he trapped Gomez leg-before.

Walcott's next partner was Denis Atkinson, for whom the English players have a healthy respect. He stayed with Walcott, still busily collecting runs, until lunch, although when he was 27 he snicked Laker hard behind the wicket. The ball hit the outside of Evans's right gauntlet. Had the wicketkeeper left the ball alone it would have gone straight to Graveney at slip. At lunch the West Indies had reduced their deficit to 37, but England held a trump card— the new ball was available one over after the interval.

In the over before it came Trueman was slashed for 13, including three hard-punched boundaries by Walcott. The new ball was taken at 252 for five, and the West Indies faced a new crisis.

Eight overs passed before England struck success, Atkinson steering an outswinger from Bailey straight into the hands of Watson at slip. He had stayed for 106 minutes.

Walcott, struck on the left wrist by Bailey when 93, was very nearly caught by a diving Compton at leg slip. Then Walcott with an on drive off Trueman—his 17th boundary—reached his century, which was one of the best of the series.

McWatt, who must have used up a fair share of his luck for the series in the first innings of the first Test on the same ground, was next to go. Laker, bowling off-spinners which were leg-breaks to the left-handed McWatt, was driven fiercely in the covers at knee height. A four looked certain but Wardle, running hard, stuck out his left hand (which to Wardle, a left-hander, was the right hand to take a catch!) and, managing to retain his balance, held on to the ball. I have seen some dazzling catches but this was one of the finest.

Wardle told me he would not have been able to get anywhere near the ball if he had not walked in as the ball was being bowled. "The longer I play the game," he said, "the more important I find it is to observe the elementary rules. When at short extra cover I can 'angle' much better if I am going towards the batsman as the ball is about to be bowled. In this particular case I saw I had a slight chance from the moment the ball left the bat as I was moving in the direction I thought the ball would go. I saw it all the way."

Walcott, troubled by the crack on his wrist which was periodically treated by gentlemen, presumably doctors, running on the field, tried to drive Laker and edged to Graveney. Thus ended as gallant an innings as there ever was. As Walcott turned towards the pavilion, many saw the beginning of the end. They were not wrong.

Even so Sobers, who again proved his ice-cool temperament, Ramadhin and King delayed the end of the West Indies innings by an hour. Ramadhin, twice dropped in Laker's first over, appreciated a strange move by Hutton, who replaced the spinners with Trueman and Bailey. Directly Hutton recalled Laker, the little East Indian from Trinidad gave a simple return catch. Ramadhin, though he opens the innings for Crompton, his League club, and is able to handle a bat a lot better than when England first knew him in 1950, hardly can be said to be a formidable batsman in Test class and he must have chuckled to himself at the gross flattery of being accorded a very deep mid-on to Laker.

Laker's four wickets were richly deserved and cost him only an addition of 39 runs which meant a full analysis for the innings of O. 50, M. 27, R. 71, W. 4. His was a splendid achievement particularly as his spinning finger became very sore towards the end.

King held up his end long enough for the tea arrangements to be postponed—if nine wickets are down the tea interval can be delayed half an hour—and Sobers, who seems likely to give England many a headache in the future, was last out.

England required 72 to win, one fewer than in the third Test at British Guiana, and if they were to get the runs on the fifth day there was one hour and a quarter left. Any suggestion of the proceedings dragging on to Monday was unpopular and the West Indies were quite prepared for the last rites to be performed. Hutton sent in Graveney and Watson, and Graveney played all over a yorker on the leg stump from King's fifth ball, an incident which was suitably celebrated and gave immense encouragement to the crowd.

Both King and Worrell using the new ball well swung and lifted and beat not only the batsmen but their own wicketkeeper as well. Of the first thirteen on the board twelve came from byes.

Watson snicked King wide of McWatt's left hand when five, but from then on with May driving beautifully there was no check on the runs and England took only 55 minutes to get to the winning run, appropriately made off Weekes by May, whose innings containing seven boundaries was a little gem.

So England, winners by nine wickets, saved the series, and as Hutton said to me afterwards, while he sipped his celebration champagne in the dressing-room, "All's well that ends well."

When Stollmeyer won the toss and England took the field minus Statham a total in the region of 400 was forecast, but England got off to a good start, the early successes kept the bowlers on top and everything went right for them. If a West Indies batsman played at the ball he got a touch—another time it could miss. Yet they batted timidly and badly and too many made nightmarish strokes.

Bailey was as surprised as the rest at the completeness of his bowling triumph on the first day. He told me he would be glad to return the same figures if he bowled on a nasty wicket in a county match let alone tumble out the crack West Indian batsmen. He thought the best ball he bowled was the one which dismissed Weekes which, being cut, came in sharply from the off and had nothing to do with the state of the wicket.

The general opinion of the players about the West Indies collapse was that it was due to the high bounce of the ball (accounted for by the hardness of the new ball on a hard surface), the extra something which bowlers always manage to pull out when they are on top, plus the presence of a little grass on the top of the wicket.

Not the least delighted at England's success and general recovery was Mr. Henry Sayen, the seventy-one-year-old dollar millionaire, who flew from Princeton, New Jersey, for the match. Last summer he went from America to England to watch the second Test at Lord's and, apart from the fact he is a generous man with a special "bonus" system for good performances, he is now regarded as an omen of good luck by the English players.

After the match they were busily persuading him to make the trip to Australia!

"I'll see if I can get to Sydney, boys," he said. And that seems one match England should not lose!

THE FIFTH TEST

Played at Kingston, Jamaica, March 30, 31, April 1, 2, 3.
England won by nine wickets.

WEST INDIES

FIRST INNINGS

J. Holt c Lock b Bailey	0
J. Stollmeyer c Evans b Bailey	9
E. Weekes b Bailey	0
F. Worrell c Wardle b Trueman	4
C. Walcott c Laker b Lock	50
D. Atkinson lbw b Bailey	21
G. Gomez c Watson b Bailey	4
C. McWatt c Lock b Bailey	22
G. Sobers not out	14
F. King b Bailey	9
S. Ramadhin lbw b Trueman	4
Extras (nb 1, lb 1)	2
Total	139

BOWLING ANALYSIS

	O.	M.	R.	W.
Bailey	16	7	34	7
Trueman	15·4	4	39	2
Wardle	10	1	20	0
Lock	15	6	31	1
Laker	4	1	13	0

ENGLAND
First Innings

L. Hutton c McWatt b Walcott	..	..	..	205
T. Bailey c McWatt b Sobers	..	..	..	23
P. May c sub b Ramadhin	..	..	..	30
D. Compton hit wkt. b King	..	..	..	31
W. Watson c McWatt b King	..	..	..	4
T. Graveney lbw b Atkinson	..	..	..	11
T. G. Evans c Worrell b Ramadhin ..	..	..	28
J. Wardle c Holt b Sobers	..	..	..	66
G. A. Lock b Sobers	..	..	..	..	4
J. Laker b Sobers	..	..	..	..	9
F. Trueman not out	..	..	..	..	0
Extras (lb 3)	..	..	..	..	3
Total ..	..	..	..	..	414

Bowling Analysis

	O.	M.	R.	W.
King	26	12	45	2
Gomez	25	8	56	0
Atkinson	41	15	82	1
Ramadhin	29	9	71	2
Sobers	28.5	9	75	4
Walcott	11	5	26	1
Worrell	11	0	34	0
Stollmeyer	5	0	22	0

WEST INDIES
Second Innings

J. Holt c Lock b Trueman	..	..	..	8
J. Stollmeyer lbw b Trueman	..	..	..	64
E. Weekes b Wardle ..	..	..	..	3
F. Worrell c Graveney b Trueman ..	..	..	29
C. Walcott c Graveney b Laker	..	..	..	116
G. Gomez lbw b Laker	..	..	..	22
D. Atkinson c Watson b Bailey	..	..	..	40
C. McWatt c Wardle b Laker	..	..	..	8
G. Sobers c Compton b Lock	..	..	..	26
S. Ramadhin c and b Laker ..	..	..	..	10
F. King not out ..	..	..	..	..	10
Extras (b 4, lb 3, w 1, nb 2)	..	..	..	10
Total ..	..	..	..	..	346

BOWLING ANALYSIS

			O.	M.	R.	W.
Bailey	..	..	..	25	11	54	1
Trueman	..	..	..	29	7	88	3
Laker	..	..	..	50	27	71	4
Lock	..	..	..	27	15	40	1
Wardle	..	..	..	39	14	83	1

ENGLAND

SECOND INNINGS

T. Graveney b King	0
W. Watson not out	20
P. May not out	40
Extras (b 12)	12
Total (one wicket)	72

BOWLING ANALYSIS

			O.	M.	R.	W.
King	..	..	..	4	1	21	1
Worrell	..	..	..	4	0	8	0
Ramadhin	..	..	3	0	14	0
Atkinson	..	..	..	3	0	8	0
Sobers	..	..	..	1	0	6	0
Weekes	..	..	..	0·5	0	3	0

CHAPTER FOURTEEN

What caused the trouble?—"Unfriendly" accusation—The facts—Bustamante and Hutton—"Crowning insult"—Hutton's letter—Bones of contention—Umpiring panel suggested—Behaviour of crowds—And of players—The Press—Bumpers—Palmer sums up—What of the future?

TO the satisfaction and added enjoyment of all, both sides took extra and special pains to ensure that the final Test went through in a true spirit of sportsmanship, without rancour or incident of any nature, and the result was an altogether healthier and calmer atmosphere. The crowd sensed, too, their measure of responsibility, and were a model of good behaviour.

Unhappily the change came a little late. Too much damage already had been done to be undone in one match. Whatever happened in the fifth Test, the series had failed lamentably to promote good-will between the countries of the opposing teams, which has always been the prime objective of every cricket tour.

Looking at the months of turmoil in retrospect, I feel rather like the Middle West farmer who, visiting a zoo and seeing a giraffe for the first time, exclaimed, "I still don't believe it's true!"

Almost from first to last a wave of prejudice, acrimony and undeniable bitterness made the tour the most unpleasant and unfortunate experience in cricket since the visit of D. R. Jardine's M.C.C. team to Australia in 1932–33, and there was no more convincing proof of the damage caused by rumour than when the team returned to Jamaica. The reception was *frigid*.

Often I heard the M.C.C. described as by far the most unpopular team ever to go to the West Indies. What was the cause of such an unwholesome description? M.C.C. were accused of taking umpiring decisions badly (though the general standard of umpiring was admitted to be a matter of concern to all), of indiscipline on the field and of "playing too hard". Rumour and plain tittle-tattle was responsible for much of the bad feeling. Even the West Indies players got hold of a story to the effect that Hutton, at the start of the tour, had called a team meeting at which it was alleged he said umpiring and opposition players were unfair. There was absolutely no foundation in the story whatsoever.

Some said the side had been chosen deliberately with the object of bumping the West Indies to defeat and so to play on the weaknesses of the batting as exposed by the Australians in Australia two years before. They were also condemned as being an "unfriendly" set of players. I think the West Indies were shocked to find an

English side arriving with the deliberate intention of winning the series. Was that so wrong?

As Sir Roger de Coverley once said, there are two sides to every question, and before the West Indies can claim any right to complain about breaches of etiquette on the part of others, they should put their own house in order.

Whatever justly can be complained about the M.C.C. team, the people of the West Indies must ask themselves if it is fair to expect visiting cricketers, who, after all, are sportsmen and not trained diplomats, to play in the conditions which exist in the West Indies and are extremely unusual and difficult.

Let us pause for one moment to summarize a few undeniable facts.

First, at Jamaica an umpire *was* shown a pistol and a knife, his wife *was* slapped in the face after he had given out J. K. Holt leg before wicket at 94, his child *was* accosted and his father threatened.

Secondly, extra police *were* drafted to the ground as a precaution to protect Jeffrey Stollmeyer, the West Indies captain, from possible demonstrations because he had not made the popular decision to enforce England to follow on. His plane to Trinidad *was* guarded overnight and the baggage of the passengers *was* thoroughly examined. I know because I was on the same plane.

All these things, however, were dismissed airily as a "domestic affair", with no malice directed towards the M.C.C.

At British Guiana the infamous bottle-throwing incident, later to be explained away as having been started by a drunk and continued by high-spirited schoolboys, *did* occur. Had this been a harmless prank would the riot squad, complete with tear gas, have been rushed to the ground?

The house of one of the umpires at Georgetown, who had given three decisions against the *home* team, *was* guarded over the week-end, and the riot squad *did* stand by presumably in case any schoolboys played truant and began another "jolly rag"!

On one ground Mr. Charles Palmer, the M.C.C. manager, took a friend into the pavilion as his guest. Asked whether his friend was a member, Palmer said, "No, I'm afraid he's not but I was just coming along to ask for him to be signed in formally." Being a first-class county Secretary himself and knowing the procedure also at Lord's, the headquarters of cricket, Palmer took for granted that the admission of his friend was a pure formality.

Apruptly and high-handedly, the reply came, "Well, he must get out."

Rather than stand on his dignity and prepared to take a personal rebuff instead of causing a scene the manager of the M.C.C. team suffered the indignity of having to find his friend a place in the public enclosure.

Technically the official probably was right, but the managers of every cricket team are accorded special privileges almost everywhere in the cricket world. Certainly had a similar thing happened at Lord's the visiting team manager's friend instantly would have been signed in for the day without any fuss or bother.

At the same ground in the West Indies complimentary tickets given by the England captain, Len Hutton, to some friends, were torn to shreds in front of Denis Compton whom the busy Hutton had asked to act as escort.

Again, one leading cricket official did not speak to the amiable Palmer from the moment Palmer arrived on the island to the moment of his departure.

The unfriendliness with which the M.C.C. were charged did not appear to be all one-sided, and a striking example of how the super-sensitive West Indies could make a veritable mountain out of a molehill occurred during the last Test at Kingston where a perfectly innocent Hutton was alleged to have snubbed Mr. Alex Bustamante, Jamaica's Chief Minister, who went to congratulate the England captain as he came in for the tea interval, after having batted practically nine hours and with his score at 205.

On entering the Kingston Cricket Club pavilion from the field, the players have to turn a sharp right and walk twenty yards or so through a crowded path of members to the dressing-room. Tired and concerned mainly with getting a shower and a change of his sweat-soaked clothing in the next twenty precious minutes, Hutton walked between the ranks of the applauding members with his head down—as do most modest cricketers when they are being showered with congratulations.

To the shouts of "Well done", Hutton repeatedly replied "Thank you".

Mr. Bustamante was one of the many who thrust out his hand Hutton, completely unaware of the presence of anyone so important did not pause.

Had he stopped to speak individually to everyone wishing to congratulate him, he might as well have gone straight back to the field.

Hutton, tired and exhausted, reached the dressing-room to take his well-earned rest, but the next thing he knew was of the door being flung open and the voice of a top-ranking official ranting at manager Palmer, "This is the crowning insult." And a lot more was said.

All Hutton and Palmer could do was to ask, "What is all this about?" When they heard Hutton was supposed to have insulted

Jamaica's Chief Minister they received a complete shock and they immediately set about putting the matter right.

A few minutes later, however, Hutton resumed his innings and, whether affected by the disturbance or not I cannot say, playing a most unHutton-like stroke, he lapsed in concentration for the first time since his innings began and lost his wicket.

Before Hutton had reached the dressing-room again, however, the pavilion seethed with various versions of the Bustamante incident and one prominent official went around describing Hutton as "ill-mannered" and "without any background".

At the end of the day a Kingston newspaper reporter went to Mr. Bustamante and, in the presence of several witnesses, said: "You have been insulted. Will you make a statement?"

The reply was: "No, I have not been insulted. Hutton is a fine young fellow and we have talked together and had a drink together. I repeat, I have not been insulted."

Again the reporter insisted that the Chief Minister had been insulted and should make a statement. So Mr. Bustamante, under pressure, dictated a statement which was taken down in longhand.

The treatment of the story in the next day's issue of the *Daily Gleaner* makes interesting reading. On the front page, under the heading "Hutton in Incident with C.M.", the following was printed:

"Len Hutton, England's captain, was involved in an unpleasant incident yesterday and later apologized to Mr. Bustamante, Chief Minister, for what had happened.

Coming back to the pavilion after scoring 205, and while the stands stood and cheered, Hutton was met as he walked in by Mr. Bustamante who had left his seat to offer his congratulations in company with Mr. Granville daCosta, president of the club.

Hutton did not pause to accept the congratulations but Mr. Bustamante held his hand saying 'Not so fast, I have come to congratulate you.'

Mr. daCosta, regarding Hutton's conduct as indicating that he did not know it was the Chief Minister, followed the skipper and impressed on him that it was the Chief Minister of Jamaica.

What Hutton said in reply is in dispute—Mr. daCosta has been pledged to secrecy—but Mr. Hutton did not then say anything more to Mr. Bustamante.

Later, upon the intervention of Mr. N. N. Nethersole, B.W.I. selector, Hutton waited on the Chief Minister and Mr. daCosta. 'I was tired and as it was a surprise to me for the Chief Minister to come to congratulate me I was nervous,' he explained."

The next morning the *Daily Gleaner* published on page eight an "olive branch" and remarkably conciliatory letter from Len Hutton in which he said:

> "I should like to assure the Chief Minister and everyone in Jamaica that never for one moment did I intend to offend the Hon. Mr. Bustamante. . . . It was most unfortunate that I was not at first aware of the Hon. Bustamante's presence at the entrance to the pavilion. After having batted for nearly nine hours and having concentrated on the cricket for nearly three days, I was extremely tired and was thinking only of the twenty minutes' respite from the game allowed by the tea interval. When returning to the pavilion through a mass of applauding spectators a batsman rarely singles out an individual and there is merely an undefined sound ringing pleasantly in his ears.
>
> Had I been forewarned of the Chief Minister's presence, I should naturally have been delighted and honoured.
>
> At the conclusion of the game I had a most friendly discussion with Mr. daCosta, the President of the Kingston Cricket Club, who was Mr. Bustamante's host on this occasion, Mr. Nethersole, representing the West Indies Cricket Board of Control, and the matter was dealt with and disposed of as between sportsmen.
>
> I think it is most regrettable that an unfortunate impression has been created and I hope this letter will make everyone realize that my team and myself have the greatest respect and admiration for the Hon. Mr. Bustamante."

Before the letter was sent Charles Palmer inserted in the third paragraph the name of Mr. Bustamante immediately before that of Mr. daCosta, but when the letter appeared in print Mr. Bustamante's name was omitted. To the reader the only inference could be that the Chief Minister and Hutton had not come together at the end of the day's play as, in fact, they had. They had a drink together in the club bar.

At the same time as manager Palmer gave the *Gleaner* representative a copy of Hutton's letter, Mr. Nethersole handed him a statement making clear that Mr. Bustamante had not been offended in any way and asked that this should be inserted underneath Hutton' letter. The Bustamante statement did not appear, but as a footnote to the letter came the paragraph:

> "Commenting on the incident on Wednesday night, Mr Bustamante told Pressmen: 'I am sure no affront was intended I accept Mr. Hutton's explanation and we have settled th whole matter in the most friendly way. We are all friends.'"

But what the *Gleaner* did *not* publish was this letter from Frank Rostron who, as the only visiting Pressman present when Mr. Bustamante gave his statement, was asked by his colleagues to write to the paper.

"As one of the visiting press correspondents who, unlike any single representative of the West Indies Press, has covered the complete tour of the M.C.C., may I make a simple request?

I ask in the interests of fair and full reporting that you publish the special statement issued in my presence to your reporter at Sabina Park by the Chief Minister himself about the alleged 'unfortunate incident' as you term it.

As an admirer and now a friend of Mr. Bustamante who has had personal kindness from him, I consider it a greater insult to your Chief Minister to badger him for a statement and then suppress it than any of the imaginary things the M.C.C. are alleged to have done.

In case your reporter should have mislaid the statement which he took down in longhand at dictation speed from Mr. Bustamante I repeat it:

Mr. Bustamante said: 'I have not been insulted. When Hutton passed me at the gate and I congratulated him he bowed and said "Thank you". Afterwards Hutton and I and Mr. daCosta all had a drink together and Hutton explained that if he had been abrupt it was nerves and surprise at seeing me where I was. But he assured me he intended no discourtesy. Mr. Hutton is a fine young player and we are a hospitable friendly young country. We are all friends.'

As a member of my profession who is as concerned about the ethics of journalism as apparently many of your writers are, I think you owe Mr. Bustamante, Hutton and the M.C.C. team and the misinformed public a straightforward publication of the statement which your correspondent requested.

As a suitable parallel, I should not dare to ask Mr. Churchill for a considered statement for publication about an incident in which he was involved and then, substituting my own account, ignore the Prime Minister's statement."

Unfortunately for the *Gleaner*, the day before the alleged "incident" took place they had carried a column-length stricture on the practices of the visiting Pressmen, flatly blaming them for the troubles of the tour. "They rake up all the mud they can find and throw it about with carelessness," said the writer of the article. There seemed to be a vast discrepancy in the minds of home and visiting journalists as to what constituted "mud" and facts.

Here is one small example of the reporting of the home journalists. At a dinner given to the M.C.C. at Trinidad Sir Errol dos Santos, President of the West Indies Cricket Board of Control, after revealing that he had written to the M.C.C. apologizing for the incidents at British Guiana, appealed "to all concerned not to magnify little incidents which may have occurred on this tour".

At least, those are the words I heard and those which I find in my shorthand notes of the speech. They are also the words which other English correspondents, also taking notes, confirm as being correct.

We must all have been wrong. The next morning the papers of the West Indies reported Sir Errol as having *appealed to the visiting Press*—which is slightly different!

What were the bones of contention in this unhappy series? Broadly, they can be listed as follows:

UMPIRING: The standard of umpiring was the basic cause of much of the trouble and controversy. Too often it lacked experience, and unfortunately inexperience is frequently linked with incompetence.

Generally in the West Indies some of the umpiring was admittedly below first-class ranking, but men like Burke and Ewart (of Jamaica) and Walcott and Jordan (of Barbados) are capable of holding their own in the best company anywhere, and Burke and Ewart and Menzies and Gillette (of British Guiana) won the admiration of both sides for their courage in the face of direct threats.

Though Hutton repeatedly repudiated any suggestion that the English team were the victims of unfair and biased umpiring the story clung like an unpleasant leech. At the end of each Test Hutton made a point of publicly thanking the umpires, and twice he said he would be more than satisfied to have the same pair for the whole series, but still the rumour persisted.

The M.C.C. team's main complaint centred in the number of *catches behind the wicket* and, on one notorious occasion at slip, which were given not out. They recognized, as all cricketers do, that leg before decisions must be a matter of the umpire's opinion and they were always prepared to accept the position.

Against the class of batsmen to be found in the opposition, and on the beautiful batting wickets of the West Indies, the bowler and fielders, perspiring in the baking rays of the tropical sun, might well be excused for thinking hard things however when they were sure world-class batsmen against them were having two innings.

Throughout the tour the conduct of the West Indian players was most creditable and they were anxious not to give offence. The one failing of some of them, in my opinion, was a reluctance to leave the crease when clearly they had been dismissed.

If a batsman is not certain that he is out he is entitled to wait for decision—I am not disputing his rights—but occasions occurred when the umpire never should have had to be asked for his opinion. I am revealing no secret when I say that the M.C.C. players did not appreciate the way some of their opponents remained at the wicket after being cleanly caught and they took exception to one man in particular. Big trees from little acorns grow!

I should like to see all batsmen follow the example of Trevor Bailey, Willie Watson and Len Hutton who, on giving catches at the wicket in the last Test, turned away without a second's delay; and without waiting for an appeal.

Len Hutton himself offered good, and very pointed, advice on the subject at the West Indies Board of Control dinner in Trinidad.

"I feel all classes of cricketers should help the umpires as much as they possibly can," he said. "Umpires do an extremely difficult job, particularly here in the West Indies, and they don't even get paid for it.

There is an old saying in Yorkshire that 'what you get for n'owt isn't worth having'. I am suggesting that if the West Indies Board of Control has any money left over in the future the umpires should be paid."

The noise which invariably accompanies cricket in the West Indies might have been a reason for umpires not hearing snicks at the wicket. Often English players, more accustomed to a degree of tranquillity, could not even hear the shouted instructions of their captain.

Three possible solutions to the umpiring question for Tests in the West Indies present themselves to me. They are:

(1) To scrap the present system, whereby each colony in which a Test is played provides the umpires for that Test, and to elect a small and select panel from which the whole series would be covered. The ideal number would be four but manager Palmer, who also favours this idea, believes the panel should consist of six. These men should be in charge of the colony matches at the start of the tour so that the visiting captain could inspect them before the Tests begin. The West Indies *have* first-class umpires—so why not use them to the best possible advantage?

(2) To appoint neutrals from countries not directly engaged in the series—say umpires for West Indies-England Tests from Australia, India or South Africa.

(3) For an English professional umpire to be brought out, or even for England to supply two umpires, both to be chosen by the West Indies.

Though it might seem a complete negation of all that cricket stands for, the scheme to engage neutral umpires would merely bring the game into line with all the other major sports. Nobody would dream of staging an international football match, of either code, without a neutral referee and I think the same custom holds in every other sport except cricket.

National prestige in cricket, however, has grown to be a matter of such importance, and in some countries the colour question inevitably arises, that perhaps neutral umpires would put an end to some of the squabbling which all too unhappily develops.

If the West Indies Board of Control agreed to the experiment of two English professional umpires being engaged, to travel separately and live apart from the teams, the officials of the West Indies team in England in 1957 could select the men they considered best fitted for the task.

A point about the selection of Test umpires which should be remembered is that in England the tour programme is so arranged that the visiting captain has at least one opportunity of seeing each of the leading candidates before the Tests start. In the West Indies Hutton was in the strange and unenviable position of having no idea of the capabilities of any alternatives should he disapprove of the men officiating in the colony match and thus regarded as almost automatic appointments for the forthcoming Test. We saw this all too clearly in British Guiana where, preferring other umpires to those who stood in the colony match, he accepted in Menzies an umpire whom he had never seen in the middle. What is the essential difference between the English umpire, whom no one would claim to be absolutely infallible, and his West Indies counterpart? believe it largely to be a question of match practice.

In England first-class cricket is played six days a week for four and a half months of the year, but only a few matches of similar ranking take place in the Caribbean.

Therefore an umpire's experience is confined in the main to week-end club matches on Saturday and Sunday afternoons.

Ken Woods, the younger umpire in the fourth Test, commend ably tries to add to his experience by attending net practices on th Trinidad Oval, and he stands at the net for hours on end as officiating in a match. Compared with the seasons of practic experience required from an English umpire of Test rank, howeve this strikes me as being hopelessly inadequate.

No one could blame young Woods but conditions of cricket an circumstances in the West Indies do not lend an opportunity f any man gaining sufficient umpiring experience early in life stand in a Test match on which so much importance is placed.

County umpires in England are hand-picked and recruited from the ranks of ex-professionals. Before they enter the first-class lists they have to go through a preliminary stage in minor counties, or second-class cricket. After each match the captains make a report about the efficiency of the two umpires engaged and at the end of the season the records are carefully studied by the Advisory County Cricket Committee on whose decision rests whether or not an umpire should be retained for the following year.

Even Frank Chester, who reigned undisputed for years as cricket's best umpire, still has a private report made about him at the end of each match and, if at the finish of the season his general standard has not been high enough, even now he would be liable to the same treatment—non-retention on the list—as a recruit in his first year.

From the confidential reports of the captains and the carefully-compiled records at Lord's the potential Test umpire is chosen. Before he can hope to get on to the select panel he must expect to spend some time gaining a practical experience, no matter how high his reputation was as a player.

Many are the famous cricketers who, on becoming umpires, have been staggered at the amount they did *not* know about the complex and difficult game of cricket.

In the first four Tests mistakes were made, as there always have been and always will be in any Test series, but they occurred at vital stages of the games. At Trinidad the claim was advanced, with truth, that in eleven days of cricket, including the colony match, only three decisions caused dissatisfaction to the fielding side. What was conveniently overlooked was the important fact that two of the three came in the first three hours of the Test and, consequently, had a large bearing on the innings and of the match. Had the time and circumstances been different and tail-enders been batting instead of such superb players as Holt and Weekes, these debatable decisions might well have passed off without so much attention and comment.

I must point out with satisfaction that in the last Test Burke and Ewart achieved the almost-impossible standard of committing no known errors, a record for which any pair might justly be proud.

Having studied the question from every angle and taking all the many tricky aspects into consideration, I sincerely urge the West Indies Board of Control to think deeply on the suggestion of a panel of umpires. I am sure it would save much heart-burning.

BEHAVIOUR OF CROWDS: Compared with English spectators, or in fact with any crowds I have come across in Australia, New

Zealand and South Africa, the West Indies are by far the noisiest and most demonstrative. The average spectator and home player becomes accustomed to the setting, no doubt because he has grown up in it. Probably he does not even hear the noise, but the visiting cricketer must be allowed some time to understand and acclimatize himself to it all.

None would deny that the West Indian loves his cricket passionately. He is versed in the lore of the game, and loves to talk about the giants of the past and matches he had seen. Frequently on leaving any ground from Kingston to Georgetown I would be followed by twenty or so enthusiasts who would pepper me with intelligent questions about English cricket.

"Why can't England find a leg-break bowler?" one would say.

"How good is Cowdrey?" would come from another.

"Why didn't they bring out Edrich?" a third would demand.

The one danger appears to lie in their enthusiasm and natural partisanship being allowed to develop into the stage of irresponsibility. The crowds vary in character as must be expected from islands so widely scattered as they are in the Caribbean.

At Kingston in the first Test the crowd made life hard for Stollmeyer. Yet they were almost quiet in the last Test; at Barbados they booed the snail-like crawl of England, but, which was far less understandable, they also showed no particular relish for some bright batting by Holt and Worrell; at British Guiana two sections of the crowd rioted on the Saturday but on the last day the spectators cheered England, the victors; and at Trinidad members booed some of the England players.

At Barbados I felt some sympathy for the crowd and most of the protests came from schoolboys, but at the same time the barracked batsman, Hutton, was justified in standing away from the wicket until the noise subsided.

Sir Errol dos Santos, the President of the West Indies Board of Control, described the British Guiana affair as having originated from the action of a drunken sot who threw the first bottle, and spoke of schoolboys joining in because they saw the affair as a jolly good rag.

Had Sir Errol, whose dismay at the scene and the harm caused to the prestige of West Indies cricket can well be imagined, been present at the match he could not possibly have pursued this line of thought.

If, as he suggested, the bottle-throwers were, in fact, schoolboys then British Guiana must boast the most advanced education system the world has ever known, one in which attendance at school until middle age is obligatory.

The plain truth of the matter is that nobody can tell who throws the first missile from a crowd, and the local officials were under no illusions about it being a schoolboys' prank. Certainly the British Guiana Board of Control Secretary, Mr. Ken Wishart, did not look upon it in that light and I know of a letter sent from a British Guiana official to a prominent West Indies Board of Control member saying that political influences were feared to be at the back of the demonstration.

The M.C.C. perfectly understood they were not the target for the bottles, but, as players in a match in which an umpire was threatened, they could not be disinterested persons.

During the fourth Test *The Clarion* blazoned the word BOO! across its front page, with the supporting headlines: "Shocking Behaviour; England On The Field: Q.P. Members in the Pavilion." Trevor Bailey was quick to parody a popular song finishing with the line, "Boo-Hoo we don't think it's True-Oo." Yet, if the facts are faced squarely, a great deal of truth was contained in the assertion of shocking behaviour.

At the end of the Test Charles Bray wrote:

"I have never witnessed a game in which tension was so strained or where there was such an undercurrent of downright hostility. Trinidad proudly boasts it has the most sporting crowd in the West Indies, and I paid tribute to its sportsmanship during the Colony game. But it was not only the English players who momentarily forgot their manners."

The attitude of the spectators at the outset of the M.C.C.'s all-too-short stay in Trinidad—eleven out of the fourteen days were spent on the cricket field—seemed to be one of determination to erase the memory of the Georgetown riot.

In the colony game the spectators were generous and impartial to a degree which previously had not been encountered. They even cat-called impatiently and protested against their own team for pausing to take refreshments during the final and match-winning stand between Watson and Compton. One of the biggest and most spontaneous cheers went to Watson when he hit a big six.

In the Test the "outer", as the Australians would describe the paying crowd, gave the impression of being fairer than the members, and easily won from the M.C.C. players the description of being the best crowd in the West Indies in front of which to play.

The duty of members is to set a standard of behaviour for the whole ground. Those who resented and booed Graveney for throwing down the ball when Holt was given not out at Trinidad were

guilty of precisely a similar breach of manners. Some of the complaints I heard in the pavilion afterwards included one that an
English amateur had raised his cap only *once* to acknowledge the
applause. I ask you!

Never in the midst of many verbal attacks about the M.C.C.'s
conduct did I hear mention of two incidents in the preceding match.
Given out caught at the wicket, one Trinidad batsman pointed to his
shirt in a way which left the onlooker in no possible doubt about
what he thought of the decision. Later he apologized to the umpire.
Another batsman stayed so long after being given out that captain
Stollmeyer made him apologize also. Two wrongs do not make a
right, but the criticism should not be one way.

BEHAVIOUR OF THE PLAYERS: The supreme tragedy of the tour from
England's point of view was that in their moments of uncontrolled
annoyance and shocked sense of injustice, they enabled the home
Press and public to turn round and, in effect, say, "You see—you,
not we, are the cause of all the trouble."

Moreover, this provided the perfect opportunity for drawing a
convenient veil over the other happenings which the M.C.C. players
insisted were at the root of the trouble.

The general tone and behaviour of the M.C.C. party was
excellent and the conduct of the overwhelming majority of players
exemplary. The charge made at Barbados that they were a "good-
time" team had no basis of fact. I heard much rumour and gossip,
but when challenged on the source of their information, the in-
variable reply of the informers was, "Well, I admit I wasn't there,
but it's what I have heard." Too many in every land are willing to
pass on scandal about sporting celebrities, and the M.C.C. were
particular sufferers. Unfounded rumours and gross distortions
of fact played all too big a part in the tour and the M.C.C.
have every reason to feel indignant at their treatment in this
matter.

Much of the censure was directed against Trueman, who, it must
be admitted, with his blunt and forthright approach to life, and his
pungent vocabulary, at times was a handful. A firmer handling of
the situation at the start of the tour might have produced better
results, but there is more good than bad in Trueman, and nobody
could have tried harder than he did. And a remarkable fact was
that Trueman would have easily topped a popularity poll with the
public, and he was much liked by both the opposition and the
umpires. I have a very soft spot for the lad. But this temper . . .!

Those who condemned the M.C.C. players conveniently seemed
to forget some of their acts of generosity—for instance, giving George

Headley a single to get off the mark in what everybody recognized would be his last Test Match.

Everywhere the players went they read condemnatory letters about them in the Press, which helped to foster an unbalanced judgment, and they were of the type which would find their way to the waste-paper basket in an English newspaper office. One letter-writer admitting he was not on the island nevertheless thought it his duty to talk of the crudeness displayed by nearly all the members of the team during their visit. I completely fail to see in what position he was to pass judgment. Of course he was in no position at all.

Many wondered if Charles Palmer was a strong enough person-ality to be the manager of such a rumour-ridden and exacting tour, but he tackled a terribly difficult job with a quiet effectiveness which had to be admired.

His only public speech of the tour, at the West Indies Board of Control dinner in Trinidad, was full of practical common sense but laced with humour.

"It would be false for me to say publicly," he declared, "that the tour has been an easy one for either side.

Test cricket in these days has unfortunately developed to such an intensity of effort, and seems to have so many extraneous influences obtruding themselves upon the game, that it frequently lacks the unruffled serenity often associated with cricket, and I am sure it is a cause for much regret on both sides that this tour has not been free from certain unpleasant occurrences.

It is incumbent upon us all to make all effort possible to resolve any troubles that may have beset us, and from my knowledge of and connection with the M.C.C. at Lord's I am sure M.C.C. will always work as it has done in the past to foster and develop the game. There is a great future for all kinds of cricket. If it is kept as a game it has enough intrinsic merits to survive any temporary doldrums into which it may fall.

A criticism of modern cricket is frequently made that the game lacks the character and characters it had in the past. May I, on behalf of modern cricket, claim that this often comes from people who tend to glamorise the past at the expense of the present.

My urge to all everywhere is to remove the rose-coloured spectacles through which we look at the past. Let us look real-istically at the past to teach us how to look at the present and future of cricket."

THE PRESS: The visiting correspondents were almost daily criticized or distorted and twisted reports, so much so that sometimes I wondered whether we were watching the same matches as the local journalists.

For instance, one West Indies cricket expert wrote that Bailey bowled leg-theory during the first innings of the last Test. The suggestion can be at once dismissed, and in fact the unanimous condemnation of leg-theory during and after the first Test effectively curbed its further use during the series. Furthermore, I read that Bailey's success in taking seven wickets for 35 was helped by the tendency of the ball to keep low. The reverse was nearer the truth for one of the reasons for Bailey's fine haul of wickets was his ability to make the good-length ball rise more than normally would be expected. Still, that was a comparatively minor matter.

Once, on being introduced to a top-ranking Civil Servant, Charles Bray was told, "You and your colleagues are the cause of all this trouble." What nonsense! I suppose the British Press attacked the umpire's wife and began the bottle-throwing!

After the British Guiana episode much of the criticism previously directed against the M.C.C. players veered towards the visiting Pressmen.

When tempers, frayed in the heat of the moment, have calmed down, nothing is easier than to blame everything on those whose job it is to tell the world what has happened in front of their eyes— and upwards of the eyes of 20,000 other people as well.

To have to record unpleasant facts or to criticize players who are often personal friends is not a pleasant duty, but not to do so is dishonest and unfair to the reading public.

If legislators feel they have a grudge against any writings on the game they should apportion the blame in the right quarter and not brand the Press as a whole.

One indefensible opinion, that England had to play 13 men— inferring the umpires were on the other side as well—was made at the end of the first Test. This was one man's view and should be remembered as such. *It was not an official opinion.* The other correspondents blamed England's defeat on bad batting and not bad umpiring and Hutton was quoted as having been satisfied.

Nearly all the most critical and controversial comments of visiting journalists were published in the West Indies—but rarely was any of the rich praise so freely accorded to the brilliant West Indies cricketers cabled back or, if so, rarely did it see the light of day. A lively and provocative column was produced in this manner almost daily but whether it did justice to the visiting Pressmen is another matter.

My other complaint is that some of the most critical comment of the M.C.C. was written by home-based West Indies journalist hundreds of miles from the scene of the play. Not one of the West Indies journalists covered all the tour, which was necessary to obtain an objective viewpoint of the cricket scene as a whole.

I have no desire or intention to begin a brickbat Press war, and I am trying to straighten out a few misunderstandings, but here is a tit-bit taken from a British Guiana publication which scarcely can be accepted as a model of accurate journalism or a contribution to the good-will of the tour.

Headed "Hooligans Bully Test Victory—Story of Bowler who Spat at Umpire", the article tells of an M.C.C. bowler (un-named) who, having been no-balled, spat at the umpire and called him the "vilest of names".

Denis Compton, it was also alleged, offered to take a British Guiana player outside and beat him up; Dick Spooner—poor, inoffensive Dick—"attacked a batsman" and Lock "hurled intimidations at umpires".

The conclusion to the story was:

"While in the record books the third Test is down as having been won by the M.C.C., in the eyes of real lovers of the game that match must be recorded as one which has been bullied by the hooligans. It is the hooligans which prevented the umpires from giving a number of decisions against them, etc."

BUMPERS: The West Indians viewed with the gravest suspicion the M.C.C.'s original selection of four fast bowlers. In the first Test with King injured they themselves had nobody able to retaliate, which was hardly England's fault, and not until the fourth Test was there any suggestion of bumpers being overdone.

After the accident to Laker in that Test, Board of Control President Sir Errol dos Santos appealed publicly to "stop these terrible bumpers" and he urged the authorities to "take steps in the immediate future to ban bumpers before some terrible tragic accident occurs".

Hutton bluntly replied: "If you don't want any more bouncers do not have any more wickets like this one (referring to the Trinidad mat). I know of no batsman who likes bouncers."

Far too many bumpers were bowled by both sides in the fourth Test and before the fifth the captains, Stollmeyer and Hutton, in a commendable attempt to avoid unnecessary trouble, suggested that the umpires, Burke and Ewart, should decide how many bouncers an over could be allowed.

The reply was two. If any bowler exceeded his allotment he was to be told quietly but firmly not to bowl any more in that over. Both King and Trueman were each warned once.

Bumpers are the answer of the fast bowler to wickets which give him precious little other chance. In the West Indies the pitches are all in favour of the batsman. They are covered throughout the duration of the cricket, even in colony matches, a procedure which, as with the preparation of wickets, is tied up with the all-important matter of finance.

The West Indies Board of Control have to make certain of recovering the heavy cost of a short tour and, to do so, they hope for six days of cricket and six large crowds at each of the five Tests. If the pitch had not been covered at Georgetown play most certainly would have been impossible on the Saturday after a deluge of the previous day and another during the night.

The preparation of Test pitches fascinated the M.C.C. players. The pitches were rolled and watered, rolled and watered, from first thing in the morning to last thing at night until they gleamed in the sunshine, and even during the intervals of the colony match preceding a Test the rolling on the adjacent strip being prepared for the bigger match went on ceaselessly until the umpires walked out again.

Apart from the financial angle, a definite case could be made out for the covering of wickets. A rain-affected West Indies pitch, like those of Australia, is almost unplayable, with the ball flying around the head from a half-volley. Moreover, it can be dangerous. Yet the side unfortunate enough to lose the toss in the present conditions is immediately placed at a big disadvantage.

The losing captain knows full well that his opponents should be capable of making a large score on a beautiful wicket and so gain a moral ascendancy. Furthermore, there must always be the chance of his side, having fielded in tropical heat for three days, not batting true to form. He realizes also that, with the wicket protected, the weather cannot come to his aid.

The last Test in the West Indies, however, contradicted all the theories and lessons of the first four. In the first two Tests Stollmeyer won the toss and the match. At Georgetown Hutton won the toss for the only time and England triumphed by nine wickets; the fourth, on the mat, came to its almost inevitable draw and the winning of the toss made little or no difference.

In the last Test everything went right for England. The West Indies collapsed inexplicably on a good batting wicket and never recovered.

I doubt whether such a thing would happen again once in fifty innings, but just as one swallow does not make a summer, so one unaccountable batting collapse does not cause any revision of the unanimous opinion that wickets in the West Indies are too much in favour of batsmen.

With West Indies wickets so good fast bowlers cannot be blamed if they resort to some bumpers, but I must write the bouncers down as a contributory factor to the tension in the Tests.

Whether the rulers of the game can offer umpires a clear defin-ition of their own interpretation of the phrase "persistent and systematic fast short-pitched balls" is a matter to which they must give serious consideration. At the moment one umpire may consider two an over to be excessive whereas another may be prepared to grant anything up to three or even four an over. To no-ball a bowler under this rule is a very serious affair and I have every sympathy with the umpires who refuse to take the initiative in an important matter which should be dealt with by those who make the laws.

May I suggest that no more than two be allowed in any one over?

In his farewell statement, made on the morning of the team's departure, the M.C.C. manager touched on most of the controver-sial points I have just raised. His words were:

"After more than three months in the West Indies we leave for England.

From a cricket point of view we go back with a better record than any previous touring side from England. We are naturally pleased about this, particularly when we remember that our efforts in the early stages were not very encouraging and we are, of course, pleased that we attained that cohesion which enabled us to square the series of Test Matches.

Both sides have played excellent cricket in hard-fought games. It is a great pity that some of the Test Matches were so tense and after such battles it is perhaps a blessing that the Test Match honours are divided.

The series has been marred by many incidents—often magnified out of all proportion by too many people—and these unfortunately produced a growing acrimony which everyone on every side must much regret. It is comforting that the last Test Match, while played keenly, was an exhilarating performance which did much to create more amicable relations. I feel that at times general feelings about the cricket got out of proportion. I do urge everyone in the West Indies to try to keep cricket as a game and to prevent extraneous influences from spoiling its essential character.

The umpiring has been the subject of much controversy. I wish to deny any allegations that we have assumed dishonesty. We have said that the standard of umpiring at times has not been good. We do not expect umpires who umpire infrequently to match the general standard attained by English umpires who do the job six days a week professionally and who are most likely old first-class cricketers of considerable experience. Furthermore, we realize that the umpiring out here is more difficult than in England because an umpire here has long periods in the sun which tends to weaken his concentration, and because in places he often works before partisan and noisy and at times even menacing crowds. By analysis we consider that mistakes have been made more against than for M.C.C. (and I repeat this does not imply dishonesty).

However, Burke and Ewart in the last Test Match must be praised very highly for fine efforts, and it is this standard of umpiring that should be uniform throughout a series of Test Matches. If I may be allowed I would like to suggest that serious consideration be given to umpiring in any future tour in the West Indies.

I realize that difficulties are inherent where the cricket areas are so widely scattered but it would to me appear desirable to create a panel of the best umpires available from *all* islands— perhaps a panel of four or six. The itinerary of the tour should be so arranged that these umpires should officiate in early minor matches and then the best, in the opinion of the two captains, should be made available for Test Matches in any island.

Representative cricket in the West Indies is not easy to organize so scattered are its 'component parts' and I would like to congratulate the West Indies Board of Control on the efforts they make to organize and foster and encourage the game. You will soon have the Australians, almost immediately after we have tried to soften them for you in Australia. In your series I very much hope you will all see great cricket.

Under Jeffrey Stollmeyer's admirable captaincy you have had a powerful and formidable team and you will no doubt have a splendid eleven next year. You will need it because the Australians are never easy to beat. We wish you good luck and a happy tour.

To the many people who have been kind to us in the West Indies we offer our sincere thanks. We are naturally looking forward to rejoining our families but we shall not forget the many fine friends we have had in the West Indies."

When Mr. Palmer made his reference to the forthcoming visit to the West Indies of the Australians presumably he was guided by a report, seemingly official, which had appeared a few days earlier in the West Indies papers. Subsequently we discovered that up to that point the Australian Board of Control had not officially accepted the tour invitation but later they did so.

THE FUTURE: From time to time during the later stages of the tour suggestions were made that few, if any, of the M.C.C. players would be willing to undertake another tour of the West Indies, and some even went so far as to advocate that the M.C.C. should cancel any tentative arrangements they had made for another tour there.

Obviously these are very grave views, but, to my mind, none of the difficulties which arose were of the kind which, with good-will, and a sensible and open-hearted approach, could not be resolved to the future benefit of all.

Rightly or wrongly, I could not escape the impression that a succession of pin-pricks, sometimes rudeness, put the tour on a wrong foot and thereafter, as event followed event, the M.C.C. came almost to expect and look for something to go wrong.

In the present circumstances I can see no alternatives to these two points:

(1) For M.C.C. to send out a team of amateur cricketers, equipped to spread the gospel of cricket without worrying overmuch about the importance of winning or losing.

(2) For M.C.C. to "toughen up" in their attitude, insist on a panel of neutral umpires; insist they have a greater say in the tour arrangements, and for them to pick the best available side to engage in a series of Tests and other matches as representatives of English cricket. Cricket ability, rather than the graces of a trained diplomat, would be the main consideration in selection.

In my view the tour of the West Indies begins wrongly in that the West Indies Board of Control virtually exercises control of the M.C.C. cricketer from first to last. The West Indies Board of Control pays the wages and expenses of the visiting players, makes all travel and hotel arrangements, takes whatever profit the tour brings in or stands any loss. And, doing all these things, they largely dictate the terms.

For instance Hutton, with previous experience of the exacting conditions of a tour in the West Indies, wanted 16 players to be in the side, apart from the manager, but he had to accept 15, a compromise being effected by the appointment of Charles Palmer as manager-player".

This custom of the West Indies being responsible for all financial matters is one which has survived from the days when countries like the West Indies and South Africa had to use their persuasive powers to induce M.C.C. to send out "missionary" teams. While fully prepared to do so, M.C.C. could not see their way to meeting any loss that such a tour might bring.

Nowadays, however, a cricket tour has assumed far more importance. With Test Matches attracting Empire-wide attention, the possibility of an M.C.C. tour resulting in a financial loss is remote.

Surely, then, M.C.C. should take a firmer line in the tour itinerary and arrangements?

As it was, had the Bermuda Cricket Association not stepped in with the offer to pay the difference between sea and air fares for the outward journey, the M.C.C. would have travelled by banana-boat both to the West Indies and home again. When the tour finished the players, anxious as they were to rejoin their families without a moment's delay, were committed to returning home the slower way, by sea. Only Laker, whose wife was not well, was granted permission to fly back. Many of his team-mates wished they could have done the same.

Secondly, the West Indies Board fixed all hotels for the M.C.C. and when at Kingston, manager Palmer indicated that his team were not happy in the accommodation provided for them—most of the players had to share tiny rooms which, when full of their baggage, became terribly cramped—they were told that no alternative could be offered.

Mr. Palmer pressed his point about the return to Kingston in March and, after some delay, the team were offered more spacious quarters for their second visit there.

Again, for another tour of the West Indies to stand a real chance of being happy and smooth M.C.C. must demand that proper recognition be given everywhere to the position of their captain and manager, as representatives of the premier cricket club in the world.

They must not allow any likelihood of a repetition of such a situation as the England captain's friends, when accompanied by an escorting M.C.C. player, being turned away, of the manager's friend, sitting next to the manager in the stand, being told to "Get out!" or of the England captain being vilified.

In what seemed to be discreditable attempts to shirk the real cause of the trouble, views were expressed that the appointment of a professional captain by M.C.C. was at the bottom of all the unpleasantness.

To me that was the worst of the anti-M.C.C. propaganda. If Hutton was a failure, and I for one stoutly deny he was, the fact of his being a professional cricketer and not an amateur had nothing to do with it. There is no knowing what might have happened had Hutton been of less equitable temperament.

Let us judge a man as a man, not by the tag attached to his name.

CHAPTER FIFTEEN

Wonderful achievement—Reasons for recovery—A common purpose unites—
Early mistakes—The greatness of Hutton—His world ranking—Who for
Australia?—Three England deficiencies—Personalities and pen-pictures.

IN THE eyes of the cricket world England achieved greater
status by holding the West Indies to a draw after being in the
apparently hopeless position of two down, with three to play, than
by defeating Australia the previous season.

Two excellent reasons could be advanced to support the popular
contention. First, England scraped through to victory over Australia
with defensive back-to-the-wall tactics in every Test, but the last;
secondly, Australia were below their usual formidable strength,
whereas, all things considered, the West Indies in their own conditions, before their own crowds, were indeed a mighty powerful
combination to face, and as always they seemed to increase in
strength and ability when they held the initiative.

Therefore, having gained a lead of two nil in the series, the
West Indies became favourites by long odds to win the rubber. After
losing at Kingston and, even more disappointingly, at Barbados,
and with everyone so rightly saying that the chances of a definite
finish on the Trinidad matting were almost non-existent, England
knew that to square the series they had to bring off the immense
task of winning at British Guiana, where the bowlers were forewarned about the reputation of the pitch, and finally at Kingston.

To the surprise of nearly everyone, England drew the rubber
by bringing off emphatic victories both at Georgetown and
Kingston, even though in the last Test they went into the field without their key bowler, Statham, who had been held back specially
for Test Matches, and also in spite of losing the toss on what, it
must be repeated, was a good batting wicket.

Several important reasons existed for the brilliant recovery made
by England. Paramount was the adjustment of Hutton's men to
the heat, the light and the crowds of the West Indies. At first many
found the climate in a tropical country much too enervating.
Acclimatization was a gradual process.

Early in the tour also an unsettled team which grew increasingly
suspicious of umpiring standards and surprised at the noise and
partisanship of the crowds, began to drop its catches and generally
failed miserably to do itself justice.

After the Barbados Test the players believed they could sense a degree of hostility towards them, and this, combined with a feeling that they were not receiving an even share of the breaks, made them into an angry side.

Previously they had not been a team in the proper sense of the word. As in moments of national crisis, however, stress brought them together, with a common purpose and a common front.

After the second Test I wrote that, though the time might seem singularly inopportune for optimism, a vast improvement for the rest of the tour could be predicted. England reached rock bottom in the first innings at Barbados, but one could almost see the side re-shaping its outlook and rekindling its resolution.

The folly of an ultra-defensive batting approach was realized, and the policy rightly rejected. The turning point of the series was reached.

Even allowing for the fact that many of the young players had not settled down, England largely could blame themselves for allowing the West Indies to win the first two Tests.

Paradoxically the worst thing that happened was for M.C.C. to beat Jamaica in the opening colony game on a fast wicket at Sabina Park.

At once they sold themselves the idea that the Test wicket necessarily also would be fast, and as a result all four quick bowlers Statham, Trueman, Moss and Bailey, were included. Instead, the pitch did not encourage speed and the attack contained no variation or real spin. As soon as two fast bowlers went off two others came on

The presence of all the pace bowlers lengthened a tail already over-long, and not until the last Test was the proper blend achieved I thought that in the two Tests in which he played, Wardle proved to be an essential member of the team. These were the two Tests which England won.

England's big men undoubtedly were Hutton, the greatest batsman of all, Trevor Bailey, who does everything well, has an unequalled intelligence for the game and inspires the side with the intensity of his effort, Statham, who made marked strides as a fast bowler, and Denis Compton, whose batting, after he had accustomed himself to the different conditions, was a revelation.

At one period, when he was not in the best of health, Hutton lost caste as a captain, but the final outcome materially strengthened his hold on the position, and I cannot see a serious competitor arising for the leadership of the tour to Australia in September.

Faults could be picked in Hutton's tactics, his field placings, on occasions even perhaps in a lack of positive direction to the team. In personality he does not compare with some of the captains of the past, and in the words of a team-mate he does not "bubble

He takes some understanding—as he himself is the first to admit. He is inclined to indulge in somewhat obscure philosophizing, and some charged him with being too tolerant of Trueman, who always gave the impression of wanting to take on the West Indians on his own.

To a section of people in the West Indies the idea of England being led by a professional captain apparently was as repugnant as it is to a minority in England; indeed, one writer laid the whole trouble of the tour at that door. Such an accusation was sheer nonsense, and completely unfair to Hutton.

In spite of all criticisms, the general emerged from his battles triumphant in the end though not unscathed, and, to my mind, England owed a lot to him for his will-power and his determination, to say nothing of his skill as a cricketer.

I thought it a sheer miracle that, with so many distractions and worries off the field, Hutton was able to stand head and shoulders above any batsman on either side and to maintain his consistency and concentration. Without him England would cut a sorry figure.

As a batsman Hutton is without peer in the world today, and his ranking among the immortals of all ages must be very high. Throughout the years, except for one lean spell in 1948, Hutton has scored a profusion of runs for England and Yorkshire on all types of pitches and often with the responsibility of being the only reliable run-getter in a weak batting side.

Hutton plays three-quarters of his cricket in England, and on county wickets which do not receive the same degree of preparation as Test pitches.

In the last few years an extra thickness of seam has been added to the ball, giving the opening bowler much more chance with the new ball and so proportionately increasing the difficulties of the opening batsman.

If I had to stake my life's savings on any batsman scoring 50 on any type of pitch, Hutton would be my unhesitating first choice. In the Test series in the West Indies, Hutton's bat seemed to grow wider and wider. If the ball beat the bat a gasp of genuine surprise would go up and long before the end of his innings of 205 in the last Test the West Indies players must have been sick and tired of the sight of Hutton. In every way he is a great batsman.

And what of England as a team? In the first two Tests they were extremely disappointing, but by the Fifth they were a powerful side, and, potentially at least, the nucleus of a strong combination to go to Australia the following winter.

Much, of course, will depend on current form in the English

home season, which will provide an excellent opportunity for Graveney and Watson to make the last step from being good county to established Test rank.

At the end of the tour in the West Indies the England team suffered from three deficiencies. It lacked an opening batting partner to Hutton, a reliable middle batsman and a leg-break bowler.

On the other hand there appeared to be an abundance of top-class candidates for the position of opening bowlers. What with Alec Bedser, Brian Statham, Trevor Bailey, Fred Trueman, the rapidly-advancing Peter Loader, of whom so many experts hold the highest possible opinion, and possibly Northamptonshire's Frank Tyson, certainly no one could complain of a shortage in this direction.

According to Surrey captain Stuart Surridge who came to the West Indies on a business trip, Tyson had greatly increased his strength and stamina by working on Surridge's tree farm, and Surridge predicted those who regarded Tyson only as an electric bowler for one or two overs were likely to be surprised.

Meanwhile my opinions of the performances and abilities of the individual M.C.C. players were:

TREVOR BAILEY. In every aspect of the game Bailey makes the maximum use of his ability and in the West Indies he was a major asset to the side. A year ago Chairman of Test Selectors Freddie Brown forecast Bailey would play an increasingly important part for England with his batting, and he would go to Australia mainly as a batsman but able to bowl a few overs to rest the shock attack.

When Watson failed as an opening batsman in the West Indies, Bailey took over for the last two Tests and he helped Hutton to give England a useful start. Like Hutton, Bailey possesses a high degree of selectivity and he scores mainly with the cut, hook and the leg glance, but he cannot drive. His grip prevents his making the stroke properly and, furthermore, he gets his body into the right position too early, the downward swing of the bat coming as a separate instead of a simultaneous action.

Hutton has advised Bailey to take up golf to help his drive, because if the bowlers concentrate on keeping the ball well up to him on the off and middle stumps, Trevor's ability to score runs is very limited.

As a bowler, Bailey suits his methods to the conditions. If the pitch is fast he bowls fast. If it is slower, but possibly more helpful to seam bowlers, he cuts down his pace.

Bailey rarely misses an opportunity of studying the opposition batsmen intently, and from his observations he works out a separate plan to bowl to each of them.

He also tries, sometimes with a singular lack of success, to work up a hatred for the opposition, knowing that if he is thinking on those lines he stands a much better chance of doing well against it.

PETER MAY. At one stage during the tour disappointment became the routine experience for a young batsman in whom England places much hope. Unfortunately after his dismissal in the first Test, May became uncertain about the type of game expected from him. He was advised to eliminate some of his most profitable scoring strokes and to concentrate on "grafting" for runs. When he tried to obey instructions and observe a style foreign to his nature he ran into trouble.

His last innings of 40 not out, on the final innings of the fifth Test, was one of the best to watch on the tour, and had he allowed himself a similar range of stroke play throughout he might well have achieved all that was expected of him.

May learned much from Hutton, and he was always a ready listener to him. I feel that the May who will fufil his rich promise is the May who goes after the bowlers and knocks them off their length. In the West Indies Hutton taught May at least one useful lesson—never to think the bowler better than himself.

As a fieldsman May made a striking advance, and his returns to the wicketkeeper were models of accuracy and speed, quite up to the high standard set for England by Jack Hobbs and Cyril Washbrook.

From 30 to 40 yards away, May threw just above stump height, and he ran out several batsmen, notably Clifford McWatt, in a crisis period of the third Test. May is obviously a future candidate for the England captaincy and, with his modest bearing and sportsmanship, he made a deep impression everywhere.

BRIAN STATHAM. Hutton makes no secret of his view that the two bowlers most likely to upset the Australians when next they visit England, in 1956, are Statham and Trueman. Statham probably will make his ability felt by the Australians even before then. He is as fast as Trueman, and to imagine better pace bowling than when he took three wickets in the first West Indies innings of the third Test, at Georgetown, would be very difficult.

England, I feel, has been slow to realize that Statham is a fast bowler of authentic speed and of world class. All the time in the West Indies he attacked the stumps and forced the batsmen to play the ball. He maintained an attacking length, and when he bowled his bouncer he never bowled it so short that the batsman had to duck and allow it to pass safely overhead. Actually Statham bowls two bumpers—a fast bumper and a slow bumper.

Brian Statham's frame is not one of rippling muscles, but his strength is deceptive, and his streamlined build won from his colleagues the nickname of "Whippet". Double-jointed all over, Brian can perform amazing feats of contortion.

So highly was Statham regarded by the team Selectors that they looked upon him as much too valuable an asset to the Test eleven to pick him to play in anything but the Tests and, after helping to beat Jamaica, Brian did not appear in another colony game.

Unfortunately for England he strained a side muscle at Trinidad —Hutton said the site of the strain was certain proof that Brian's bowling action was perfect—and he had to withdraw from the match, and not participate in the fifth and all-important Test.

Throughout the tour the West Indies batsmen showed a healthy respect for Statham's speed, accuracy and ability to swing the ball either way.

In brief Statham was a distinct success and he is now an essential member of the English attack.

WILLIE WATSON. Watson was an enigma. In colony matches he saw the ball the size of one of the footballs he kicked for England and Sunderland, and the West Indies wickets seemed to have been specially prepared for him. He hit the ball beautifully off the back foot and on the rise, and his placing and timing were as brilliant as anything I have seen from Australia's Neil Harvey.

Unhappily for England, although he scored a century in the Test at Sabina Park, Watson could not produce his superb form in the remaining four Tests. The experiment of turning him into an opening batsman did not work.

In the Tests he showed a pronounced frailty against the swinging ball coming through quickly. Yet he made centuries against Jamaica, Trinidad and British Guiana (a double century), and a good score against Barbados.

Apparently Hutton has not abandoned the idea of using Watson as an opening batsman, because he sent him in first in the second innings of the fourth and fifth Tests, even though in the first innings of the two games Watson had batted at number five.

To try to make any player accustomed to batting in the middle of the order into an opener takes a long time, and Watson may yet provide the answer to England's big need. He possesses an unruffled temperament and is the master of snatching sharp singles. His partners, from Hutton downwards, had complete faith in his judgment and not once in the West Indies was there even a suggestion of a close call when he set off for a run.

Willie Watson's father played Soccer for Huddersfield Town and a brother was also a professional Soccer footballer, his last club being Oldham. Like all the best type of sportsmen, Watson is quiet and unassuming.

DENIS COMPTON. Denis Compton's tour began in doubt and uncertainty and finished in triumph. To the second innings of the second Test Compton was a struggling cricketer with his confidence sapped, and that the final days of his Test career were rapidly approaching seemed all too unhappily apparent.

Denis himself must have felt this way because when he went to the wicket at Barbados for his fourth Test innings of the tour, after failures in three, he bore the air of a man who had just seen a ghost or was walking to his own execution.

Then Denis pulled himself together, fought as resolutely as he ever has done in his cricketing life, and won through. He never looked back.

Denis told me that he had discovered one bad fault in his long innings, to overcome which he cut out his leg "tickle" to the ball pitched on the leg stump and concentrated instead in hitting it in the direction of mid-on and mid-wicket. Such was his improvement that in reliability he became second only to Hutton.

Moreover, Denis Compton's fielding improved out of all recognition and was better than it had been for some time. No longer could there be any question of regarding him as something of a passenger in the field. In spite of the hard grounds he kept fit, and was a keen and loyal supporter of Hutton.

To my mind, however, Denis was not given enough bowling. Holt, for one, could not pick out his "chinaman" from his googly, but Compton all too rarely received a chance of bowling at him.

In every way Denis could look back upon the tour as one of distinct personal success. He looked to have ensured his place in the side going to Australia a few months later.

TOM GRAVENEY. When the tall, graceful Graveney batted against Jamaica in the first colony match at Kingston he was nothing short of brilliant, and a tour as successful as he made of India two years earlier was predicted for him.

Unfortunately Graveney did not maintain his early promise, and he still has some way to go before he can be regarded as a certain choice for an England team.

When he is well set, Tom looks a beautiful batsman—as, indeed, do so many—but his strokes are mainly confined to driving, and the opposition is able to plan accordingly to restrict his scoring.

Graveney is deficient of the "killer" instinct which made his Gloucestershire predecessor, Wally Hammond, with whom he has been compared and in whose footsteps so many have expected him to follow, devastating.

Tom is still capable of much development. Earlier in his career I thought he could not miss reaching the highest flight of batsmen, but unless he begins to bridge the gap between being a good player and a very good player soon, I shall begin to have doubts.

I feel in batting Graveney too often suffers from lapses of concentration, but as a makeshift slip fieldsman he did a very good job for England in the West Indies, particularly in the third and fifth Tests. Until the tour began he had not fielded in the slips, except for very occasional periods.

Tom Graveney has one unusual distinction—Hutton sometimes cannot remember his name! Hutton forgot it when the England team was being presented to the Queen at Lord's and in the West Indies he introduced him to one Governor as Tom Goddard—who, of course, is the former Gloucestershire off-break bowler.

FREDDIE TRUEMAN. One person may do more to prevent Freddie Trueman from realizing his main ambition in life to become the best fast bowler in the world. His name is Freddie Trueman—Trueman's own worst enemy.

West Indies crowds alternately booed and cheered Trueman, but usually the biggest cheer was raised for him when he went striding out to bat. Potentially he is a great fast bowler, and in the last Test at Jamaica, when his run-up was smooth, he turned in a fine performance.

Umpire Tom Ewart told me Trueman was three times better in the last Test than when he first saw him at Sabina Park in January.

If he is wise, Freddie Trueman will have learned much from the tour of the West Indies. He has many loyal and good points, and he must ensure that they remain uppermost in his make-up and approach to life. Apart from his bowling ability he has a prodigious throw, but he is rather unwise to advertise it as much as he does —he glories in his strength and aim—and he would be well advised not to show it to new batsmen too often.

GODFREY EVANS. Godfrey was not really fit until the final Test, in which he kept wicket with his old zest, purpose and skill, and in which he batted with more concentration than he had previously applied.

Early in the tour he was troubled by boils, starting with a carbuncle on his shoulder and ending with a boil on the ankle which kept him out of the fourth Test. His fingers were full of sores also, and to add to his ailments and disabilities he chipped a bone in the fourth finger of his left hand at Grenada. As a result of being generally run down, Godfrey was not his normal cheery self until towards the end of the tour, and as a consequence the team missed not only Evans, the peer of present-day wicketkeepers, but the liveliness and vivacity of Evans the man.

JIM LAKER. Laker at the start of the tour was too often taken out of the attack before he had bowled sufficient overs to do himself justice. All slow bowlers must be given some time to work out their theories, especially when pitting their wits against some of the world's best batsmen on good wickets.

Just as he bowled so well against Australia in the Fifth Test, at The Oval, the previous summer, so once again he reserved his best effort to the last game, when his bowling in the second innings provided a vital contribution to England's victory.

After being hit in the eye by a bouncer from Frank King in the fourth Test, Laker was rather apprehensive about his ability to pull his full weight in the fifth, because his vision undoubtedly had been impaired. Hutton, however, conscious of the need for Laker, persuaded him that a three-quarter fit Laker might be sufficient to turn the scales in England's favour. His bowling was regarded as much too valuable to be lost, even though he might fail to make many runs and would be troubled to follow the ball all the way in the field. Luckily for England Laker played.

Laker has a quiet, but strong sense of humour, and he showed a remarkable aptitude for forecasting scores and the number of wickets to fall during the various spells of play. He was rarely wrong and was within 20 of getting the total correct in the West Indies second innings of the last Test.

TONY LOCK. Hutton placed more faith in Lock than any of his other slow men, but the Surrey left-arm slow bowler took some time to adjust himself to the conditions. Particularly was this so in fielding, and understandably at first the West Indians simply could not understand why Lock had gained such a reputation in the short-leg and leg-slip positions.

Towards the end of the series they knew why. In bowling, for too long a period Lock tried to hit the stumps every ball as though he was using a turning wicket in England, but eventually he realized that he had to beat the batsman through the air by flight.

As soon as Lock began to vary his bowling by flighting the ball higher and slower on the off stump and inviting the batsmen to drive him into the packed covers, and to change his pace, he became much more impressive.

After being no-balled for throwing at Kingston and Bridgetown, he eliminated the faster ball to eliminate all suspicion of his action. Even though it robbed him of his surprise weapon and thereby lessened his potential danger it was a prudent measure.

CHARLES PALMER. Many occasions must have arisen on this wearing tour when Charles Palmer wished he was in the West Indies solely as a player without the additional duties of team manager. As a matter of fact I do not think he was given enough cricket, and his inclusion in the second Test, when he was out of match practice —he did not play in the preceding colony game—seemed illogical to me.

Palmer played one magnificent innings in the colony match on the Trinidad matting, but West Indies crowds saw this neat little batsman in action all too seldom.

I doubt whether Palmer would care to repeat his experience as manager of this troublesome tour. At times it must have been a nightmare to him, but he acquitted himself well, even if some thought he was too conciliatory to too many people. My end of tour report on the ex-schoolmaster is: Very satisfactory!

DICK SPOONER. The opportunities of Dick Spooner, as second string to Godfrey Evans, necessarily were restricted. He kept wicket very well in the British Guiana colony match, and with Evans not well and consequently out of form he might easily have won a place in the third Test.

Spooner came in for the fourth Test, when Evans was kept out by boils, but he stood down for the fifth. His batting never reached its Warwickshire level, but he found scant chance of running into form. Not only were his match innings few and far between, but he rarely seemed to be able to obtain sufficient net practice for him to settle down. He was a useful reserve and an excellent team man.

KEN SUTTLE. Suttle, a left-handed batsman, burst into prominence by scoring a century against Middlesex at Lord's. After acknowledging deafening applause from a large Whitsuntide crowd, he walked down the wicket to the next ball and hit it for six, which is typical of Ken Suttle.

At one period in the early part of the tour, when things were not going very well for him, this, by nature, rather highly-strung young man wanted to walk down the pitch to discuss every ball with his partner.

He made a poor start in the West Indies and did not recover properly, but his cheerfulness never departed and he never worried about his leg being pulled by his colleagues, as it so often was.

I doubt whether any single member of the party enjoyed the tour more than Suttle. When he batted, however, his bat was at a crooked angle on the leg stump, but if he can learn to add sounder defensive technique to his good eye for the ball, he could make a lot of runs in many places.

If a bowler worried Suttle he was inclined to sink everything in one terrific hit-or-miss gamble.

He fielded very well, ran fast, and was a reliable catcher, but I would not commend his habit of throwing in on the turn without looking or taking aim—an action for which he was often applauded by the West Indies crowds. Almost invariably the throw would be wide of the wicket and in one or two instances a fair chance of a run out was thrown away. The extra second occupied in turning round and ensuring an accurate return would not have been wasted.

ALAN MOSS. Another type of touring cricketer who always did what was asked of him, Moss went through his first overseas experience very creditably. He collected his quota of wickets and reached his peak with a spell of real hostility on the Trinidad mat.

From first to last Moss was a great trier but sometimes, when hit, he showed a tendency to try to bowl beyond his natural speed, a fair sign of inexperience.

Moss did not play cricket in any form until he was sixteen years old, when he joined West Willesden, a North London rambling club without a home of their own. He owed his chance to the *Evening News* London Colts' scheme. Having had the importance of aiming at the stumps drummed into him, he was seldom guilty of inaccurate bowling.

JOHNNY WARDLE. A high dignitary of the Church, with many years of experience of the Caribbean behind him, told me that every Governor in the West Indies should be a Charlie Chaplin with a working knowledge, at least, of cricket.

The average West Indian dislikes sarcasm in any form, and cannot appreciate subtle humour, but has a wonderful sense of the ridiculous.

Wardle caught the moods of the crowds better than any other

player, and he was the clown prince of the party. Strangely, and in marked contrast, off the field he was very quiet and kept much to himself.

Johnny Wardle baffled a surprising number of the West Indies batsmen with his left-arm "Chinamen" and googlies, probably because nobody in the islands bowls this type of ball, and therefore many of the batsmen found themselves playing against it for the first time in their lives.

Wardle often laughed to himself at the way he could bemuse some of the batsmen.

The biggest hitter on the England side, Wardle enjoyed considerable crowd appeal, and in each of his two Tests appearances he was on the winning side. His catch off McWatt in the last Test was as good as any in the entire series.

CHAPTER SIXTEEN

Power of West Indies—And their weaknesses—Many all-rounders—Walcott tops W formation—Regard for Atkinson—Stollmeyer an astute captain—Discovery of Sobers—Problem of The Leagues—The cauldron simmers down.

DISAPPOINTING as it must have been for the West Indies to have to concede half the prize which at one time was within their grasp, their big consolation was to retain the proud record of never having lost a series of Tests at home.

The cricket of the West Indies remains powerful and virile, with all its special national characteristics, but I do not think the players as a whole possess that capacity to fight back with unyielding tenacity which is typical of Australians. Certainly, many of them quickly revealed their restlessness when they were tied down at the crease for any length of time.

The West Indian is essentially an attacking cricketer and, when he is succeeding, he is wonderful to watch. His fielding can be devastating, but is inclined to droop if things go wrong.

Internationally, of course, the West Indies definitely belong to the upper bracket. Batting strength is contained down to number eight or nine; they have genuine all-rounders in Atkinson, Gomez, Worrell and Walcott; and most of the recognized eleven can bowl at a pinch—or for that matter, even keep wicket.

In fact, versatility is essentially their strong point, and offhand I can think of Walcott and Christiani who have not only bowled and batted in Test cricket but kept wicket as well.

In the last stages of the fourth Test wicketkeeper McWatt went on to bowl and took a wicket, and leg-break bowler Ferguson kept wicket in a manner that would make him a certainty for the position in a number of sides.

Unquestionably the three W's are the idols of the islands, so much so that I was surprised that the West Indies stamps and currencies did not carry their imprints! Against England, however, Worrell did not cause as many headaches as might have been expected. He was stale, never found his touch, although he made two big scores, and was vulnerable to the pace bowlers.

How long Everton Weekes will be able to stand up to six-day Test cricket because of his severe muscular trouble is in the lap of the gods, but he enjoyed a good season, and Walcott's reputation, already very high, was raised by several points.

The English players considered Walcott the most difficult of the three W's to dismiss, and he went from strength to strength. Walcott is a great player who hits as hard as any man alive, and I should not be surprised to find him nominated for the West Indies captaincy at some future date. I would be prepared in the end to see his Test figures better than either Weekes or Worrell.

Denis Atkinson, of Barbados, is an all-rounder of refreshing keenness and no small ability. Denis Compton, for one, thought he was the most difficult of all the West Indies bowlers, and the best tribute I can pay him is to wish that he was available for England.

With the honourable Test career of Gerry Gomez inevitably approaching its end the all-round strength of Atkinson, a really happy warrior, will be of immense value to the West Indies.

Captain Jeffrey Stollmeyer did not score as many runs as he always looked capable of making, but he remained as good to watch as ever, with particular emphasis on the leg-side strokes.

Stollmeyer won much admiration for his strength of mind and purpose during the first Test when the crowd were angry at his decision not to make England follow on.

He is a good and painstaking captain, whose team were behind him solidly. His meticulous field-placings, when he insisted that every player took up his position to almost a half-inch, revealed his close study of the game, and he did little either in tactics or in strategy which could be faulted. He was always on top of the situation, and he never allowed the match to "run away" from him. I thought he made an admirable skipper.

Of the bowlers Frank King definitely became hostile in the last two Tests, but clearly Ramadhin and Valentine are more suited to English conditions than their home pitches. Once England's batsmen had overcome the Valentine-Ramadhin complex, which seemed to be a hangover from 1950, the two slow bowlers were forced to work hard and pay heavily for their wickets.

The biggest West Indies discovery was Garfield Sobers, who, making his Test début at the age of 17 years and 245 days, became the second youngest cricketer to play in International cricket. His left-arm slow bowling shows much promise, but I should not be surprised if he makes more of a name for himself as a batsman than as a bowler.

Clifford McWatt was a dependable and at times excellent wicketkeeper, and the England team were always pleased to see the back of him as a batsman. A possible successor to McWatt is young Hendricks, who kept well for Jamaica in the second colony match. Another youngster who may well come to the fore is Reggie Scarlett, Jamaican off-spinner.

Altogether West Indies look likely to be able to field a very fine side for a number of years to come, and I expect that most of those who played against Hutton's team in 1954 will return in the party coming to England in 1957.

I am looking forward to renewing their acquaintance, and I am sure that English crowds will thoroughly appreciate not only their skill but also their zest for the game.

Cricket-lovers in the West Indies often complain about the "poaching" of their star men by the English League clubs, and they quote Frank Worrell as an example of the detrimental effect the bright one-day cricket can have on technique and approach to the first-class game. On the other hand Walcott has enhanced rather than lost his skill. Much depends on the individual.

The backbone of the West Indies side are the professionals, Weekes, Worrell, Walcott, Ramadhin and Valentine, and judging from letters and verbal appeals made to me to help them by other colony players, the ambition of most cricketers in the Caribbean is to obtain an engagement in the League in England.

Until comparable livelihoods can be offered them at home, the trek of West Indies cricketers to England will continue.

For this reason I was pleased to see a growing practice of offering coaching engagements in the West Indies to celebrities like Weekes and Worrell. Only good can come from such a development.

·   ·   ·   ·   ·

The cauldron boiled, and bubbled over. Now it can simmer down. We must see that it is not allowed to become over-heated again.

Complete List of all Matches Played by M.C.C. during the Tour

Played in Bermuda. M.C.C. won by an innings and 28 runs.

FIRST MATCH *v.* PICK OF THE LEAGUES

PICK OF THE LEAGUES

FIRST INNINGS			SECOND INNINGS		
E. Brown c Graveney b Wardle..		17	c Evans b Trueman	..	2
A. A. Madeiros lbw b Moss	..	33	lbw b Wardle	..	23
A. F. Mello not out	..	10	c Evans b Laker ..	..	9
E. Raynor lbw b Moss ..	..	1	b Wardle ..	..	0
P. Mulder lbw b Moss ..	..	0	b Laker ..	..	44
R. Perinchief b Trueman	..	0	c Suttle b Laker ..	..	0
E. Madeiros lbw b Laker	..	0	lbw b Wardle	..	6
P. Blee c Wardle b Laker	..	0	c Graveney b Laker	..	3
E. Simons b Wardle ..	..	1	c and b Laker ..	..	8
G. Ferreira c and b Wardle	..	4	b Trueman	..	3
R. Smith c May b Wardle	..	0	not out ..	..	0
Extras	..	7	Extras	..	6
Total	..	73	Total ..	..	104

Bowling Analysis

	O.	M.	R.	W.	O.	M.	R.	W.
Trueman ..	10	2	27	1	8	1	16	2
Moss ..	8	3	7	3	5	2	9	0
Laker ..	14	7	16	2	13·1	4	35	5
Wardle ..	12·2	7	16	4	11	3	39	3

M.C.C.

FIRST INNINGS

L. Hutton c Ferreira b Mulder	..	..	..	0
W. Watson c Raynor b Mulder	..	..	..	9
P. B. H. May c Blee b Mulder	..	..	..	7
D. C. S. Compton b Smith	..	..	..	18
T. W. Graveney b Perinchief ..	..	..	..	52
K. Suttle lbw b Perinchief	..	..	..	12
J. H. Wardle b Perinchief	..	..	..	3
J. C. Laker b Simons ..	..	..	..	67
T. G. Evans b Simons ..	..	..	..	24
F. S. Trueman b Mulder	..	..	..	1
A. E. Moss not out ..	..	..	..	0
Extras	..	..	..	12
Total	..	..	..	205

Bowling Analysis

	O.	M.	R.	W.
Mulder	15	3	49	4
Simons	9·4	2	27	2
Smith	12	2	40	1
Perinchief	14	3	54	3
Raynor	5	0	18	0
Blee	3	1	5	0

Played in Bermuda.   Match drawn.

SECOND MATCH *v.* BERMUDA

M.C.C.

FIRST INNINGS		SECOND INNINGS	
L. Hutton b Woods	49	lbw b Hazel	10
D. Compton c Bean b Symonds..	41	b Woods	3
P. May c W. Simmons b Woods	33	c Bean b Edwards ..	48
K. Suttle lbw b Woods	0	lbw b Edwards	10
T. Graveney b Woods	0	b Symonds	28
T. Bailey c C. Simmons b Hazel	11	not out	22
R. Spooner lbw b Woods ..	0	c Smith b Edwards ..	0
J. Laker c W. Simmons b Symonds	6	not out	35
G. Lock c McD. Simmons b Symonds	3		
F. Trueman b Symonds	0		
B. Statham not out	0		
Extras	5	Extras	10
Total	148	Total (six wkts. dec.)	166

Bowling Analysis

	O.	M.	R.	W.		O.	M.	R.	W.
Woods ..	16	3	49	5		13	2	29	1
Hazel ..	10·2	2	28	1		12	0	41	1
Edwards ..	6	1	20	0		14	4	41	3
Symonds ..	14	3	29	4		14	4	32	1
C. Simmons ..	5	0	17	0		4	2	13	0

BERMUDA

First Innings			Second Innings		
W. Edwards lbw b Statham	..	5	c and b Lock ..	..	9
W. Wilson lbw b Statham	..	19	c Spooner b Statham	..	4
N. Hazel b Lock	..	17	lbw b Statham ..	..	5
W. Simmons c Statham b Lock		7	c Spooner b Laker	..	29
A. S. Bean c and b Lock	..	4	c Statham b Laker	..	3
McD. Simmons lbw b Lock	..	27	not out	..	12
W. Smith c Hutton b Lock	..	27	c Spooner b Compton	..	5
C. Symonds not out	..	11	not out	..	16
C. Simmons b Lock ..	..	4			
C. Wade c Spooner b Lock	..	2			
E. E. Woods c Statham b Lock	..	0			
Extras	..	10	Extras ..	..	7
Total	..	133	Total (six wkts.)		90

Bowling Analysis

		O.	M.	R.	W.		O.	M.	R.	W.
Statham	..	15	2	29	2		3	0	13	2
Trueman	..	5	0	16	0		5	2	13	0
Lock	..	20·4	5	54	8		8	4	13	1
Laker	..	10	2	24	0		8	2	26	2
Compton	..	—	—	—	—		8	2	18	1

Played in Bermuda. Match drawn (rain).

THIRD MATCH *v.* BERMUDA

BERMUDA

W. Edwards b Lock ..	..	..	..	..	28
A. Madeiros c Moss b Wardle	..	..	..	9
W. Smith lbw b Lock ..	..	..	..	25
W. Simmons lbw b Lock	..	..	..	21
N. Hazel lbw b Wardle ..	..	..	..	3
C. Symonds c Hutton b Lock ..	..	..	..	6
McD. Simmons c Moss b Lock	..	..	..	13
P. Mulder c Bailey b Lock	..	..	..	0
A. Hughes c Moss b Lock	..	..	..	9
C. Simmons not out ..	..	..	..	4
E. Woods c Evans b Wardle	..	..	..	8
Extras	..	..	..	7
Total	..	..	..	133

Bowling Analysis

	O.	M.	R.	W.
Bailey	6	3	8	0
Moss	10	1	40	0
Wardle	12·2	2	43	3
Lock	17	3	35	7

M.C.C.

L. Hutton c Madeiros b Edwards	67
W. Watson not out	55
P. May not out	5
Extras	8
Total (for one wkt.)	135

Played at Inswood, Jamaica, December 30 and 31. Match drawn.

FOURTH MATCH *v.* COMBINED PARISHES

COMBINED PARISHES

FIRST INNINGS		SECOND INNINGS	
M. Frederick c Moss b Lock ..	85	b Graveney	40
V. Allen c Trueman b Moss ..	4	c Spooner b Trueman ..	6
G. Headley c Lock b Moss ..	1	c Spooner b Moss ..	12
G. Charlton c Spooner b Lock ..	7	not out	15
R. Robison b Laker ..	8		
S. Hinds c Laker b Wardle ..	15	not out	15
A. Charvis b Moss ..	0		
L. Mullings lbw b Lock ..	24		
H. Dallas not out	6		
H. Tavares b Lock ..	0		
H. Pryce b Trueman ..	4		
Extras	14	Extras	1
Total	168	Total (three wkts.)	89

Bowling Analysis

	O.	M.	R.	W.	O.	M.	R.	W.
F. Trueman..	10·5	4	43	1	7	2	24	1
A. Moss ..	10	4	15	3	4	0	21	1
T. Bailey ..	5	1	16	0	3	0	8	0
G. A. Lock ..	14	7	25	4	—	—	—	—
J. Laker ..	10	3	31	1	—	—	—	—
J. Wardle ..	7	2	24	1	4	1	4	0
T. Graveney	—	—	—	—	5	0	17	1
D. Compton	—	—	—	—	2	1	14	0

P

M.C.C.

FIRST INNINGS

T. Graveney b Mullings	23
T. Bailey c Robison b Tavares	78
P. May b Mullings	0
D. Compton c Mullings b Pryce	73
R. Spooner not out	36
K. Suttle not out	43
Extras	22
Total (four wkts. dec.)	275

Bowling Analysis

	O.	M.	R.	W.
H. Pryce	18	3	46	1
R. Robison	8	2	21	0
A. Charvis	16	2	45	0
G. Charlton	1	0	11	0
G. Headley	2	0	4	0
L. Mullings	15	4	38	2
H. Tavares	16	3	50	1
H. Dallas	14	3	38	0

Played at Kingston, Jamaica, January 2, 3, 5 and 6.   M.C.C. won by an innings and 21 runs.

FIFTH MATCH *v.* JAMAICA

JAMACIA

FIRST INNINGS		SECOND INNINGS	
A. F. Rae run out	4	b Trueman	15
M. Frederick c Evans b Bailey ..	60	lbw b Statham ..	10
J. K. Holt, Jnr., c Watson b Lock	39	lbw b Trueman ..	6
K. Rickards lbw b Bailey ..	75	c Hutton b Laker	35
N. Bonitto c Laker b Statham ..	32	b Statham.. ..	20
A. P. Binns c Hutton b Trueman	17	b Trueman ..	43
R. E. Scarlett lbw b Bailey ..	3	lbw b Trueman ..	0
R. Miller lbw b Trueman ..	12	c Bailey b Statham	19
S. Goodridge b Statham	2	c Statham b Trueman	3
A. L. Valentine b Lock ..	5	b Statham ..	10
E. S. Kentish not out	4	not out	0
Extras..	13	Extras	9
Total	266	Total	170

Bowling Analysis

	O.	M.	R.	W.	O.	M.	R.	W.
F. Trueman..	25·5	9	75	2	21	8	45	5
B. Statham ..	21	3	46	2	20·5	8	35	4
G. A. Lock ..	28	11	59	2	14	5	30	0
T. Bailey ..	14	6	38	3	6	3	6	0
J. Laker ..	11	2	35	0	10	2	33	1
T. Graveney	—	—	—	—	2	0	12	0

M.C.C.

FIRST INNINGS

L. Hutton c Holt b Scarlett	41
W. Watson c Goodridge b Miller	161
P. B. H. May c Binns b Scarlett	9
D. C. S. Compton c Scarlett b Kentish	56
T. Graveney b Kentish	82
T. G. Evans st Holt b Scarlett	0
J. C. Laker c Goodridge b Scarlett	33
T. E. Bailey not out	21
G. A. Lock not out	40
Extras	14
Total (seven wkts. dec.)	457

Bowling Analysis

	O.	M.	R.	W.
S. Goodridge	18·5	6	65	0
E. S. Kentish	22	2	70	2
R. Miller	23	1	54	1
R. E. Scarlett	40	3	155	4
A. L. Valentine	18	1	99	0

Played at Kingston, Jamaica, January 8, 9, 11 and 12.   Match drawn.

SIXTH MATCH *v.* JAMAICA
JAMAICA

FIRST INNINGS		SECOND INNINGS	
A. F. Rae c Evans b Moss ..	28	c Evans b Laker	53
M. Frederick c Moss b Bailey ..	58	lbw b Laker	30
J. K. Holt, Jnr., c Evans b Moss	33	st Spooner b Compton ..	152
K. Rickards lbw b Wardle ..	0	b Bailey	1
G. Headley c Suttle b Trueman..	5	not out	53
N. Bonitto b Bailey	7	not out	5
R. Miller b Moss	8		
R. E. Scarlett b Wardle ..	3		
J. Hendricks b Bailey	24		
E. S. Kentish b Moss	4		
A. H. P. Scott not out	3		
Extras	14	Extras	34
Total	187	Total (four wkts. dec.)	328

Bowling Analysis

	O.	M.	R.	W.	O.	M.	R.	W.
F. Trueman ..	11	5	26	1	17	6	55	0
A. Moss ..	18	7	47	4	16	1	67	0
T. Bailey ..	11·5	4	29	3	17	10	21	1
J. Wardle ..	19	3	54	2	21	9	54	0
J. Laker ..	8	4	17	0	30	12	54	2
D. C. S. Compton—	—	—	—	—	9	1	29	1
C. Palmer ..	—	—	—	—	15	11	14	0

M.C.C.

FIRST INNINGS		SECOND INNINGS	
R. T. Spooner c Hendricks b Kentish	0	c Hendricks b Holt ..	1
J. Laker c Hendricks b Scarlett ..	31		
P. B. H. May c Bonitto b Scott ..	124	not out	13
D. C. S. Compton b Kentish ..	47		
K. Suttle lbw b Scott	1	not out	19
C. H. Palmer lbw b Scarlett ..	33		
T. E. Bailey c Frederick b Scarlett	14		
T. G. Evans c Frederick b Scarlett	0		
J. Wardle lbw b Kentish ..	4		
F. Trueman b Headley	12		
A. Moss not out	7		
Extras	13	Extras	1
Total	286	Total (one wkt.)	34

Bowling Analysis

	O.	M.	R.	W.		O.	M.	R.	W.
E. S. Kentish ..	33	6	79	3		3	2	1	0
J. K. Holt, Jnr.	8	2	22	0		4	1	7	1
R. O. Scarlett	43	13	69	4		5	1	10	0
A. H. P. Scott	23	3	73	2		7	1	15	0
G. Headley ..	13·3	3	30	1		—	—	—	—

Played at Antigua, January 23 and 25. M.C.C. won by an innings and 56 runs.

EIGHTH MATCH *v.* LEEWARD ISLANDS

LEEWARD ISLANDS

FIRST INNINGS		SECOND INNINGS	
L. Clarke run out	0	c Wardle b Graveney ..	15
J. Maynard st Spooner b Laker ..	0	lbw b Compton	2
P. Gonsalves b Wardle	0	b Laker	21
B. Ross b Laker	0	lbw b Laker ..	47
C. Roberts b Laker	2	lbw b Compton ..	0
A. G. Eddy b Laker	20	st Spooner b Graveney ..	47
E. Matthews st Spooner b Wardle	1	b Wardle ..	15
S. Walling c Graveney b Wardle	6	st Spooner b Compton ..	7
W. Riley b Wardle	4	b Compton ..	2
S. Thompson not out	2	st Spooner b Compton ..	0
G. Edwards b Wardle	1	not out	0
Extras	2	Extras	11
Total	38	Total	167

Bowling Analysis

	O.	M.	R.	W.		O.	M.	R.	W.
Moss	3	3	0	0		—	—	—	—
Bailey	2	2	0	0		—	—	—	—
Laker	10	1	29	4		17	5	34	2
Wardle ..	9·5	4	7	5		21	7	39	1
Palmer ..	—	—	—	—		4	1	16	0
Compton ..	—	—	—	—		13	1	50	5
Graveney ..	—	—	—	—		15·2	9	17	2

M.C.C.

FIRST INNINGS

Hutton c Clarke b Gonsalves	82
Watson b Eddy	17
Suttle b Eddy	0
Compton lbw b Gonsalves	22
Bailey b Roberts	20
Palmer lbw b Roberts	1
Spooner lbw b Eddy	5
Laker run out	8
Graveney st Thompson b Matthews	50
Wardle not out	43
Moss lbw b Matthews	8
Extras	5
Total	261

Bowling Analysis

	O.	M.	R.	W.
Roberts	13	2	38	2
Edwards	9	0	23	0
Riley	8	0	31	0
Eddy	17	7	43	3
Matthews	10·4	0	40	2
Gonsalves	13	2	45	2
Ross	7	2	25	0
Clarke	2	0	11	0

Played at Bridgetown, Barbados, January 29, 30, February 1, 2 and 3.   M.C.C. won by one wicket.

NINTH MATCH *v.* BARBADOS

BARBADOS

FIRST INNINGS		SECOND INNINGS	
Smith c and b Lock ..	25	run out	22
Lucas c Spooner b Moss ..	1	lbw b Lock	28
Walcott c Graveney b Laker ..	25	c Compton b Lock ..	0
Weekes b Lock	17	b Lock	47
Sobers st Spooner b Compton ..	46	b Laker	27
Atkinson b Moss	151	b Lock	1
Goddard b Lock	8	lbw b Laker ..	5
Griffith c Trueman b Moss ..	15	c Graveney b Lock ..	11
DePeiza not out	44	not out	16
Hoad b Trueman	16	c Moss b Laker ..	11
Mullins lbw b Lock	22	c Suttle b Laker ..	1
Extras	19	Extras	10
Total	389		173

Bowling Analysis

		O.	M.	R.	W.		O.	M.	R.	W.
Trueman	..	28	9	63	1		12	3	45	0
Moss ..	..	22	8	56	3		4	1	14	0
Lock ..	..	52·3	20	119	4		21	9	57	5
Laker	..	40	7	101	1		13·4	2	47	4
Compton	..	9	1	31	1		1	0	6	0

M.C.C.

FIRST INNINGS				SECOND INNINGS		
Watson c and b Hoad	..	..	53	lbw b Goddard ..	..	24
Suttle b Atkinson ..	..	..	96	c Walcott b Goddard	..	62
May run out	..	..	57	c DePeiza b Goddard	..	0
Graveney b Goddard	..	..	17	lbw b Goddard ..	..	22
Compton c DePeiza b Walcott	..	..	41	lbw b Mullins ..	..	15
Spooner c Atkinson b Walcott	..	..	3	c and b Atkinson	..	28
Laker b Walcott ..	..	..	15	c Lucas b Goddard	..	0
Hutton not out	..	..	59	b Atkinson	..	3
Lock lbw b Sobers	..	..	4	b Sobers ..	..	18
Moss c Smith b Atkinson	..	..	16	not out	..	0
Trueman b Walcott	..	..	1	not out	..	9
Extras	..	..	11	Extras	..	15
Total	..	..	373	Total (nine wkts.)		196

Bowling Analysis

		O.	M.	R.	W.		O.	M.	R.	W.
Mullins	..	19	2	54	0		8	2	15	1
Griffith	..	7	2	14	0		3	0	18	0
Sobers	..	34	6	103	1		19	9	36	1
Hoad	..	10	0	54	1		—	—	—	—
Atkinson	..	35	15	72	2		36·2	17	46	2
Goddard	..	10	5	23	1		27	13	43	5
Walcott	..	18·3	8	42	4		12	6	23	0

Played at Georgetown, British Guiana, February 17, 18, 19, 20 and 22. M.C.C. won by an innings and 98 runs.

ELEVENTH MATCH *v.* BRITISH GUIANA

M.C.C.

First Innings

W. Watson c Dyer b Hector	257
L. Hutton c G. Gibbs b Hector	0
P. May c Gibbons b Hector	9
D. Compton b L. Gibbs	18
T. Graveney c Christiani b L. Gibbs	231
K. Suttle run out	39
R. Spooner not out	20
J. Wardle c Christiani b G. Gibbs	4
G. A. Lock b G. Gibbs	4
A. Moss c Camacho b G. Gibbs	0
F. Trueman c Seafforth b Gibbs	20
Extras	5
Total	**607**

Bowling Analysis	O.	M.	R.	W.
R. Hector	30	2	136	3
G. Camacho	12	1	52	0
S. Seafforth	22	2	82	0
L. Gibbs	41	8	126	2
Basdeo	5	0	32	0
N. Thomas	3	0	22	0
G. Gibbs	32	2	122	4
R. J. Christiani	6	0	30	0

BRITISH GUIANA

First Innings		Second Innings	
G. Gibbs c Graveney b Moss	34	b Moss	
A. Gibbons b Wardle	38	b Wardle	2
G. Camacho c Graveney b Wardle	24	c Trueman b Lock	3
R. J. Christiani c Trueman b Wardle	75	c Compton b Trueman	8
C. A. McWatt c and b Wardle	29	c Graveney b Wardle	
N. Thomas run out	26	lbw b Wardle	3
H. Dyer run out	5	c Trueman b Compton	
R. Hector b Lock	13	c Compton b Trueman	
L. Gibbs b Wardle	1	not out	1
S. Seafforth b Wardle	2	b Moss	1
Basdeo not out	0	c Graveney b Moss	
Extras	15	Extras	
Total	**262**	**Total**	**24**

Bowling Analysis

	O.	M.	R.	W.		O.	M.	R.	W.
F. Trueman*..	12	3	34	0		11	3	24	2
A. Moss ..	17	8	25	1		10·5	1	45	3
J. Wardle ..	39	17	77	6		28	9	82	3
G. A. Lock ..	28·5	11	55	1		18	6	47	1
D. Compton ..	18	5	56	0		14	5	41	1
T. Graveney ..	—	—	—	—		6	6	0	0

* Bowled three no-balls in second innings.

Played at Grenada, March 6 and 8. Match drawn.

THIRTEENTH MATCH *v.* WINDWARD ISLANDS

M.C.C.

First Innings			Second Innings	
Suttle st Thomas b Mason	..	19	c Johnson b Mason ..	0
May c Johnson b Mason	..	13	not out	93
Bailey c Mason b Gresham	..	14	c Neverson b Crick ..	0
Hutton c Thomas b Barrow	..	82		
Watson c Johnson b Barrow	..	30		
Graveney c Johnson b Barrow	..	6	not out	11
Evans not out	..	26		
Wardle b Dasilva	.. ..	1	c Johnson b Gresham ..	66
Lock not out	..	5		
Extras	..	9	Extras	7
Total (seven wkts. dec.)		205	Total (three wkts.)	177

Bowling Analysis

	O.	M.	R.	W.		O.	M.	R.	W.
Mason ..	14	4	23	2		8	3	41	1
Crick ..	7	2	29	0		6	1	17	1
Dasilva ..	15	3	39	1		5	1	20	0
Barrow ..	9	0	45	3		3	0	42	0
Gresham ..	7	1	45	1		4	0	11	1
Johnson ..	2	0	15	0		3	0	18	0
Roberts ..	—	—	—	—		1	0	11	0
Thomas ..	—	—	—	—		2	0	10	0

WINDWARD ISLANDS

FIRST INNINGS

Neverson not out	..	..	..	..	..	90
Barrow b Trueman	..	..	..	..	..	13
Deterville c May b Trueman		..	..	..	..	0
Roberts run out ..	..	..	..	..	..	2
Gresham c Evans b Trueman	..	..	..	..	43
Fletcher lbw b Trueman		..	..	..	..	1
Thomas b Trueman	..	..	..	..	..	12
Crick c Watson b Trueman	..	..	..	..	4
Johnson c and b Trueman	..	..	..	..	3
Mason c May b Lock ..	..	..	..	..	5
Dasilva lbw b Lock	..	..	..	..	..	0
Extras	..	..	..	..	..	21
Total ..	..	..	..	..	..	194

Bowling Analysis

				O.	M.	R.	W.
Trueman ..	..	..		24	3	69	7
Moss	..	..	..	10	2	30	0
Wardle ..	..	..		10	4	23	0
Graveney	..	..		5	1	20	0
Lock	..	..	..	22·5	13	23	2
Bailey	..	..	..	3	1	8	0

**Played at Port of Spain, Trinidad, March 10, 11, 12, 13 and 15.
M.C.C. won by seven wickets.**

FOURTEENTH MATCH *v.* TRINIDAD

TRINIDAD

FIRST INNINGS			SECOND INNINGS		
N. Asgarali c Suttle b Bailey	..	33	lbw b Trueman ..	..	65
J. Stollmeyer b Trueman	..	89	c Spooner b Moss	..	48
R. Legall lbw b Compton	..	42	c and b Wardle ..		8
R. Tang Choon c Spooner b Moss		29	run out ..	..	0
G. Gomez c and b Trueman	..	91	not out ..	..	25
B. Kanhai c Lock b Trueman	..	1	st Spooner b Wardle	..	13
C. Sampath b Moss	..	1	c Wardle b Trueman	..	2
C. Furlonge c Trueman b Moss	..	18	c Statham (sub) b Trueman	32
W. Ferguson c Trueman b Lock		8	b Trueman	..	18
O. Demming c Spooner b Moss	..	5	run out ..	..	4
J. Taylor not out ..	..	0	b Wardle	..	0
Extras	..	..	12	Extras	..	17
		---			---
Total ..	..	329	Total ..	..	232

Bowling Analysis

	O.	M.	R.	W.		O.	M.	R.	W.
F. Trueman ..	27·3	6	75	3		21	2	47	4
A. Moss ..	19	5	63	4		19	2	59	1
T. Bailey ..	14	2	43	1		7	3	15	0
J. Wardle ..	26	7	60	0		24	9	55	3
G. Lock ..	16	4	58	1		15	4	35	0
D. Compton ..	3	1	18	1		—	—	—	—
C. Palmer ..	—	—	—	—		2	1	4	0

M.C.C.

FIRST INNINGS		SECOND INNINGS	
P. May b Demming	0	b Asgarali	4
K. Suttle c Demming b Ferguson	20	c Ferguson b Taylor ..	14
W. Watson lbw b Gomez ..	141	not out	32
G. Lock c Demming b Ferguson	8		
D. Compton b Ferguson	15	not out	90
C. Palmer c Legall b Asgarali ..	87		
R. Spooner c Gomez b Taylor ..	6		
T. Bailey not out	28	c Stollmeyer b Demming	90
J. Wardle c Taylor b Ferguson ..	18		
F. Trueman not out	1		
Extras	7	Extras	3
Total (for eight wkts. dec.)	331	Total (for three wkts.)	233

Bowling Analysis

	O.	M.	R.	W.		O.	M.	R.	W.
D. Demming	20	3	49	1		21	2	91	1
Taylor ..	15	5	32	1		17	4	35	1
W. Ferguson ..	26	1	119	4		2	0	10	0
R. Kanhai ..	10	1	41	0		4	0	19	0
G. Gomez ..	21	4	45	1		—	—	—	—
Stollmeyer ..	6	0	19	0		—	—	—	—
A. Asgarali ..	7	3	19	1		22	6	71	1
C. Furlonge ..	—	—	—	—		3	0	4	0

Played at Montego Bay, Jamaica, March 27 and 28. Match drawn. (No play first day—rain.)

SIXTEENTH MATCH *v.* JAMAICA COUNTRY XI

M.C.C.

T. E. Bailey c Richards b Dallas	55
K. Suttle b Pryce	0
P. May b Pryce	0
W. Watson retired hurt	31
T. Graveney lbw b Dallas	0
R. Spooner b Minott	1
J. Wardle c Frederick b Marriott	25
C. H. Palmer b Minott	5
G. A. Lock not out	0
F. Trueman lbw b Marriott	0
A. Moss c Forbes b Marriott	6
Extras	12
Total	135

Bowling Analysis

	O.	M.	R.	W.
Pryce	9	4	14	2
Minott	5	1	10	2
Forbes	5	0	26	0
Smith	6	0	33	0
Dallas	5	0	34	2
Marriott	1	0	6	3

JAMAICA COUNTRY XI

E. McMorris lbw b Wardle	13
B. Lawrence b Wardle	7
E. Frederick c Trueman b Wardle	8
D. Thorburn b Moss	37
C. Richards c Suttle b Lock	14
C. Smith b Moss	3
H. Dallas not out	10
G. Batts not out	3
Extras	1
Total (six wkts.)	96

Bowling Analysis

	O.	M.	R.	W.
Trueman	5	2	11	0
Moss	8	1	24	2
Wardle	10	3	43	3
Lock	13	6	11	1
Bailey	3	1	6	0

AVERAGES IN THE TESTS

ENGLAND

BATTING

	Inns.	Not out	Runs	Highest score	Average
L. Hutton	8	1	677	205	96·71
D. Compton	7	0	348	133	49·71
P. May	10	1	414	135	46·00
T. Bailey	7	2	193	49	38·60
T. Graveney	10	3	265	92	37·86
W. Watson	10	2	224	116	28·00
F. Trueman	4	1	38	19	12·67
T. G. Evans	6	0	72	28	12·00
J. Laker	5	1	44	27	11·00
B. Statham	6	2	28	10*	7·00
G. A. Lock	7	1	31	13	5·17

Also batted: J. Wardle 38 and 66; C. Palmer 22 and 0; R. Spooner 19 and 16; A. Moss 0 and 16.

* Indicates not out.

BOWLING

	O.	M.	R.	W.	Average
B. Statham	153	24	460	16	28·75
T. Bailey	182	51	459	14	32·79
J. Laker	218·1	84	469	14	33·50
F. Trueman	133·2	27	420	9	46·67
J. Wardle	83·3	23	187	4	46·75
G. A. Lock	292·5	87	718	14	51·29

Also bowled: A. Moss 36—5—114—2; D. Compton 27·4—3—144—2; T. Graveney 8—0—59—0; C. Palmer 5—1—15—0; L. Hutton 6—0—43—0.

WEST INDIES

BATTING

	Inns.	Not out	Runs	Highest score	Average
C. Walcott	10	2	698	220	87·25
E. Weekes	8	1	487	206	69·57
J. Holt	9	1	432	166	54·00
F. Worrell	8	1	334	167	47·71
D. Atkinson	7	1	259	74	44·75
C. McWatt	8	2	198	54	33·00
J. Stollmeyer	9	0	256	64	28·44
B. Pairaudeau	3	0	76	71	25·33
G. Gomez	7	1	126	47*	21·00
F. King	3	1	24	10*	12·00
S. Ramadhin	6	0	23	10	3·83
A. Valentine	4	1	0	0*	—

Also batted: G. Headley 16 and 1; R. Christiani 25 and 11; M. Frederick 0 and 30; W. Ferguson 8* and 44; G. Sobers 14* and 26; E. Kentish 0.

* Indicates not out.

BOWLING

	O.	M.	R.	W.	Average
E. Kentish	43	15	72	5	14·40
G. Sobers	29·5	9	81	4	20·25
C. Walcott	53	24	94	4	23·50
J. Stollmeyer	23	4	72	3	24·00
S. Ramadhin	304·3	133	559	23	24·30
F. King	110	41	247	8	30·87
G. Gomez	128	37	263	7	37·57
D. Atkinson	177	71	314	8	39·25
A. Valentine	190·5	81	378	7	54·00

Also bowled: F. Worrell 70—10—193—2; W. Ferguson 47—17—155—1; C. McWatt 4—1—16—1; G. Headley 5—0—23—0; R. Christiani 1—0—2—0; B. Pairaudeau 1—0—3—0; E. Weekes 8—0—39—0.

M.C.C. AVERAGES—ALL FIRST CLASS MATCHES

BATTING

		Inns.	Not out	Runs	Highest score	Average
L. Hutton ..	.. ..	12	2	780	205	78·00
W. Watson	.. ..	16	3	892	257	68·62
T. Graveney	.. ..	14	3	617	231	56·09
T. Bailey ..	.. ..	11	4	346	90	49·43
D. Compton	.. ..	14	1	630	133	48·46
K. Suttle ..	.. ..	7	1	251	96	41·83
P. May ..	.. ..	18	2	630	135	39·37
C. Palmer ..	.. ..	4	0	142	87	35·50
J. Wardle ..	.. ..	5	0	130	66	26·00
J. Laker ..	.. ..	9	1	123	33	15·37
F. Trueman	.. ..	9	3	81	20	13·50
R. Spooner	.. ..	8	1	93	28	13·29
G. A. Lock	.. ..	12	2	105	40*	10·50
A. Moss ..	.. ..	6	2	39	16	9·75
T. G. Evans	.. ..	8	0	72	28	9·00
B. Statham	.. ..	6	2	28	10*	7·00

* Indicates not out.

BOWLING

		O.	M.	R.	W.	Average
B. Statham ..	..	194·5	35	541	22	24·59
A. Moss ..	..	161·5	38	490	18	27·22
T. Bailey ..	..	251·5	79	611	22	27·77
J. Wardle ..	..	240·3	77	569	18	31·61
F. Trueman ..	..	319·4	81	909	27	33·66
J. Laker ..	..	330·5	113	756	22	34·36
G. A. Lock ..	..	486	157	1,178	28	42·07
D. Compton ..	..	81·4	16	325	6	54·17

Also bowled: C. Palmer 22—13—33—0; T. Graveney 16—6—71—0;
L. Hutton 6—0—43—0.

M.C.C. AVERAGES—ALL MATCHES IN BERMUDA AND WEST INDIES

BATTING

			Inns.	Not out	Runs	Highest score	Average
L. Hutton ..	..	..	18	2	1,070	205	66·87
W. Watson	..	..	21	5	1,034	257	64·63
D. Compton	..	..	19	1	787	133	43·72
T. Graveney	..	..	22	4	787	231	43·72
T. Bailey ..	..	..	18	5	546	90	42·00
P. May ..	..	..	26	4	829	— 135	37·68
J. Wardle ..	..	..	10	1	268	66	29·78
K. Suttle ..	..	..	15	2	335	96	25·77
C. Palmer ..	..	..	6	0	148	87	24·67
J. Laker ..	..	..	13	2	239	67	21·73
T. G. Evans	..	..	10	1	122	28	13·56
R. Spooner	..	..	13	2	135	36*	12·27
G. A. Lock	..	..	15	4	113	40*	10·27
F. Trueman	..	..	12	3	82	20	9·11
A. Moss ..	..	..	9	3	53	16	8·83
B. Statham	..	..	7	3	28	10*	7·00

* Indicates not out.

BOWLING

			O.	M.	R.	W.	Average
J. Wardle	..	..	335·5	110	807	38	21·24
B. Statham	..	..	212·5	37	583	26	22·42
A. Moss	..	..	219·5	54	636	27	23·56
J. Laker	..	..	412	137	951	38	25·03
G. A. Lock	..	..	581·3	195	1,339	51	26·25
F. Trueman	..	..	394·3	97	1,128	39	28·92
T. Bailey	..	..	273·5	87	657	22	29·86
D. Compton	..	..	99·4	18	407	12	33·92
T. Graveney	..	..	41·2	16	125	3	41·67

Also bowled: C. Palmer 26—14—49—0; L. Hutton 6—0—43—0.

THE PAVILION LIBRARY

New Titles

Cricket Cauldron
Alex Bannister

Masters of Cricket
Jack Fingleton

Backlist

Cricket All His Life
E. V. Lucas

The Cricket Captains of England
Alan Gibson

Farewell to Cricket
Don Bradman

Jack Hobbs
Ronald Mason

In Celebration of Cricket
Kenneth Gregory

The Best Loved Game
Geoffrey Moorhouse

Bowler's Turn
Ian Peebles

Lord's 1787-1945
Sir Pelham Warner

Lord's 1946-1970
Diana Rait Kerr and Ian Peebles

Through the Caribbean
Alan Ross

Two Summers at the Tests
John Arlott

Double Century Vol II
Marcus Williams (ed.)

In Search of Cricket
J. M. Kilburn

Double Century Vol I
Marcus Williams (ed.)

Sort of a Cricket Person
E. W. Swanton

End of an Innings
Denis Compton

Ranji
Alan Ross

Batter's Castle
Ian Peebles

The Ashes Crown the Year
Jack Fingleton

Life Worth Living
C. B. Fry

Cricket Crisis
Jack Fingleton

P. G. H. Fender
Richard Streeton

Hirst and Rhodes
A. A. Thomson

Crusoe on Cricket
R. C. Robertson-Glasgow